· JONATHON · GREEN ·

# FAMOUS LAST WORDS

SILVERDALE BOOKS

For C. S.

*Book design by*
Pearce Marchbank

*Layout and origination by*
Ben May, Studio Twenty, London

*Photographs courtesy of*
National Portrait Gallery
(PAGE 6, 144)
Hulton Getty
(PAGES 24, 42, 45 TOP, 52, 60,
62 TOP RIGHT, 70, 80 BOTTOM RIGHT,
81 BOTH, 97, 98,120,127, 128,
131 BOTTOM RIGHT, 132, 143 TOP,
147 TOP, 148, 150 )
Pearce Marchbank
(PAGES 33, 65)

Published by SILVERDALE BOOKS
an imprint of Bookmart Ltd
Registered Number 2372865
Trading as Bookmart Ltd
Desford Road
Enderby
Leicester LE9 5AD

First published in Great Britain in 1999 by
Kyle Cathie Limited

ISBN 1 85626 577 9

FIRST PUBLISHED IN GREAT BRITAIN BY
OMNIBUS PRESS, 1979

A C.I.P. CATALOGUE RECORD FOR THIS TITLE
IS AVAILABLE FROM THE BRITISH LIBRARY

PRINTED AND BOUND IN SINGAPORE BY
KYODO PRINTING

# I am just going outside and I may be some time.

This is a new and expanded edition of *Famous Last Words*, first published in 1979. I have added another three hundred sign-offs and broadened the 'mini-biographies' in the hope of giving a little background to some of the less easily recognised. Otherwise the essence of the book remains the same: the last words of kings, queens, courtiers, doctors, lawyers, poets, painters, philosophers, priests, saints, villains, murderers, martyrs and sportsmen... a panorama, in their own words, of the way some of the better-known members of humanity have faced their own extinction.

Two factors have made these final sentences famous. Usually the person has been sufficiently well known in life for whatever reason, good or bad, for there to have been general interest in his or her parting words to the attendant world. On the other hand, there are some final phrases that have brought their originator a fame in death that they never achieved in life.

There are infinite ways of dying, and the last words included here reflect them all. Nevertheless, certain moods, certain styles do persist, and this book has been divided into eighteen loosely generalised sections that show these ranges of feeling.

People face their death in many ways. Some, the professional phrase-makers, seem to have rehearsed a number of quotable last words all their life. Others, in the main clergymen, are content to fall back on the established formulae of their creed. Yet more, inevitably, call for their mother. Military men seem brave or patriotic; villains prefer bravado; the aristocracy try to maintain their hauteur, even on the scaffold; saints reveal qualities that duly bring them canonisation.

The pitfalls of such a book, obviously, are the omissions. While every effort has been made to gather as many last words as possible, and to set them in context and chronology, gaps inevitably appear. Quite simply, all too many famous names, with no thought for posterity, have died silently or unrecorded. To note just a few personal losses, why were Evelyn Waugh, John Lennon, P. G. Wodehouse, Raymond Chandler and Lenny Bruce reluctant to leave something for an attendant public? And what of all those show-business unfortunates, whose lives fascinated millions but whose lifestyle has laid them off prematurely? More importantly, what of the unsung heroes and heroines of countless battlefields, prison camps and similar hells? The well-attended deathbed, which encourages stirring farewells, is a thing of the past. Most die in hospital now, and a busy nurse has no time for taking notes.

Fortunately there remain many who did remember to sign off in style, and it is they who have found some small and posthumous fame here.

In an era when death is perhaps the supreme taboo, we can draw some comfort in the way these men and women have coped with their impending demise. They fill these pages with fear, resignation, exultation, anger, arrogance, surprise, their last words shouted or murmured: some have shivered in the face of the inevitable, some embraced it with fond relief.

One might not look forward to death, one might well wish profoundly to avoid it, but when it arrives all that one can hope, like so many of the people included here, is at least to do it well. *Jonathon Green*

*Facing page: The most famous last words of all? Lawrence Oates' farewell to Captain Scott on his ill-fated expedition to the South Pole in 1912; (Scott is at the centre of the photograph, with Oates to his left). See page 40.*

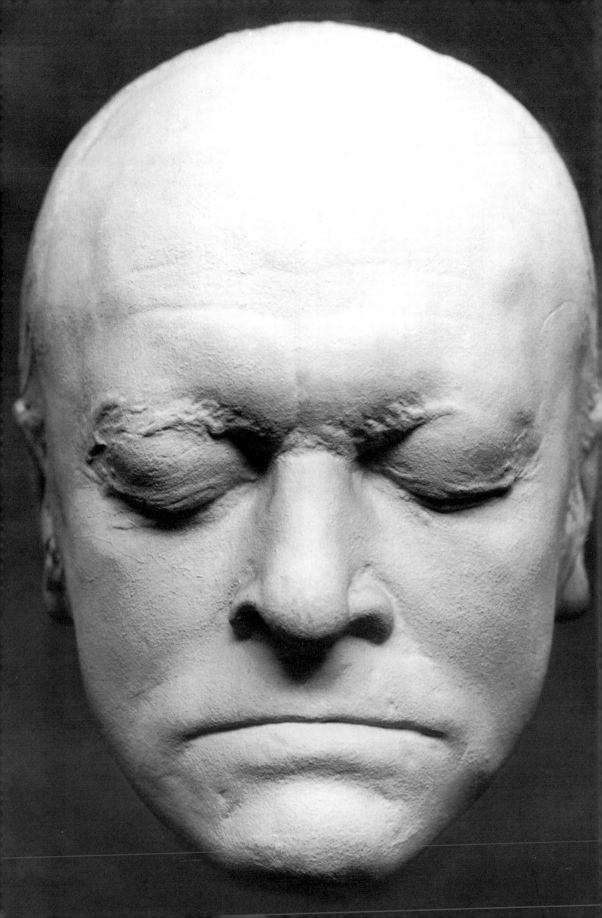

# A FOND FAREWELL

*One-way family favourites.*

### Fifth Earl Of Aberdeen
*British aristocrat, died 1864.*
*Asked how he felt...*
Perfectly comfortable.

### Abigail Adams
*Letter writer and wife of American President John Adams, died 1818.*
Do not grieve my friend, my dearest friend. I am ready to go. And John, it will not be long.

### Alice Adams
*Lover, but never wife, of American revolutionary Nathan Hale, died c.1775.*
Where is Nathan?

### John Quincy Adams
*American President, died 1848.*
This is the last of earth. I am content.

### Joseph Addison
*British essayist, co-founder of The Spectator magazine, died 1719.*
See in what peace a Christian can die.

### Thomas B. Aldrich
*American author and journalist, died 1907.*
In spite of it all, I am going to sleep.

### Vittorio Alfieri
*Italian dramatist, died 1803.*
Clasp my hand, dear friend, I am dying.

### John Peter Altgeld
*Governor of Illinois, died 1902.*
*To his last visitor...*
How d'you do, Cushing. I am glad to see you.

### Viscount Amberley
*Father of Bertrand Russell, died 1931.*
It is all done. Goodbye my little dears for ever.

### Anaxagoras
*Greek philosopher, died 428 BC.*
*Asked what he felt would be his best memorial...*
Give the boys a holiday.

### Agrippa D'Aubigne
*Huguenot leader and poet, died 1630.*
*A final verse...*
It comes at last the happy day.
Let there be given
To God in heaven
While we learn pleasure in His way.

### John Bachman
*Lutheran minister, died 1874.*
I love her. I love you all.

### Richard Harris Barham
*British clergyman and humorist, author of The Ingoldsby Legends, died 1845.*
*The final line of his final poem...*
Here is rest.

### Maurice Baring
*British novelist, died 1945.*
*Asked what he wanted for lunch...*
Anything you would like me to have.

### Isaac Barrow
*British scholar and preacher, died 1677.*
I have seen the glories of the world.

*The poster for John Barrymore's first talkie, made in 1929.*

### John Barrymore
*American actor, died 1942.*
*To his brother Lionel...*
You heard me, Mike.
*And to his old friend, the scriptwriter Gene Fowler...*
Tell me Gene, is it true that you're the illegitimate son of Buffalo Bill?

*Facing page: the death mask of poet and artist William Blake.*

### Sir Charles Bell

*British anatomist and discoverer of the distinct functions of the nerves, died 1842.*
*To his wife...*

Hold me in your arms.

### General Ludwig von Benedek

*German soldier, died 1881.*
*A telegraph message to his wife...*

Relieved to hear you feel better. I had a very bad night. Am now strong.
Your poor Louis.

### Anthony Benezet

*American teacher, abolitionist and social reformer, died 1784.*
*To his wife...*

We have lived long in love and peace.

### Park Benjamin

*American journalist, died 1864.*
*His wife asked him 'Do you know me?'...*

Why should I not know you, Mary?

### Monsignor Robert Benson

*British Catholic writer and apologist, died 1914.*

Arthur! Don't look at me. Nurse, stand between my brother and me! Jesus, Mary and Joseph, I give you my heart and soul.

### Jeremy Bentham

*British political theorist, the creator of 'Utilitarianism', died 1832.*

I now feel that I am dying. Our care must be to minimise pain. Do not let the servants come into the room and keep away the youths. It will be distressing to them and they can be of no service.

### Hector Berlioz

*French composer, best known for his 'Symphonie fantastique', died 1869.*

One thousand greetings to Balakirev.

### Theodore Beza

*German Protestant theologian, died 1605.*
*Still worrying about Geneva, the home of his faith...*

Is the city in full safety and quiet?

### William Blake

*British poet, died 1827.*
*To his wife, who asked whose songs he was singing...*

My beloved, they are not mine, no, they are not mine.

### Gebhard von Blücher.

*Prussian general, died 1819.*
*To an aide...*

Nostitz, you have learned many a thing from me. Now you are to learn how peacefully a man can die.

### Edwin Booth

*American actor, died 1893.*
*Asked how he felt by a grandson...*

How are yourself, old fellow?

### William Booth

*British lay preacher and founder of the Salvation Army, died 1912.*
*To his son, William Bramwell Booth...*

I am leaving you a bonnie handful. Railton will be with you.

### Alexander Borodin

*Russian composer, died 1887.*
*Writing to his wife about a ball to which he was going and at which he would die...*

I shall say no more about it and leave the description of the festivity to the more expert pen of other correspondents.

### Henry Bowditch

*Divine, died 1911.*
*Asked whether he suffered...*

No dear. Wish that the end would come.

### Saul Bowles

*American journalist, died 1915.*
*To his nurse...*

You may be sure that in another world there is always one soul praying for you.

### Johannes Brahms

*German composer, died 1891.*
*Enjoying his last glass of wine...*

Ah, that tastes nice. Thank you.

### Anne Brontë

*British novelist, author of The Tenant of Wildfell Hall, died 1849.*
*To her elder sister...*

Take courage Charlotte, take courage!

### Sir James Brooke

*Raja of Sarawak, died 1868.*
*Starting a letter that he could not finish...*

My dear Arthur...

### Rupert Brooke

*British poet, died 1915.*
*Greeting a final visitor...*

Hello.

### Robert Brookings

*American businessman and philanthropist, founder of the Brookings Institute, died 1932.*

I have done everything I wanted to do. This is the end.

*Right:*
*Johannes Brahms*

## Elizabeth Barrett Browning
*British poet, died 1861.*
*Asked how she was feeling...*
Beautiful.

## Robert Browning
*British poet, died 1889.*
*Hearing that his last volume of poems –*
*Asolando – was proving popular...*
How gratifying.

## Johann Bücher
*German jurist, died 1892.*
Now farewell. Permit me to close my tired eyes and sleep.

## William Cecil, Lord Burghley
*Elizabethan statesman, died 1598.*
*Leaving his affairs in the hands of his Steward...*
I have ever found thee true to me and now I trust thee with all.

## Aaron Burr
*American politician, died 1836.*
Madame.

## Feruccio Busoni
*Italian pianist and composer, died 1924.*
*To his wife...*
Dear Gerda, I thank you for every day we have been together.

## William Cadogan
*Second Earl of Cadogan, died 1797.*
*To his servants...*
I thank you all for your faithful services. God bless you.

## Edmund Campion
*British Jesuit martyr, executed 1581.*
*Asked on the scaffold for which queen – Protestant Elizabeth or Catholic Mary – he prayed...*
Yes, for Elizabeth, your Queen and my Queen, whom I wish a long quiet reign with all prosperity.

## Charles Carroll
*American patriot leader, longest surviving signer of the Declaration of Independence, and the only Roman Catholic to sign that document, died 1832.*
Thank you, doctor.

## Alice Cary
*American poet, died 1871.*
I want to go away.

## Miguel de Cervantes
*Spanish writer, author of Don Quixote, died 1616.*
*To his patron...*
Already my foot is in the stirrup. Already, great Lord and master, the agonies are upon me as I send these lines. Yesterday they administered to me the Last Rites. Today I am writing this. Time is short. Agony grows. Hope lessens. Only the will to live keeps me alive. Would that life might last until I might kiss the feet of your excellency. Seeing your excellency back in Spain, hale and hearty, might restore me to life. But if it be decreed that I must die, heaven's will be done. May your excellency know at least what my wish was and know also that he had in me a servant so faithful as to have wished to have served your excellency even after death.

## Thomas Chalmers
*Scottish divine, died 1847.*
A general good night.

## Philip Stanhope, fourth Earl of Chesterfield
*British statesman and writer, died 1773.*
*Known for his manners, he remained attentive to the needs of others even on his deathbed...*
Give Dayrolles a chair.

## Henry Clay
*American politician, died 1852.*
I believe, my son, that I am going. Now I lay me down to sleep.

## Francis Cobbe
*Irish philanthropist and religious writer, died 1904.*
*His last letter...*
I am touched by your affectionate words, dear Blanche, but nobody must be sorry when that time comes, least of all those who love me.

## George M. Cohan
*American showman and entertainer, died 1942.*
*His last words were of his wife...*
Look after Agnes.

## Samuel Taylor Coleridge
*British poet, died 1834.*
*Making provision for his favourite servant...*
I beg, expect and would fain hope of them [his family] according to their means such a contribution as may suffice collectively a handsome Legacy for that most faithful, affectionate and disinterested servant Harriet Macklin. Henry can explain. I have never asked for myself. Samuel Taylor Coleridge.

## Calvin Coolidge
*American President, died 1933.*
Good morning, Robert.

## Sir Arthur Conan Doyle
*British writer, the creator of Sherlock Holmes, died 1930.*
*To his wife...*
You are wonderful.

### Sir Astley Cooper
*British surgeon, died 1841.*
Goodbye, God bless you.

### John J. Crittenden
*American politician, died 1863.*
*To a servant...*
Tom, come and raise me up and arrange my pillow. That's right Tom.

### Herbert Croft
*Bishop of Hereford, died 1691.*
*His last words allude to his lying next to Dean Benson, at the bottom of whose gravestone are these words, 'In morte non divisi;' the two tombstones having hands engraved on them, reaching from one to the other, to signify the lasting friendship which existed between these two divines...*
In life united.

### John Wilson Croker
*British politician and essayist, died 1857.*
*To a servant...*
Oh, Wade...

### John Crome
*British landscape artist, died 1821.*
*His dying words were of his famous Dutch peer...*
Oh Hobbema, Hobbema, how I do love thee.

### Harvey Cushing
*American neurosurgeon, died 1939.*
*To his nephew who was adjusting his bedclothes...*
Pat, you have the touch. You're a good doctor.

### John A. Dahlgren
*American armaments inventor, died 1870.*
*To his wife...*
Madeline, I will take nothing more until you go to your breakfast, which you must require.

### Marie, Marquise du Deffand
*French literary hostess, died 1780.*
*Refusing to accept a priest as confessor...*
I shall confess to my friend, the Duc de Choiseul.

*Charles Dickens, portrait courtesy of the Bank of England.*

### Thomas Denton
*British counterfeiter executed for petty treason (possessing the implements for coining) 1789.*
*His last letter...*
Dear Father and Mother, When you receive this I shall be gone to that country 'from whence no traveller returns'. Don't cast any reflections on my wife – the best of mothers, and the best of women; and, if ever woman went to heaven, she will. If I had taken her advice I should not have been in this situation. God bless my poor Dick [his son]! The bell is tolling. Adieu. T. Denton.

### Walter Devereux
*First Earl of Essex and second Viscount Hereford, died 1576.*
*Referring to Sir Philip Sidney...*
I wish him well – so well that, if God move their hearts, I wish that he might match with my daughter. I call him son – he is so wise, virtuous, and godly. If he go on in the course he hath begun, he will be as famous and worthy a gentleman as ever England bred.

### Charles Dickens
*British writer, died 1870.*
*These words were quoted in the Times obituary...*
Be natural, my children. For the writer that is natural has fulfilled all the rules of art.

### Rudolf Diesel
*German engineer, one of the pioneers of the internal combustion engine, died 1913.*
*His last letter...*
Greetings and a kiss. In fondest love, Your father.

### Grace Dodge
*American philanthropist, died 1914.*
*Asking after some guests whom she was too ill to meet herself...*
And were they happy?

### Stephen A. Douglas
*American politician, died 1861.*
*His final advice to his sons...*
Tell them to obey the laws and respect the Constitution of the United States.

### Ernest Dowson
*British poet, died 1900.*
*To Mrs. Robert Sherard who had nursed him...*
You are like an angel from heaven. God bless you!

### Michael Drayton
*British poet, died 1631.*
*To his patron's daughter, Anne Rainsford...*
So all my thoughts are pieces but of you
Which put together make a glass so true

As I therein no other's face but yours can view.

### Edward Edwards
*British pioneer of public libraries, died 1886.*
*To his landlady, who had just bathed his feet...*
I am much obliged to you – very...

### Sir Charles Eliot
*British diplomat and colonial administrator who initiated the policy of white supremacy in Kenya, died 1931.*
I see Mother.

### John Lovejoy Elliott
*British founder of the Ethical Culture Movement, died 1925.*
The only things I have found worth living for, and working for, and dying for, are love and friendship.

### Ralph Waldo Emerson
*American philosopher and poet, died 1882.*
Goodbye, my friend.

### Epicurus
*Greek philosopher, died 270 BC.*
Now farewell, remember all my words.

### Christmas Evans
*Welsh preacher, died 1838.*
Goodbye. Drive on.

### Paolo Farinato
*Italian painter, died 1606.*
Now I am going.
*His sick wife joined him in death, saying:*
I will bear you company, my dear husband.

### Wilbur Fisk
*American educator and Methodist clergyman, died 1839.*
*Asked by his wife if he recognised her...*
Yes, love, yes.

### Marjory Fleming
*British child prodigy, died eight years old, 1811.*
Oh mother, mother...

### Edwin Forrest
*American actor, died 1872.*
God bless you, my dear and much valued friend.

### Georg Forster
*German explorer and scientist, died 1794.*
*His last letter home...*
It's true, isn't it, my children, that two words are better than none? I haven't strength to write more. Goodbye. Keep away from illness. A kiss for my little darlings.

### Stephen Collins Foster
*American composer, died 1864.*
The creator of 'ragtime' music, died in poverty. This note was found in his pocket...
Dear friends and gentle hearts.

### Margaret Fox
*British wife of George Fox, the Quaker leader, died 1702.*
*To her daughter...*
Take me in thy arms, I am in peace.

### Anatole France
*French scholar and satirist, died 1924.*
So this is what it is like to die. It takes a long time. Maman!

### Simon Fraser, twelfth Baron Lovat
*Jacobite plotter, executed 1747.*
*His last words were lengthy.*
*Watching a grandstand fall, which caused the deaths of several people...*
The more mischief the better sport.
*Noting the immense crowds gathered around the scaffold...*
Why should there be such a bustle about taking off an old grey head that cannot get up three steps without two men to support it?
*Before placing his head on the block he, with characteristic appropriation of the noblest sentiments, repeated the line from Horace...*
Dulce et decorum est pro patria, mori.
*He then said a prayer, after which he called his solicitor and agent in Scotland, Mr. W. Fraser, and gave him his gold-headed cane...*
I deliver you this cane in token of of my sense of your faithful services, and of my committing to you all the power I have upon earth.
*Finally he addressed his friend James Fraser...*
My dear James, I am going to heaven, but you must continue to crawl a little longer in this evil world.

### Leon Gambetta
*French politician, died 1882.*
When a visitor fainted at seeing him so near the end...
Good heavens, has he hurt himself?

### Count Agenor de Gasparin
*French nobleman, died 1871.*
*To his wife who wished to walk up the steps behind him...*
No, you know I like to have you go before me.

### Anne Gilbert
*Author of children's books, died 1904.*
*Kissing her daughter twice after she had arranged her mother's hair...*
That's for thank you...That's for goodnight.

### Mary Gooch
*Killed herself, 1823.*
*The successful half of a double suicide attempt...*
My dear, pray give me that blue muslin handkerchief that I may have it in my hand when I die. Pray don't you take anything, but let me die and you will get over.

### Ulysses S. Grant
*American President, died 1885.*
It is raining, Anita Huffington.

### Thomas Gray
*British poet, author of Elegy In A Country Churchyard, died 1771.*
Molly, I shall die.

### Anthony Norris Groves
*British missionary, died 1853.*
*To his son...*
Now my precious boy, I am dying; be a comfort to your beloved mother, as your dear brothers Henry and Frank have been to me. And may the Lord Himself bless you and make you His own. May the Lord give you the peace and joy in Himself that He has given me, for these are true riches. What would thousands of gold and silver be to me now? Now I give you a father's blessing.

### Joseph J. Gurney
*British Quaker philanthropist, died 1847.*
*Speaking to his wife...*
I think I feel a little joyful, dearest.

### Rev. James Hackman
*British clergyman, hanged, 1779.*
*Executed for a crime of passion: murdering Miss Ray, the mistress of Lord Sandwich. He shot her at Covent Garden Theatre and simultaneously tried to shoot himself. He failed and was arrested. His last letter...*
My dear Frederic, When this reaches you I shall be no more; but do not let my unhappy fate distress you too much: I have strove against it as long as

*U.S.Grant,*
*U.S.President.*

possible, but its flow overpowers me. You well know where my affections were placed: my having by some means or other lost hers (an idea which I could not support) has driven me to madness. The world will condemn me, but your good heart will pity me. God bless you, my dear Frederic! Would I had a sum to leave you, to convince you of my great regard! You was my only friend. I have hid one circumstance from you, which gives me great pain. I owe Mr. Knight, of Gosport, one hundred pounds, for which he has the writings of my houses; but I hope in God, when they are sold, and all other matters collected, there will be nearly enough to settle our account. May Almighty God bless you and yours with comfort and happiness; and may you ever be a stranger to the pangs I now feel! May Heaven protect my beloved woman, and forgive this act, which alone could relieve me from a world of misery I have long endured! Oh! if it should ever be in your power to do her an act of friendship, remember your faithful friend,
J. Hackman.

### James Hall
*British servant and murderer, hanged, 1741.*
*He murdered his master for money. In a last letter to his wife, penned the night before his execution...*

My Dear, I am very sorry we could not have the liberty of a little time by ourselves when you came to take your leave of me; if we had, I should have thought of many more things to have said to you than I did; but then I fear it would have caused more grief at our parting. I am greatly concerned that I am obliged to leave you and my child, and, much more, in such a manner as to give the world room to reflect upon you on my account; though none but the ignorant will, but rather pity your misfortunes, as being fully satisfied of your innocency in all respects relating to the crime for which I am in a few hours to suffer. I now heartily wish, not only for my own sake, but the injured person's, yours, and my child's, that I was as innocent as you are, but freely own I am not, nor possibly can be in this world; yet I humbly hope, and fully trust, through God's great mercy, and the merits of my blessed Saviour, Jesus Christ, to be happy in the next. After I parted with you I received the holy sacrament comfortably, which Mr. Broughton was so good as to administer to me, who has also several times before taken a great deal of pains to instruct me, and so have some others of his acquaintance, by whose assistance, and my own endeavours, I hope God will pardon all my sins for Christ's sake, and admit me into his heavenly kingdom. My dear, some of my latest prayers will be to God, to direct and prosper you and my child in all good ways, so long as he pleases to let you live here on earth; that afterwards he may receive you both to his mercies to all eternity. I hope I shall willingly submit to my fate, and die in peace with all men. This is now all the comfort I can give you in this world, who living was, and dying hope to remain, Your loving and most affectionate husband, James Hall.

### Frank Harris
*Irish-born American editor and bon viveur, died 1931.*
*To his wife...*
Nellie, my Nellie ... I'm going!

### Héloïse
*Wife of the theologian and philosopher Pierre Abelard, died 1164.*
In death, at last, let me rest with Abelard.

### Edwin P. Hood
*American Congregationalist, divine and author, died 1885.*
Oh God! Oh God! My wife! My wife!

### Sir Elijah Impey
*British judge, died 1809.*
*Apologising for leaning too heavily on a nurse who was helping him into bed...*
Did I hurt you, my dear?

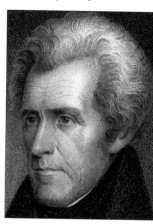

### Andrew Jackson
*American President, died 1845.*
Oh do not cry. Be good children and we shall all meet in heaven.

### Marshal Joseph Joffre
*French general, died 1931.*
*To his confessor...*
I have not done much evil in my life and I have sincerely loved my wife.

### Samuel Johnson
*British essayist, lexicographer and critic, died 1784.*
*To his step-daughter...*
God bless you, my dear.

### (Emily) Margaret Jourdain
*British authority on English furniture and decoration, died 1951.*
*She lived with Ivy Compton-Burnett from 1919 until she died...*
Don't let Day [their maid] eat all the Elvas plums.

### Francis Adrian van der Kemp
*Died 1847.*
*Last letter...*
Now I must close. I can scarcely distinguish one letter from another. Whatever may happen I know you remain unalterably my friend, as, so long as I draw breath, I shall be yours. Once again, farewell.

### James Kent
*American jurist, died 1847.*
Go, my children. My object in telling you this is that, if anything happens to me, you might know, and perhaps it would console you to remember, that on this point my mind is clear; I rest my hopes of salvation on the Lord Jesus Christ.

### Thomas King
*British Unitarian minister, died 1864.*
*Taking a last look at his son...*
Dear little fellow, he is a beautiful boy.

### Richard Knill
*British dissenting minister, died 1857.*
*To his daughter...*
How are you, Mary?

### Alexander Korda
*Hungarian-born British film producer, died 1956.*
*His last words were to his doctor...*
If I say goodnight to you now my friend, will you promise that I won't wake up again?

### Madame de Lafayette
*French writer, died 1693.*
*To her husband...*
Is it then true? You have loved me? How happy I am! Kiss me! What a blessing. How happy I am to be yours!

### Edward Lear
*British author of 'nonsense' verses, died 1888.*
*To his servant...*
I cannot find words sufficient to thank my good friends for the good they have always done me. I did not answer their letters because I could not write, as no sooner did I take a pen in my hand than I felt as if I were dying.

### Alphonse Legros
*French painter and etcher, died 1911.*

Referring to his fellow-artist and architect Alfred Stevens...

Il a été reconnu. (He has been recognised.)

## Princess Dorothea de Lieven
*Russian diplomat, died 1857.*
*A note to her friend François Guizot...*

I thank you for twenty years of affection and happiness. Don't forget me. Goodbye. Goodbye.

## Lord Lonsdale
*British sporting grandee, died 1944.*
*A last letter to his daughter...*

Life has been such lovely fun.

## George, first Baron Lyttleton
*British patron of the arts, died 1773.*
*Final advice to his son-in-law...*

Be good, be virtuous, my Lord. You must come to this.

## O.O. McIntyre
*American newspaper columnist, died 1938.*
*To his wife...*

Snooks, will you please turn this way. I like to look at your face.

## Sir Morell Mackenzie
*British laryngologist, died 1892.*
*Referring to his brother, a doctor...*

Yes, send for Stephen.

## Dolly Madison
*Wife of American President James Madison, died 1849.*

My poor boy.

## Maurice Maeterlinck
*Belgian poet and dramatist, died 1949.*

For me this is quite natural. It is for you that I am concerned.

## Ottmar Mergenthaler
*German inventor of Linotype printing, died 1899.*
*To his attendant family...*

Emma, my children, my friends, be kind to one another.

## Frank Merlo
*American secretary to playwright Tennessee Williams, died 1963.*
*Williams asked if he should go away...*

Oh no. I'm used to you.

## Sir John Everett Millais
*British painter, died 1896.*
Millais, who, when the power of speech had left him during his last illness in 1896, wrote on a slate the words (referring to George Smith, founder of *The Dictionary of National Biography*)...

I should like to see George Smith, the kindest man and the best gentleman I have had to deal with.

## Henry Miller
*Theatre manager, died 1874.*
*To his son...*

Gilbert, poor Dodd.

## William Morris
*British poet, decorator, printer and socialist, died 1896.*
*In a letter to Lady Burne-Jones...*

Come soon, I want a sight of your dear face.

## Rev. William Muhlenberg
*American clergyman, died 1877.*
*To his last visitor...*

Good morning.

## Ed Murrow
*American broadcaster, died 1965.*
*To his wife...*

Well, Jan, we were lucky at that.

## Waclav Nijinsky
*Russian ballet dancer, died 1950.*

Mamasha!

## Alfred Harmsworth, Lord Northcliffe
*British press magnate, died 1922.*
*Final orders for his funeral and obituary...*

I wish to be laid as near Mother as possible at North Finchley. I do not wish anything erect from the ground or any words except my name, the year I was born and this year on the stone. In *The Times* I should like a page reviewing my life work by someone who really knows, and a leading article by the best man available on the night.

## John Boyle O'Reilly
*Irish revolutionary and author, died 1890.*

Yes, Mamsie dear, I have taken some of your sleeping medicine. I feel tired now, and if you will let me lie down on that couch, I will go to sleep right away...Yes my love! Yes, my love!

## Sir William Osler
*British professor of medicine, died 1919.*
*Talking to his doctor as if he were still a child...*

Nighty-night, a-darling.

## Bass Outlaw
*American gunfighter, died 1894.*

Gather my friends around me, for I know that I must die.

## Charles Stewart Parnell
*Irish patriot, died 1891.*
*The mythical speech ran...*

Let my love be given to my colleagues and to the Irish people.
*But Parnell actually said...*

Kiss me, sweet wifie, and I will try to sleep a little.

## Sophia Peabody
*Wife of Nathaniel Hawthorne (American writer, died 1864).*
*To her husband...*

I am tired...too tired...I am glad to go...I only wanted to live...for you...and Rose...Flowers, flowers.

## Springett Penn
*American, son of William Penn of Pennsylvania.*

Let my father speak to the doctor and I'll go to sleep.

## George Lawrence Pilkington
*British explorer in Uganda.*

Thank you my friends, you have done well to take me off the battlefield. Now give me rest.

## James K. Polk
*American President, died 1849.*
*To his wife...*

I love you Sarah. For all eternity, I love you.

## Noah Porter
*American lexicographer, died 1892.*
*To a child...*

Go call your mother, wake her. I want to consult with her.

## William H. Prescott
*American historian, died 1849.*
*Amused that his wife could remember the name of a diplomat that he had forgotten...*

How came you to remember?

## Marcel Proust
*French novelist, author of* À la recherche du temps perdu, *died 1922.*
*Dictating to his housekeeper. Death came a day later...*

Celeste, I think what I have made you take down is very good. I shall stop now. I can't go on.
*To his brother who asked if he were hurting...*

Yes, Robert dear, you are.

## Giacomo Puccini
*Italian opera composer, best known for* La Bohème *and* Tosca, *died 1924.*

My poor Elvira, my poor wife.

## Alexander Pushkin
*Russian novelist, author of* Boris Godunov, *died 1837.*

Farewell, my friends.

### John Radcliffe

*Physician to Queen Anne, died 1714. Letter to his sister...*

I have nothing further than to beseech the Divine Being who is the God of the living to prosper you and all my relations with good and unblameable lives, that when you shall change the world you are now in for a better, we may all meet together in glory and enjoy these ineffable delights which are promised to all that love Christ's coming. Till then, my dear, dear Milly, take this as a last farewell from your Affectionate and Dying Brother, J. Radcliffe. N.B. The Jewels and Rings in my gilt cabinet, not mentioned in my will, I hereby bequeath to you.

### John Ray

*British naturalist and collector of proverbs, died 1705.*

When you happen to write to my singular friend Dr. Hotton, I pray tell him that I received his most obliging and affectionate letter for which I return thanks and acquaint that I am not able to answer it.

### Thomas Read

*American poet, died 1872.*

Sweet are the kisses of one's friends.

### Thomas William Robertson

*British actor and dramatist, died 1871. To his son...*

Goodbye, my son, and God bless you. Come and see me tomorrow. If I don't speak, don't be frightened, and don't forget to kiss your father.

### Edwin Arlington Robinson

*American poet, died 1935.*

We'll have our cigarettes together...Goodnight.

### John Wilmot, Earl of Rochester

*British aristocrat, rake, playwright and poet, died 1680.*

Has my friend left me? Then I shall die shortly.

### Rose Rodin

*Wife of the sculptor Auguste Rodin, died 1917.*
*Given her husband's promiscuity, her worries were possibly rather naive...*

I don't mind dying, but it's leaving my man. Who will look after him? What will happen to the poor thing?

### Gioacchino Rossini

*Italian composer of operas, died 1868. He called his wife's name...*

Olympe.

### Benjamin Rush

*American Revolutionary leader, died 1813. To his son...*

Be indulgent to the poor.

### George Sand (Amandine Dupin)

*French novelist, died 1876. To her family...*

Farewell, I am going to die. Goodbye Lina, goodbye Maurice, goodbye Lolo, good...

### Sappho

*Greek poetess, died c. 580 BC. A farewell poem to her daughter...*

For it is not right that in the house of song there be mourning. Such things befit not us.

### Jess Sarber

*American sheriff of Lima, Ohio. Shot by gunmen who were freeing John Dillinger from his jail, 1933. To his wife Lucy who had watched the shootout...*

Mother, I believe I'm going to have to leave you.

### Clara Schumann

*German pianist, died 1896.*

You two must go to a beautiful place this summer.

### Johann Gottfried Seume

*German poet, died 1910. When asked if he wanted anything...*

Nothing, dear Weigel. I only wanted to tell you that you shouldn't be annoyed if I say some things I wouldn't say in a different situation. I take a guilt with me. You I cannot repay. My eyes grow dim.

### Severus

*Roman nobleman, died 390. To his wife and daughter, who had already been buried in the family mausoleum...*

My dear ones, with whom I have lived in love for so long, make room for me, for this is my grave and in death we shall not be divided.

### Tobias George Smollett

*British novelist, died 1771. His last words were spoken to his wife...*

All is well, my dear.

### Konstantin Stanislavsky

*Russian dramatic theorist, died 1938. He was talking about his sister...*

I've lots to say to her, not just something. But not now. I'm sure to get it all mixed up.

### Harriet Beecher Stowe

*American writer, author of* Uncle Tom's Cabin, *died 1896. To her nurse...*

I love you.

Rossini.

### Robert A. Taft
*American senator, died 1953.*
*To his wife...*

Well, Martha! Glad to see you looking so well.

### William Desmond Taylor
*Hollywood star, died 1922.*
*Taylor died in mysterious circumstances. Fellow star Mary Miles Minter alleged she heard his corpse speak from the coffin...*

I shall love you always, Mary!

### Sir Godfrey Tearle
*British actor, died 1954.*
*To his girlfriend, the actress Jill Bennett....*

You are my sunshine.

### Irving Thalberg
*Hollywood producer, died 1936.*

Don't let the children forget me.

### General Regis de Trobriand
*American soldier, commander of the Army of the Potomac.*
*Letter to an aide...*

You will understand, dear Bonnaffan, that in such condition it is out of the question for me to receive any visit, or even to designate any possible time of meeting, as by that time it is as likely that I may be underground as on it. Farewell then, or au revoir, as the case may turn. Anyhow, I remain, Yours faithfully, R. de Trobriand.

### Maarten Tromp
*Dutch admiral, died 1653.*
*To his family...*

Take courage, children. Act so that my end will be glorious, as my life has been.

### Marie Tussaud
*Founder of Madame Tussaud's waxworks, died 1850.*
*To her two sons...*

I divide my property equally between you, and implore you, above all things, never to quarrel.

### Mark Twain (Samuel L. Clemens)
*American humorist, died 1910.*
*To his daughter, Clara...*

Goodbye. If we meet...

### Jules Verne
*French novelist, author of* Around the World in Eighty Days, *died 1905.*
*To his children...*

Honorine, Mechel, Valentine, Suzanne – are you here?

### Louisa, Marchioness of Waterford

Oh darling Adelaide, goodness and beauty, beauty and goodness those are ever the great things!

*Cardinal Wolsey.*

### Walt Whitman
*American poet and socialist, died 1892.*

Oh dear, he's a good fellow.

### Sir William Wilde
*Irish surgeon, father of Oscar Wilde, died 1876.*
*Listening to the noise from his son's party...*

Oh those boys, those boys!

### Alfred Williams
*British poet, died 1905.*
*To his wife...*

My dear, this is going to be a tragedy for us both.

### Woodrow Wilson
*American President, died 1924.*
*He spoke his wife's name...*

Edith.

### Thomas Wolfe
*American novelist, author of* Look Homeward, Angel, *died 1938.*
*Greeting his late wife...*

All right Mabel, I am coming.

### Cardinal Wolsey
*British clergyman, died 1530.*
*Unlike many of those who opposed Henry VIII's desire to break with Rome, Wolsey died in his bed.*

Master Kingston, farewell. My time draweth on fast. Forget not what I have sent and charged you withal. For when I am dead you shall, peradventure, understand my words better.

### Grant Wood
*American painter, died 1942.*
*His last word was his sister's name...*

Nan.

### William Wordsworth
*British Romantic poet, died 1850.*
*Asking for his sister...*

God bless you. Is that you, Dora?

### William Wycherly
*British dramatist, died 1716.*
*Asked by his young wife what were his last wishes...*

My dear, it is only this: you will never marry an old man again.

### William Yancey
*American southern politician, died 1863.*
*To his wife...*

Sarah!

# THE KING IS DEAD

*How the mighty are fallen.*

### Abimelech
*King of Judaea.*
Draw thy sword and slay me, that men say not of me 'A woman slew him'.

### Agesilaus II
*King of Sparta, died 361.*
If I have done any honourable exploit, that is my monument. But if I have done none, then all your statues will signify nothing.

### Agis
*King of Sparta, strangled to death 240.*
Weep not for me.

### Albert, Prince of Saxe-Coburg-Gotha
*Prince Consort to Queen Victoria, died 1861.*
*A private farewell...*
Good little woman.
*And a public one...*
I have had wealth, rank and power, but if these were all, how wretched I should be. Rock of ages cleft for me. Let me hide myself in thee.

### Albert I
*King of Belgium, killed in a climbing accident 1934.*
*To his companions as he set off on his own route...*
If I feel in good form I shall take the difficult way up. If I do not, I shall take the easy one. I shall join you in an hour.

### Alexander I
*Czar of Russia, died 1825.*
What a beautiful day.

### Alexander II
*Czar of Russia, assassinated 1881.*
I am sweeping through the gates, washed in the blood of the lamb.

### Alexander the Great
*King of Macedon and conqueror of the then known world, died 323 BC.*
To the strongest!

### Alexander
*King of Judaea, died 78 BC.*
Fear not true Pharisees, but greatly fear painted Pharisees.

### Pope Alexander VI (Roderigo Borgia)
*Italian pontiff, died 1503.*
I come. It is right. Wait a minute.

### Alfonso XIII
*King of Spain, died 1941.*
Spain, My God!

### Ali Pasha
*Turkish leader, 'The Lion of Janina', assassinated 1822.*
Go my friend, dispatch poor Vasiliky, that these dogs may not profane her beauteous form.

### Andronicus I
*Roman Emperor of the Commeni Dynasty, assassinated 1185.*
Lord have mercy on me! Wilt thou break a bruised reed?

### Anne of Austria
*Queen consort of Louis XIII of France and regent during the opening years of the reign of Louis XIV, died 1666.*
M. de Montaigu, consider what I owe to God, the favour He has shown to me and the great indulgence for which I am beholden to Him.

### Anne
*Queen of England, died 1714.*
*While handing the staff of the Treasury to Lord Shrewsbury...*
Use it for the good of my people.

### Antoninus Pius
*Roman Emperor, died 161.*
Tranquility.

### Arta xerxes I
*King of Persia, died 424 BC.*
*To Cyrus the Younger...*
Oh most unjust and senseless of men, who are the disgrace of the honoured name of Cyrus, are

*Facing page: King Charles I of England, complete with head.*

you come here leading the wicked Greeks on a wicked journey to plunder the good things of the Persians, and this with the intention of slaying your Lord and brother, the master of ten thousand times ten thousand servants that are better men than you, as you shall see this instant. For you shall lose your head here before you look upon the face of the King.

### Titus Pomponius Atticus
*Roman knight and patron of letters, best remembered for his connection with the orator Cicero, died 132 BC.*
I have determined on ceasing to feed the disease, as by the food and drink I have taken during the last few days I have prolonged life only so as to increase my pains, without hope of recovery. I therefore entreat you, in the first place to approve my resolution, and in the next, not to labour in vain trying to dissuade me from executing it.

### Augustus
*Roman Emperor, died 1 AD.*
Forty young men are carrying me off.
To his wife...
Live on, mindful of our wedlock, and farewell!

### Aurangzeb
*Emperor of Hindustan, last of the great Mughal emperors of India, died 1707.*
Soul of my soul, now I am going alone. I grieve for your helplessness. But what is the use. Every torture that I have inflicted, every sin that I have committed, every wrong that I have done I carry the consequences with me. Strange that I came with nothing into the world and now go away with this stupendous caravan of sin, wherever I look I see only God. I have greatly sinned and I know not what torment awaits me. Let not Muslims be slain and the reproach fall upon my useless head. I commit you and your sons to God's care and bid you farewell.
Your sick mother, Udaipur, would fain die with me. Peace.

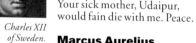
*Charles XII of Sweden.*

### Marcus Aurelius
*Roman emperor, best known for his* Meditations, *died 180.*
Go to the rising sun, for I am setting. Think more of death than of me.

### Babar
*The first Mughal Emperor of India, died 1530. His prayer, for the life of his son, was answered when he, and not Hamayan, died...*
Oh God, if a life may be exchanged for a life, I Babar, give my life and my being for Hamayan.

### Beatrix
*Grand Duchess of Bavaria, died 1447.*
Noble prince, dear brother, it is proper that you should know that we fell ill last Monday and though we had hopes of getting the better of our infirmity, we notice that the weakness and sickness is going from bad to worse. We beg you in all friendliness to send one or two of your councillors here so that if God Almighty calls us, your brotherly affection may know what sort of departure we made.

### Cambyses
*King of Persia, died 521 BC.*
I charge you all that you do not tamely allow the kingdom to go back to the Medes. Recover it one way or another, by force or fraud. By fraud if it is by fraud that they have seized it, by force if force has helped them in their enterprise. Do this and then may your land bring you forth fruit abundantly and your wives bear children and your herds increase and freedom be your portion for ever. But do it not, make no brave struggle to regain the kingdom and then may my curse be on you and may the opposite of all these things happen to you and not only so, but may you one and all perish at last by such a fate as mine.

### Caroline
*Queen and wife of George II of England, died 1737.*
Pray louder that I may hear.

### Caroline
*Princess of Brunswick-Luneburg, consort of George IV of England, died 1821.*
I would spare you the affliction of seeing me die. Pray…

### Caroline Sophia
*Wife of George III of England, died 1818. Told that 'There is a better life'...*
Very true.

### Catherine of Aragon
*First wife of King Henry VIII of England, died 1536. His desire to divorce her led to the creation of the Church of England.*
Lord into Thy hands I commend my spirit.

### Charlemagne (Charles the Great)
*Holy Roman Emperor, died 814.*
Into Thy hands, Oh Lord, I commend my spirit.

### Charles I
*King of England, executed 1649.*
I die a Christian, according to the profession of the Church of England, as I found it left me by my father. I needed not to have come here, and therefore I tell you, and I pray God it may not be laid to your charge, that I am the Martyr of the People.

### Charles II
*King of England, died 1685. Thinking of his mistress, Nell Gwynn...*
Let not poor Nelly starve.

### Charles V
*King of France, died 1380.*
I find that Kings are happy but in this that they have the power of doing good.

### Charles VIII
*King of France, died 1498.*
I hope never again to commit a mortal sin, not even a venial one, if I can help it.

### Charles IX
*King of France, died 1574.*
Ah my nurse, my dearest nurse, what blood and murders. I have had but wicked counsel. Oh my God forgive me all that and so it please Thee, have mercy on me.

### Charles XII
*King of Sweden, killed 1718.*
Don't be afraid.

### Charlotte Augusta
*Princess of Wales, died 1817. Calling for her adviser Baron Stockmar...*
They have made me tipsy. Stocky, Stocky!

### Charmion
*Maid of Queen Cleopatra of Egypt, committed suicide 30 BC. Asked how her mistress, who committed suicide, had died...*
Extremely well, and as became the descendant of many kings.

## Christina
*Queen of Sweden, died 1689.*
*Dictating the inscription that was to be placed on her gravestone...*

Queen Christina lived LXIII years.

## Cleopatra
*Queen of Egypt, committed suicide 30 BC.*
*On finding the poisonous asp in a bowl of fruit...*

So here it is!

## Cxi Cxi (Tz'u-hsi)
*Empress Dowager of China, died 1908 BC.*

Never again allow a woman to hold the supreme power in the State. It is against the house-law of our dynasty and should be forbidden. Be careful not to allow eunuchs to meddle in government matters. The Ming dynasty was brought to ruin by eunuchs, and its fate should be a warning to my people.

## Cyrus the Great
*King of Persia, died 529 BC.*

Remember my last saying: show kindness to your friends then you shall have it in your power to chastise your enemies. Goodbye my dear sons, bid your mother goodbye for me. And all my friends, who are here or far away, goodbye.

## Cyrus the Younger
*King of Persia, killed 401 BC.*

Clear the way, villains, clear the way!

## Darius III
*King of Persia, died 330 BC.*

But Alexander, whose kindness to my mother, my wife and my children, I hope the Gods will recompense, will doubtless thank you for your humanity to me. Tell him therefore in token of my acknowledgement, I give him this right hand.

## Didius Julianus
*Roman Emperor, killed 193.*

What harm have I done? Have I put anybody to death?

## Saint Edmund
*King of East Anglia, killed for refusing to abjure his religion 870.*

Jesus, Jesus!

## Edward I
*King of England, died 1307.*
*His son disobeyed his dying commands, and he was buried in Westminster Abbey.*

Carry my bones before you on your march. For the rebels will not be able to endure the sight of me, alive or dead.

## Edward II
*King of England, died 1327.*

I thank Thee, O Lord, for all Thy benefits. With all my power I ask for Thy mercy that Thou wilt forgive me for all the sins that I, in my wrongdoing, have committed against Thee. And I ask with my whole heart the grace of pardon from all men whom I have knowingly or unwittingly offended.

## Edward III
*King of England, died 1377*

Jesu.

## Edward VI
*King of England, died 1553*

Lord take my spirit.

## Edward VII
*King of England, died 1910.*

No, I shall not give in. I shall go on. I shall work to the end.

## Edward VIII
*King of England and latterly Duke of Windsor, died 1972.*
*To the Duchess of Windsor (formerly Wallis Simpson), who had offered to sit up with him...*

No darling, I shall soon be asleep. Get some rest please.

## Elizabeth I
*Queen of England, died 1603.*
*To her courtier Robert Cecil, who had foolishly suggested that the Queen 'must'...*

Must! Is must a word to be addressed to princes? Little man, little man! Thy father, if he had been alive, durst not have used that word. All my possessions for one moment of time.

## Elizabeth Christine
*Wife of Frederick the Great, died 1797.*

I know you will not forget me.

## Madame Elizabeth
*Sister of Louis XVI of France, guillotined, as had been her brother, 1794.*

In the name of modesty, cover my bosom.

## Epaminondas
*King of Thebes, killed 362 BC.*

Now is the time to die. The victories of Leuctra and Mantinea are daughters enough to keep my name alive.

## Farouk
*King of Egypt, died 1965.*
*Farouk, a notable playboy and bon viveur, made this comment on losing his throne in 1952...*

There will soon be only five Kings left: the Kings of England, Diamonds, Hearts, Spades and Clubs.

## Franz Ferdinand
*Archduke of Austria, killed 1914.*
*His assassination at Sarajevo set in motion the events that launched the First World War. To his duchess, also a victim of the attack...*

Sophie, don't die, live for the children.

## Franz Joseph
*Emperor of the Holy Roman Empire, died 1916.*

God preserve the Emperor!

## Frederick the Great
*King of Prussia, died 1786.*

I am tired of ruling over slaves. We are over the mountain, we shall go better now.

## Frederick William
*King of Prussia, died 1746.*
*In reply to the priest's words 'Naked came I out of my mother's womb and naked shall return'...*

No, not quite naked, I shall have my uniform on.

## Frederick V
*King of Denmark, died 1776.*

It is a great consolation to me in my last hour that I have never wilfully offended anyone and that there is not a drop of blood on my hands.

## Frederick III
*King of Germany, died 1888.*
*To his daughter...*

Remain as noble and good as you have been in the past. This is the last wish of your dying father.

### Servius Selpicius Galba
*Roman Emperor, killed 69 AD.*
What's all this, comrades? I am yours and you are mine. Strike, if it be for the good of Rome!

### George IV
*King of England, died 1830.*
To his page Sir Walter Waller...
Wally, what is this? It is death, my boy. They have deceived me.

### George V
*King of England, died 1936.*
To his Privy Councillors while having difficulty signing his initials...
Gentlemen, I am sorry for keeping you waiting like this. I am unable to concentrate.
*His patriotic farewell was...*
How is the Empire?
*But popular tradition claims that, on hearing the suggestion that he might soon be well enough to visit his favourite resort of Bognor Regis...*
Bugger Bognor!

### Gianger
*Son of Suleyman the Magnificent, the Ottoman Emperor, committed suicide 1553. To his father, who had just killed another son, Mustapha, and offered Gianger his brother's spoils.*
Fie of thee, thou impious and wretched dog, traitor, murderer – I cannot call thee father – take the treasure, the horse and armour of Mustapha to thyself.

### Gustavus Adolphus II
*King of Sweden, killed 1632.*
On the battlefield of Lutzen, to the Duke of Lauenberg...
I have enough, save thyself brother.
*However, the traditionally patriotic version runs...*
I seal with my blood my religion and the liberties of Germany.

### Hadrian
*Roman Emperor, died 138.*
O blithe little soul, thou, flitting away,
Guest and comrade of this my clay,
Whither now goest thou, to what place
Bare and ghastly and without grace?

*Joseph II, Holly Roman Emperor.*

Nor, as thy wont was, joke and play.

### Harun Al-Rashid
*Caliph of the Abbasid dynasty, ruler of Islam and patron of the arts, died 809.*
Sahl, remember in a moment like this what the poet has said: 'Descended from a race so great, I firmly bear the hardest fate'.

### Henri IV
*King of France, assassinated 1610.*
It is nothing.

### Henrietta Anne
*Duchess of Orléans, died 1670. Asked by the attending abbé, 'Madame, you believe in God? You hope in God? You love God?'*
With all my heart.

### Henry IV
*King of Germany and Holy Roman Emperor, died 1106.*
O how unhappy I am who squandered such great treasures in vain, how happy I could have been if I had given these things to the poor! But I swear before the eye of the All-Knowing that all my efforts have been for the advancement of my church.

### Henry II
*King of England, died 1189.*
Shame, shame on a conquered king.

### Henry IV
*King of England, died 1413. When told that the chamber in which he was lying sick was known as 'Jerusalem'...*
Lauds be given to the Father of Heaven, for now I know that I shall die here in this chamber, according to the prophecy of me declared, that I should depart this life in Jerusalem.

### Henry V
*King of England, died 1422.*
Into Thy hands, O Lord...

### Henry VIII
*King of England, died 1547.*
Monks! Monks! Monks!

### Henry, Prince of Wales
*Son of James I, died 1612.*
I would say somewhat, but I cannot utter it.

### Catherine Howard
*Wife of Henry VIII, executed 1542.*
I die a Queen, but I would rather die the wife of Culpepper. God have mercy on my soul. Good people, I beg you. Pray for me.

### Humbert I
*King of Italy, assassinated 1900.*
It is nothing...

### Isabella
*Queen of Spain, died 1504.*
Do not weep for me, nor waste your time in fruitless prayers for my recovery, but pray rather for the salvation of my soul.

### James II
*Exiled King of England, died 1701. To Louis XIV of France, who had given him a home in France and who visited his deathbed...*
Grateful, in peace.

### James V
*King of Scotland, died 1542.*
The Devil do with it! It will end as it began, it came with a lass and it will go with a lass.

### Jehoram
*King of Judaea, assassinated 849 BC.*
There is treachery, O Ahaziah.

### John
*King of England, died 1216.*
I commit my soul to God and my body to Saint Alstane.

### Joseph II
*Holy Roman Emperor, died 1790.*
Let my epitaph be: Here lies Joseph, who was unsuccessful in all his undertakings.

### Josephine de Beauharnais
*Empress of France, wife of Napoleon, died 1814.*
Napoleon! Elba! Marie Louise!

## Jugurtha
*King of Numidia, died 104 BC.*
*Jugurtha had fought to free his North African kingdom from Roman rule but died a prisoner in a freezing underground cell.*

Oh Hercules, how cold your bath is!

## Julius Caesar
*Roman Emperor, assassinated 44 BC.*
*To Marcus Junius Brutus, leader of the conspirators who stabbed him to death...*

Et tu Brute?

## David Kalakua
*King of the Hawaiian Islands, died 1891.*
*He had his dying message recorded...*

Tell my people I tried to restore our Gods, our way of life…

## Abdur Rahman Khan
*Amir of Afghanistan, died 1901.*

My spirit will remain in Afghanistan, though my soul shall go to God. My last words to you, my son and successor, are never trust the Persians.

## Konradin
*King of Sweden, executed 1268.*

Oh my mother, how deep will be thy sorrow at the news of today.

## Marie-Thérèse-Louise, Princesse de Lamballe
*French aristocrat, torn to pieces by a mob 1792.*
*Accused of intriguing against the Revolution with Queen Marie Antoinette, when asked by the crowd to cry 'Vive la nation!' she replied...*

Fie on the horror!

## Leopold I
*King of Belgium, died 1865.*
Don't leave me.

## Leopold II
*King of Belgium, died 1909.*
I am hot.

## Lothar I
*King of the Franks, died 885.*

What manner of king is He above who thus doeth to death such great kings?

## Louis I
*King of France, died 840.*
Out, out!

## Saint Louis
*King Louis XI of France, died 1270.*
I will enter now into the house of the Lord.

## Louis XIII
*King of France, died 1643.*
Dinet! Thoughts arise which trouble me. Well, my God, I consent with all my heart.

## Louis XIV
*King of France, 'Le Roi Soleil', died 1715.*
Why weep you? Did you think I should live forever? I thought dying was harder.

## Louis XV
*King of France, died 1774.*
*Referring to the text of his public apology to his subjects...*
Repeat those words, Monsieur Almoner, repeat them.

## Louis XVI
*King of France, guillotined 1793.*
I shall drink the cup to the last dregs.

## Louis XVII
*Ten-year-old son of Louis XVI, died in prison 1795.*

I have something to tell you. I suffer much less. The music is so beautiful. Listen, listen, in the midst of all those voices I recognise my mother's!

## Louis XVIII
*King of France, died 1824.*
*Trying to rise from his bed...*
A king should die standing up.

## Louis I de Bourbon, Prince de Condé
*French aristocrat, killed at the battle of Jarnac 1569.*
*To his friend D'Argence, who told him, 'Hide your face'...*

Ah, D'Argence, D'Argence! You will not be able to save me.

## Louis II de Bourbon, Prince de Condé
*French aristocrat, leader of the Frondist uprising and later one of Louis XIV's most valued generals, died 1688.*
*The devotedly godless Louis supposedly underwent a deathbed conversion, but few really believed it.*

In Thy justice free me.

## Louis the Dauphin
*Son of Louis XV, died 1765.*
*Taking the hand of the Bishop of Verdun...*
Lay it on my heart, you have never left it…
*When the doctor took his pulse...*
Ah! take the bishop's. What fortitude he has!

## Madame Louise
*Daughter of Louis XV, died 1800.*
Hurry! At a gallop! To Paradise!

## Louise
*Queen of Prussia, died 1820.*
I am a Queen but I have no power to move my arms.

## Margaret of Austria
*Regent of the Netherlands, died 1530.*
*Her final letter was to her nephew, the future Holy Roman Emperor Charles V...*

I have made you my universal and sole heir, recommending you to fulfil the charges in my will. I leave you your countries over here which, during your absence, I have not only kept as you left them to me at your departure, but have greatly increased them, and restore to you the government of the same, of which I believe to have loyally acquitted myself, in such a way as I hope for divine reward, satisfaction from you, monseigneur, and the goodwill of your subjects, particularly recommending to you peace, especially with the Kings of

*Louise, Queen of Prussia.*

*Mary I, Calais in her heart.*

France and England. And to end, monseigneur, I beg of you for the love you have been pleased to bear this poor body, that you will remember the salvation of the soul, and the recommendation of my poor vassals and servants. Bidding you the last adieu, to whom I pray, monseigneur, and give you prosperity and a long life. From Malines, the last day of November 1530. Your very humble aunt, Margaret.

### Margaret
*Queen of Scotland, died 1445.*
Fin de la vie! Qu'on ne m'en parle plus. (Death. Don't talk to me about it any more.)

### Margaret of Valois
*Queen of France, died 1594.*
Farewell and remember me.

### Maria Theresa of Austria
*Archduchess of Austria, queen of Hungary and Bohemia and wife of the Holy Roman Emperor Francis I, died 1780.*

I could sleep, but must not give way to it. Death is so near, he must not be allowed to steal upon me unawares. For fifteen years I have been making ready for him, and must meet him awake.

### Maria Theresa
*French aristocrat, died 1683.*
*It was raining outside...*
Yes, it is indeed frightful weather for a journey as long as the one before me.

### Marie Antoinette
*Queen consort of King Louis XVI of France, guillotined 1793.*
*Having tripped over the executioner's foot...*
Monsieur, I beg your pardon. I did not do it on purpose.

MARY QUEEN OF SCOTS.

### Mary I
*Queen of England, died 1558.*
*Calais, once a British possession, was lost during her reign...*
When I am dead and opened, you shall find 'Calais' lying in my heart.

### Mary II
*Queen of England, died 1694.*
*To Archbishop Tillotson, who broke down while praying for her...*
My Lord, why do you not go on? I am not afraid to die.

### Mary, Queen of Scots
*Executed for treason on the orders of her sister Elizabeth I 1587.*
Do not cry, I have prayed for you. In You, Lord, I have faith, and You shall protect me for ever. Into Thy hands, O Lord, I commend my spirit.

### Maximilian
*Emperor of Mexico, died 1867.*
*He murmured his wife's name...*
Lotte!

### Montezuma II
*The last Aztec Emperor, died 1520.*
*Forgiving his old enemy Cortes...*
For all my misfortunes, Malinche, I bear you no ill will.

### Joachim Murat
*'The King of Naples', executed by a firing squad 1815.*
Soldiers, do your duty. Aim for the heart but spare the face. I have too often faced death to fear it.

### Napoleon II
*Only son of Napoleon Bonaparte and Duke of Reichstadt, died of tuberculosis 1832.*
Call my mother! Call my mother! Take the table away. I don't need anything any more...Poultices.

### Napoleon III
*King of France, died 1873.*
*Dying in exile, he recalled his last disastrous battle, which failed to stop his deposition and the installation of the Third Republic...*
Were you at Sedan?

### Oscar
*King of Sweden, died 1901.*
Don't let them shut the theatres for me.

### Marcus Salvius Otho
*Roman Emperor, committed suicide 69 AD.*
*Otho fell on his sword in front of the Army, although the troops begged him to live...*
Deny me not the glory of laying down my own life to preserve yours. The more hope there is left, the more honourable is my early retirement, since it is by my death alone that I can prevent the further effusion of Roman blood, and restore peace and tranquillity to a distracted empire, by being ready to die for its peace and security.
*To one of his freedmen...*
Go then and show yourself to the soldiers, lest they should cut you to pieces for being accessory to my death.

### Pericles
*Athenian statesman, died 429 BC.*
No Athenian, through my means, ever wore mourning.

### Prince Peter of Portugal
*Brother of Prince Henry the Navigator, died 15th century.*
Oh, body of mine! I feel that you can do not more, and you my spirit, why should you tarry here? Fight on, comrades! And you, you villains, do your worst!

### Peter the Great
*Czar of Russia, died 1725.*
*His final words were written...*
Give back all to...

## Peter III
*Czar of Russia, strangled on the orders of his wife Catherine the Great, 1792.*

It was not enough to prevent me reigning over Sweden and to tear from my head the crown of Russia! They must have my life besides!

## Philip II
*King of Spain, died 1598.*

I die like a good Catholic. In faith and obedience to the Holy Roman Church.

## Philip III
*King of Spain, died 1621.*

Oh would to God I had never reigned. Oh that those years in my kingdom I had lived a solitary life in the wilderness. Oh that I had lived alone with God. How much more secure should I have died. With how much more confidence should I have gone to the throne of God, what doth all my glory profit but that I have so much the more torment in my death.

## Richard I
*King of England, killed in a skirmish by one Bertrand de Gourdon 1199.*

Youth, I forgive thee. Take off his chains, give him 100 shillings and let him go.

## Richard III
*King of England, killed 1485.*

I will die King of England, I will not budge a foot! Treason! Treason!

## Rudolf of Hapsburg
*Crown Prince of Austria, committed suicide 1889.*
He formed a suicide pact with his lover Marie Vetsera; this was a last letter to his wife...

Dear Stephanie, You are freed henceforward from the torment of my presence. Be happy, in

your own way. Be good to the poor little girl who is the only thing I leave behind. Give my last greetings to all my acquaintances, especially to Bombelles, Spindler Latour, Nowo, Gisela, Leopold etc., etc. I face death calmly, death alone can save my good name. With warmest love from your affectionate Rudolf.

## Saladin (Salah Ad-Din Yusuf Ibn Ayyub)
*Muslim sultan of Egypt, Syria, Yemen and Palestine, founder of the Ayyubid dynasty, and the most famous of Muslim heroes, died 1193.*
On hearing the passage, 'He is God than whom there is no other God who knoweth the unseen and the seen, the Compassionate, the Merciful'...

True.

## Saul
*King of Israel, died c. 1000 BC.*

Stand, I pray thee, upon me, and slay me, for anguish is come upon me, because my life is yet whole in me.

## Septimus Severus
*Roman Emperor, died 211.*

Little urn, you will soon hold all that will remain of him whom the world could not contain.

## Stanislaus I
*King of Poland, died of burns from his cloak catching fire 1766.*

You gave it me to warm me, but it has kept me too hot.

## Tamburlaine
*Turkic ruler, who spread his conquests from India and Russia to the Mediterranean Sea, died 1405.*

Never yet has death been frightened away by screaming.

## Theodoric
*Merovingian King, died c. 534.*
Disappearing on a strange coal-black steed...

I am ill-mounted. This must be the foul fiend on which I ride. Yet will I return, if God wills and Holy Mary.

## Titus
*Roman Emperor, died 81 AD.*

My life is taken from me though I have done nothing to deserve it. For there is no action of mine which I should repent but one.

## Vespasian
*Roman Emperor, died 79 AD.*

Dear me, I must be turning into a God.

## Marie Vetsera
*Austrian baroness, who died in a suicide pact with Rudolf of Hapsburg 1889.*
A last letter to her friend Marie Larisch...

Dear Marie, Forgive me all the trouble I have caused. I thank you so much for everything you have done for me. If life becomes hard for you, and I fear it will after what we have done, follow us. It is the best thing you can do. Your Mary.

## Victor Emmanuel II
*King of Italy, died 1878.*

How much longer will it last? I have some important things to attend to.

## Victoria
*Queen of England, died 1901.*
She cried out to her son and successor Edward VII...

Oh that peace may come. Bertie!

## Vitellius
*Roman Emperor, executed 69 AD.*
To his executioner...

Yet I was once your Emperor.

## William the Conqueror
*King of England, died 1087.*

I commend myself to the blessed Lady Mary hoping by Her intercessions to be reconciled to Her most dear Son, Our Lord Jesus Christ.

## William II
*King of England, killed in a shooting accident 1100.*
To Walter Tirel, who duly shot, but not the deer...

Shoot, Walter, shoot, as if it were the devil.

## William III
*King of England, died 1702.*
Can this last long?

## William the Silent
*Founder of the Dutch Republic, assassinated 1584.*
Asked 'Do you trust your soul to Jesus Christ?'...

Yes. May God have mercy upon my soul and upon this poor people.

# DULCE ET DECORUM

*Old soldiers never die, they just keep talking on.*

### Sir Ralph Abercromby
*British soldier, died at the battle of Aboukir Bay 1801.*
Finding that a soldier had given up his blanket to put under his wounded body...
Only a soldier's blanket? Make haste and return it to him at once!

### Anaxabius
*Greek soldier, killed in an ambush.*
Men, it is good for me to die on this spot where honour bids me, but you hurry and save yourselves before the enemy can close with us.

### General Lewis Armistead
*American Civil War leader, killed 1863.*
Give them the cold steel, men!

### General George Bayard
*American Civil War leader, killed at the battle of Fredericksburg 1862.*
My black mare and sorrel horse I give to you, father. There are about $60 in my pocket book. There are papers in my trunk to be turned over to the Quarter-Master's department to settle. One more goodbye, beloved father, mother, sisters all. Ever yours...

### Brevet-Brigadier-General Lewis Benedict
*American Civil War leader, killed at the battle of Pleasant Hill 1864.*
Giving his last order...
Colonel, rally your men and advance as soon as possible.

### Colonel G. E. Benson
*British officer in the Boer War killed at Bakenlaagte 1899.*
Benson specialised in night marches and surprise attacks. He died with 161 out of a force of 178 men...
We shall do no more night marching. It is all day now. Goodbye and God bless you.

### Edward Braddock
*British soldier, died 1755.*
He was killed fighting Indians in America, near Fort Duquesne.
We shall know better how to deal with them next time.

### Sir Isaac Brock
*British soldier, killed at Queenstown, 1812.*
Never mind me, push on the York volunteers.

### Marcus Junius Brutus
*Roman general, killed at the battle of Philippi 42 BC.*
Oh wretched valour, thou wert but a name, and yet I worshipped thee as real indeed. But now it seems thou wert but fortune's slave.

### Marshal Robert Bugeaud de la Piconnerie
*French general and imperialist, killed 1849.*
It is all over with me.

### Major Henry Ward Camp
*American Civil War leader, killed at the battle of Richmond 1861.*
Come on boys! Come on!

### Marshal Pierre Cambronne
*Commander of the Old Guard at Waterloo, killed 1815.*
Rejecting a demand for surrender...
Merde! The Old Guard dies but does not yield!

### Sir George Cathcart
*British soldier; died during the attack on Mt. Inkerman during the Crimean War, 1854.*
His last words were to his favourite staff officer, Major Maitland and then he fell dead from his horse, shot through the heart...
I fear we are in a mess.

### Gene Raljean Championnet
*French soldier, died 1800.*
Dying in bed he regretted surviving all his battles...
My friends, take care to console my mother. Would that I had been able to die like Joubert.

### General Auguste Colbert
*French general, killed 1809.*
To an aide...
You are then very much afraid of dying today?

### General George Custer
*American soldier, killed with his men, at Little Bighorn, 1876.*
His last message...
Benteen, come on. Big Village. be quick, bring packs.

*Facing page:
Rittmeister
Manfred Freiherr
von Richthofen,
'The Red Baron'.*

### Admiral George Dewey
*American sailor, died 1917.*
Gentlemen, the battle is done. The victory is ours!

### Dieneces
*Greek warrior.*
*Hearing that the Medean archers were so many that their arrows would darken the sky...*
Our Trachinian friend brings excellent tidings. If the Medes darken the sun we shall have our fight in the shade.

### Colonel Charles Dreux
*American Civil War leader, killed at the battle of Newport News.*
Steady boys, steady!

### Captain George Duff
*British sailor, killed at the battle of Trafalgar 1805.*
*From his last letter to his wife...*
My dearest Sophia, I have just had time to tell you that we are going into action with the Combined Fleets. I hope and trust in God that we shall all behave as becomes us and that I may yet have the happiness of taking my beloved wife and children in my arms. Norwich [his son, who would witness his father's death] is quite well and happy. I have, however, ordered him off the quarter deck. Yours ever and most truly, Geo. Duff.

### Viscount Dundee ('Bonnie Dundee')
*Scottish soldier, killed at the battle of Killiecrankie 1689.*
*Asked how the battle went and having been told 'Well for King James bad for you'...*
If it goes well for him it matters less for me.

### Colonel Henry Egbert
*Killed during the American invasion of Manila 1899.*
Goodbye General. I am done. I'm too old.

### Eucles
*Greek soldier, killed 490 BC.*
*Eucles had brought with his last breath the famous message of victory from the battle of Marathon when a tiny Greek force defeated the Persians...*
Rejoice, we rejoice!

### Wing Commander Paddy Finucane
*British fighter pilot, killed in the Battle of Britain 1940.*
*His plane was shot down over the Channel...*
This is it, chaps.

### General Charles 'Chinese' Gordon
*British general, killed at the siege of Khartoum 1885.*
*His last words were of the enemy...*
Where is Mahdi?

*General Charles 'Chinese' Gordon.*

*He also penned a last letter [to his sister]...*
I am quite happy, thank God, and, like Lawrence, I have tried to do my duty.
*And a last diary entry...*
I have done the best for the honour of my country.

### Lieutenant-Colonel John Greble
*American Civil War officer, killed at the battle of County Creek 1861.*
Sergeant, take command! Go ahead!

### Bertrand du Guesclin ('The Eagle of Brittany')
*Constable of France, killed besieging an enemy fortress 1380.*
Remember that your business is only with those that carry arms. The churchmen, the poor, the women and children are not your enemies. I commend to the King, my wife, my brother... farewell... I am at an end.

### Captain Haggard
*British officer in the Royal Welch Fusiliers, killed at Ypres 1915.*
Stick it, the Welch!

### William, Duke of Hamilton
*Killed at the battle of Worcester 1651.*
*Hamilton was kiled fighting for Charles II, although he had opposed Charles I...*
I believe that though in the last hour of the day I have entered into my Master's service, yet I shall receive my penny.

### Sir Henry Havelock
*British commander during the Indian mutiny, died of dysentery at the Siege of Lucknow 1857.*
Come, my son, and see in what peace a Christian can die.

### General Jean Humbert
*French soldier, died 1921.*
I die far from my country, too far, alas! To rest one day in the cemetry of my village, beside my poor parents...there I should have wished to die. Ah, my friends. Let the will of God...

### General Thomas 'Stonewall' Jackson
*American Civil War leader, killed in error by his own troops at Chancellorsville 1863.*
Let us cross over the river and sit in the shade of the trees.

### Albert S. Johnston
*American Civil War general, killed 1862.*
*Asked if he was wounded...*
Yes. And I fear seriously.

### Jean Lannes, Duc de Montebello
*Marshall in Napoleon's army, killed at the battle of Aspern, Esseling 1809.*
*On the operating table he still believed that Napoleon was supernatural.*
Save me, Napoleon!

### Karl Theodor Koerner
*German patriotic poet of the war of liberation against Napoleon. He became a national hero after he was killed in battle, aged 22, 1813.*
*Referring to his wounds...*
There I have one but it doesn't matter.

### Sir William de Lancey
*British soldier, killed at Waterloo 1815.*
Magdalene, my love, the spirits.

### Captain James Lawrence
*American sailor, killed 1813.*
*Lawrence commanded the US Chesapeake against the HMS Shannon...*
Don't give up the ship.

### Otto Lilienthal
*German flying pioneer, died in an air crash 1896.*
Sacrifices must be made.

### Marshal de Moncey, Duc de Conegliano
*Soldier in French Revolutionary and Napoleonic armies, died 1842.*
Let everyone fulfil and close his course like me.

### Marquis de Montcalm
*Commander of the French forces in Canada, killed at Quebec 1759.*
So much the better. I shall not then live to see the surrender of Quebec.

### Simon de Montfort
*British aristocrat, killed at the battle of Evesham 1265.*
*To his supporters...*
Commend your souls to God, for our bodies are the foe's.

## Captain James Mugford
*Captain of the schooner* Franklin,
*killed during the American War of
Independence 1776.*

Don't give up the ship! You will
beat them off!

## Captain Lewis Nolan
*British officer, killed during the Charge of
the Light Brigade 1854.*
*Nolan took the fateful message to Lord
Lucan. When Lucan seemed unwilling to
obey it, Nolan urged him to charge…*

Lord Raglan wishes the cavalry
to advance rapidly to the front,
and try to prevent the enemy
carrying away the guns.
Troops of horse artillery may
accompany. French cavalry is on
your left. Immediate.
There are the enemy, my Lord,
and there are the guns!

## Charles Peguy
*French poet and philosopher, killed at the
first battle of the Marne 1914.*

Keep firing.

## Rittmeister Manfred Freiherr von Richthofen 'The Red Baron'
*German air ace, shot down 1918.*
*To his mechanics, who were worrying as to
his safety…*

Don't you think I'll be back?

## Lieutenant Aloysius Schmitt
*American Navy chaplain, killed at Pearl
Harbor 1941.*
*Schmitt was chaplain of the USS* Oklahoma,
*bombed by the Japanese. He insisted on
being last through the porthole to safety. His
shoulders stuck…*

Go ahead boys, I'm all right.

## Count von Sedgwick
*Prussian soldier, hit by a cannonball 1757.*
Let all brave Prussians follow me!

## General Sedwick
*American Civil War commander; one of
around 27,000 men killed at the battle of
Spotsylvania 1864.*
*Looking foolishly over the parapet at the
enemy lines…*

They couldn't hit an elephant at
this dist…

## Sir Philip Sidney
*British soldier, killed at the battle of
Zutphen 1586.*
*Passing his water bottle to another wounded
man…*

Thy necessity is yet greater than
mine.

## Simonides
*Greek soldier, died c. 468 BC.*
*His verse glorified the Spartan dead who
held the pass of Thermopylae against the
Persians in 480 BC.*

Go stranger and to Lacedaemon
tell
That here, obedient to her laws,
we fell.

## General J. E. B. Stuart
*American Civil War soldier, killed at the
battle of Yellow Tavern 1864.*
I am resigned, if it be God's will.

## General William Penn Symons
*British general in the Boer War, killed at the
siege of Ladysmith 1899.*
*Symons ignored warnings when he stood on
a rampart to survey the scene…*
I am severely… mortally…
wounded in the stomach.

## Tecumseh
*Shawnee chief, orator and military leader,
died fighting American troops 1813.*
Brother warriors, we are about to
enter an engagement from which
I will not return. My body will
remain on the field of battle.

## Christopher Tennant
*British soldier, killed by shrapnel 1917,
after just three weeks in France.*
*To his batman…*
Oh Hobbes, I'm hit in the eye!

## William B. Travis
*Commander of the Alamo, killed there
1836.*
I am besieged by one thousand
or more of the Mexicans under
Santa Ana. I have sustained a
continuous bombardment for
twenty-four hours and have not
lost a man. The enemy have
demanded a surrender and I have
answered the summons with a
cannon shot and our flag still
waves proudly from the walls.

## Lieutenant-Commander Sakuma Tshuhmu
*This note was found in his submarine…*
12.30 I feel great pain in
breathing. I thought I had blown
out gasoline, but I have been
intoxicated by gasoline.
Commander Nakano. It is now
12.40.

## Vicomte de Turenne
*French soldier, killed at the battle of
Salzback 1675.*
I did not mean to be killed today.

## 'Mad Antony' Wayne
*American Revolutionary soldier, killed
1786.*
This is the end. I am dying. I
can't bear up much longer. Bury
me here on the hill by the
flagpole.

## General James Wolfe
*British soldier, killed as his men took
Quebec from the French 1759.*
*His rival, General de Montcalm, also died in
the battle. The last words of his order ran…*
The officers and men will
remember what their country
expects from them, and what a
determined body of soldiers are
capable of doing against five
weak battalions, mingled with a
disorderly peasantry. The
soldiers must be attentive to
their officers, and resolute in the
execution of their duty.
*After he had been wounded he told
attendant soldiers…*
Go one of you, my lads, with all
speed to Colonel Burton and tell
him to march Webb's regiment
down to the St. Charles River
and cut off the retreat of the
fugitives from the bridge. Don't
grieve for me [he said to one of
them], I shall be happy in a few
minutes. Take care of yourself, as
I see you are wounded. Now,
God be praised, I die happy.

*'Stonewall' Jackson:
shot by his own men.*

# MY COUNTRY 'TIS OF THEE

*Patriotism, the last refuge for many.*

**John Adams**
*American President, died 1826.*
*Suggesting his own epitaph...*
Here lies John Adams – who took upon himself the responsibility of peace with France in the year 1800.

**Dr John Adams**
*American clergyman, died 1862.*
*Final entry in his diary, saddened by the outbreak of the Civil War...*
This day I enter my ninety-first year. The year just closed has been one of trial and deep solicitude. My country, oh my country! I do not expect to see peace restored during the short remainder of my stay but I am earnestly looking forward to the everlasting rest which remaineth to the people of God. God reigns. He will accomplish all his purposes. Amen and Amen.

**Anonymous Vietcong soldier**
It is the duty of our generation to die for our country.

**Seigneur de Bayard**
*'Chevalier sans peur et sans reproche',*
*killed at the battle of Romagnano 1524.*
Let me die facing the enemy.

**Count Otto von Bismarck**
*German statesman, died 1898.*
I do not want a lying official epitaph. Write on my tomb that I was the faithful servant of my master, the Emperor Wilhelm, King of Prussia.
*When his daughter wiped his brow...*
Thank you my child.

**Robert Blum**
*French Socialist, shot 1848.*
He refused the traditional blindfold...

I want to look death in the eye. I die for freedom. May my country remember me. I am ready. Let there be no mistake and no delay.

NAPOLEON

**Napoleon Bonaparte**
*Emperor of France, died 1821.*
France! Army! Head of the Army! Josephine!

**John Wilkes Booth**
*Assassin of President Abraham Lincoln,*
*executed 1865.*
Tell my mother that I died for my country. I thought I did it for the best. Useless! Useless!

**Marcos Bozzari**
*Greek patriot and friend of Lord Byron,*
*died in the War of Independence 1823.*
Oh, to die for liberty is a pleasure and not a pain!

**General Karl Brandt**
*Nazi war criminal, hanged 1946.*
It is no shame to stand on this scaffold. I served my fatherland as others before me.

**John Brown**
*American abolitionist, hanged 1859.*
*A final remark as he rode to the gallows,*
*seated on his coffin...*
This is a beautiful country.

**Robert the Bruce**
*King of Scotland, died 1329.*
*To Sir James Douglas...*
I will that as soon as I shall be dead, you take my heart from my body and have it well embalmed. You will also take as much money from my treasury as shall appear to you sufficient to perform your journey as well as for all those more whom you shall choose to take with you in your train and you will then deposit your charge at the Holy Sepulchre where our Lord was buried. Gallant knight, I thank you. You promise it me then...Thanks be to God for I shall now die in peace, since I know that the most valiant, accomplished knight of my kingdom will perform that for me which I am unable to perform for myself.

**James Buchanan**
*American President, died 1868.*
Whatever the result may be, I shall carry to my grave the consciousness that I at least meant well for my country.

*Facing page:*
*Vietnamese student*
*Nhat Chi Mai*
*burns himself to*
*death in Saigon*
*in 1967.*

### Arthur Buckminster Fuller

*American clergyman and Union Army chaplain, killed at the battle of Fredericksburg 1862.*
*Fuller grabbed a musket and asked his company commander...*

Captain, I must do something for my country. What shall I do?

### John C. Calhoun

*American politician, died 1850.*

The South, the poor South! God knows what will become of her.

### Callicrates

*Greek general, died at the battle of Plataea 148 BC.*

I grieve not because I have to die for my country, but because I have not lifted my arm against the enemy or done any deed worthy of me, much as I have desired to achieve something.

### Luis de Camoens

*Portuguese poet, died 1580.*

So I shall conclude my life and all will see how I was so attached to my country that I was not satisfied to die in it, but to die with it.

### George Canning

*British Prime Minister, died 1827.*

Spain and Portugal.

### Michael Carmody

*A journeyman weaver of County Cork, Ireland, executed 1734.*
*His business, based on wool, had failed through growing popularity of cotton and he had turned to crime. The prisoner was dressed in cotton, as was the hangman, and the gallows were similarly adorned...*

Give ear, good people, to the words of a dying sinner! I confess I have been guilty of many crimes that necessity obliged me to commit, which starving condition I was in, I am well assured, was occasioned by the scarcity of money that has proceeded from the great discouragement of our woollen manufacturers. Therefore, good Christians, consider, that if you go on to suppress your own goods by wearing such cottons as I am now clothed in, you will bring your country into misery, which will consequently swarm with such unhappy malefactors as your present object is, and the blood of every miserable felon that will hang, after this warning from the gallows, will lie at your doors. And if you have any regard for the prayers of an expiring mortal, I beg you will not buy of the hangman the cotton garments that now adorn the gallows, because I can't rest quiet in my grave if I should see the very things that brought me to misery, thievery and this untimely end, all which I pray of the gentry to hinder their children and servants, for their own characters' sakes, though they have no tenderness for their country, because none will hereafter wear cottons, but oyster-women, criminals, hucksters, and common hangmen.

### Edith Cavell

*British nurse, shot for spying 1915.*

I realise that patriotism is not enough. I must have no hatred or bitterness towards anyone.

### Camillo Cavour

*Italian patriot, died 1861.*

Italy is made – all is safe!

### Jacques Cazotte

*French author, guillotined 1792.*

I die as I have lived. Faithful to God and my king.

### Georges Clemenceau

*French premier, died 1929.*

I wish to be buried standing facing Germany.

### Augustin Cochin

*French academic, died 1916.*

The Republic has been killed by her own children. The odious 1793, the foolish 1848. 1870 has carried her to her grave. She was killed by Robespierre, by Marat and then by all the word-mongers who have dealt in plots, in debts and foolish actions and who have three times ascended this chariot of the people.

### Anthony Collins

*British deist writer, died 1729.*

I have always endeavoured to the best of my ability to serve God, my King and my country. I go to the place God has designed for those who love Him.

### Crantor

*Greek philosopher, died 275 BC.*

Sweet in some corner of native soil to rest.

### Leon Czogolsz

*Assassin of American President Garfield, hanged 1901.*

I killed the President because he was the enemy of the good people, the good working people. I am not sorry for my crime.

### Richard Harding Davis

*American war correspondent, died 1916.*
*His last communiqué...*

That France and her Allies succeed should be the hope and prayer of every rightful American. The fight they are waging is for the things the real unhyphenated American is supposed to hold most high and most dear. Incidentally they are fighting his fight, for their success will later save him, unprepared as he is to defend himself from a humiliating and terrible thrashing. And every word and act of his now that helps the Allies is a blow against frightfulness, against despotism and on behalf of a broader civilisation, a nobler freedom and a much more pleasant world in which to live.

### Sir James Douglas ('The Good Douglas')

*Scottish patriot, killed 1330.*
*Douglas set off with Robert the Bruce's heart, encased in a golden casket, to Jerusalem, but was killed by the Moors in Andalusia, while fighting for King Alfonso of Castile. As he died he threw the casket in front of him towards the Holy Land...*

Now pass thee onward as thou wast wont, and Douglas will follow thee or die.

### Marcus Livius Drusus

*Roman politician, died 109 BC.*

Will the Republic again find a citizen like me?

## Louis-Antoine-Henri, Duc d'Enghien
*French prince, shot 1804.*
*His execution, generally seen as an atrocity but justified by false rumours of his treason, ended all hope of reconciliation between Napoleon and the royal house of Bourbon.*
Let's go my friends, I die for my King and for France.

## Hans Frank
*German war criminal, Governor-General of Poland during the Nazi occupation, hanged 1946.*
A thousand years will pass and the guilt of Germany will not be erased.

## Giuseppe Garibaldi
*Italian patriot, died 1882.*
*Talking about two birds that came to his window, rather than the more noble concept 'the people of Italy'...*
Feed them when I am gone.

## Gopal Godse Narayan Apal
*Assassins of Mahatma Gandhi, hanged 1948.*
India united!

## Samuel Gompers
*American labour leader, died 1924.*
God bless our American institutions, they grow better day by day.

## John Carteret, Earl Granville
*British statesman, died 1763.*
*On seeing a draft of the Treaty of Paris, which brought to an end the Seven Years War between France and Britain...*
It has been the most glorious war and it is now the most honourable peace.

## Sir Richard Grenville
*Elizabethan sailor, killed 1591.*
Here I die, Richard Grenville, with a joyful and quiet mind, for that I have ended my life as a good soldier ought to, who has fought for his country, Queen, religion and honour. Wherefore my soul most joyfully departeth out of this body...but the others of my company have done as traitors and dogs, for which they shall be reproached all their lives and leave a shameful name for ever.

## James Guthrie
*Scottish Presbyterian divine, hanged for high treason 1661.*
The covenants, the covenants, shall yet be Scotland's reviving!

## Nathan Hale
*American Revolutionary officer, shot by the British as a spy 1776.*
What a pity it is that we can die but once to serve our country.

## Philip Hamerton
*British artist and essayist, died 1894.*
If I indulge my imagination in dreaming about a country where justice and right would always surely prevail, where the weak would never be oppressed, nor an honest man incur any penalty for his honesty – a country where no animal would ever be ill-treated or killed, otherwise than in mercy that is truly ideal dreaming because, however far I travel, I shall not find such a country in the world, and there is not any record of such in the authentic history of mankind.

## Patrick Hamilton
*Scottish martyr, killed 1528.*
How long, Lord, will darkness overwhelm this kingdom? How long wilt Thou suffer this tyranny of men? Lord Jesus, receive my spirit!

## John Hampden
*Opponent of Charles I, killed at the battle of Chalgrove Field 1643.*
Oh Lord save my country! Oh Lord be merciful to…

## Lazare Hoche
*French revolutionary general, died 1797.*
Goodbye my friends, goodbye. Tell the government to keep a sharp eye in the direction of Belgium. Goodbye my friends.

## Sam Houston
*Texan patriot, died 1863.*
Texas, Texas, Margaret…

## General Herman Hoeffle
*Nazi war criminal, hanged 1945.*
Dear Germany.

## Agustin de Iturbide
*Mexican caudillo (military chieftain) and briefly, as Agustin I, Emperor of Mexico, shot 1824.*
I am no traitor! Such a stain will never attach to my children or to their descendants.

## Helen Hunt Jackson
*American novelist, died 1885.*
*A letter to President Cleveland...*
Dear Sir, From my deathbed I send you message of heartfelt thanks for what you have already done for the Indians. I ask you to read my 'Century of Dishonour'. I am dying happier in the belief that it is your hand that is destined to strike the first steady blow toward lifting this burden of infamy from our country and righting the wrongs of the Indian race. With respect and gratitude, Helen Jackson.

## Jacob
*Biblical patriarch.*
I am to be gathered unto my people. Bury me with my fathers in the cave that is in the field of Ephemeron the Hittite, in the cave that is in the field of Machpelah, which is before Mares in the land of Canaan which Abraham bought with the field of Euro the Hittite for a possession of a burying place. There they buried Abraham and Sarah his wife, there they buried Isaac and Rebecca his wife and there I buried Leah. The purchase of the field and of the cave that is therein was from the children of Heth.

## Thomas Jefferson
*American President, died on Independence Day 1826.*
Is it the Fourth? I resign my soul to God and my daughter to my country.

## Louis Kossuth
*Hungarian patriot, died 1914.*
*He died outside Hungary, in Turin, and complained to his sister...*
It grieves me that I have to perish in exile.
*She told him that he was 'the most popular Hungarian'...*
Only your vanity holds this.

## Pierre Laval
*France's collaborationist Premier, shot 1945.*
Vive la France!

## Sir Henry Lawrence
*Indian administrator, died 1857.*
*Choosing his epitaph...*
'Here lies Henry Lawrence who tried to do his duty'. This text I should like: 'To the Lord our God belong mercies and forgivenesses, though we have rebelled against Him'. Is it not in Daniel? It was on my dear wife's tomb.

## Carl Lody
*German spy, shot 1914.*
*His last letter to his family...*
My Dear Ones, I have trusted in God and He has decided. My hour has come, and I must start on the journey through the Dark Valley like so many of my comrades in this terrible war of nations. May my life be offered as a humble offering on the altar of the Fatherland. A hero's death on the battlefield is certainly finer, but such is not to be my lot and I die here in the enemy's country silent and unknown, but the consciousness that I die in the service of the Fatherland

*Agustin de Iturbide: Emperor of Mexico.*

makes death easy. The Supreme Court Martial in London has sentenced me to die for military conspiracy. Tomorrow I shall be shot in the Tower. I have had just judges and I shall die as an officer, not as a spy. Farewell, God bless you, Hans.

### Francisco Lopez
*Paraguayan dictator, died 1870.*
I die with my country!

### Mao Zedong
*Chairman of the People's Republic of China, died 1976.*
*Two versions of Mao's last instructions exist, their different interpretations call for opposing theories of China's future...*
Act according to the principles laid down.
Act in accordance with past principles.

### José Marti
*Cuban patriot, died 1895.*
*He was writing a letter which was never finished...*
There are some affections which involve such delicate points of honour...

*Right: Nazi foreign minister Joachim von Ribbentrop photographed in 1946 prior to his war-crimes trial.*

### Count Metternich
*Austrian statesman, died 1859.*
I was a rock of order.

### Draza Mihailovic
*Yugoslav freedom fighter, shot 1946.*
I found myself in a whirl of events and intrigues. I found Destiny was merciless to me when it threw me into the most difficult whirlwinds. I wanted much, I began much – the whirlwind, the world whirlwind, carried me and my work away.

### Nhat Chi Mai
*Vietnamese student who burnt himself to death in Saigon 1967.*
*This final verse served as a note...*
I offer my body as a torch to dissipate the dark to waken love among men to give peace to Vietnam.

### Lord Horatio Nelson
*British admiral, killed at the battle of Trafalgar 1805.*
*Despite popular mythology, Nelson's last words were not 'Kiss me Hardy', but...*
Thank God I have done my duty.

### William Pitt the Elder
*British statesman, died 1778.*
*To his son...*
Go my son, whither your country calls you. Let her engross all your attentions. Spare not a moment which is due to her service in weeping over an old man who will soon be no more.

### William Pitt the Younger
*British Prime Minister, died 1806.*
*There are many versions of Pitt's last words. All of them, including the less grandiose, but most likely, are well-supported.*
Oh my country, how I leave thee.
Oh my country, how I love thee.
My country, oh my country.
I think I could eat one of Bellamy's veal pies.

### Thomas Pride
*Best known for 'Pride's Purge', his expulsion of the Presbyterians from the House of Commons in 1648, died 1658.*
I am very sorry for these three nations, whom I see in a most sad and deplorable condition.

### 'Bill the Butcher' Poole
*American gang leader, killed 1855.*
*This deathbed repentance of the leader of New York's 'Bowery Boys' inspired many melodramas which climaxed on a tableau of The Butcher wrapped in the Stars and Stripes...*
Goodbye boys, I die a true American!

### Red Jacket
*Chief of the Seneca Indians, died 1830.*
Bury me among my people. I do not wish to rise among pale faces.

### Joachim von Ribbentrop
*German foreign minister, hanged as a Nazi war criminal 1946.*
God save Germany! My last wish is that Germany rediscover her unity and that an alliance is made between East and West and that peace reign on earth.

### Harold Harmsworth, Viscount Rothermere
*British newspaper magnate, died 1940.*
There is nothing more I can do to help my country now.

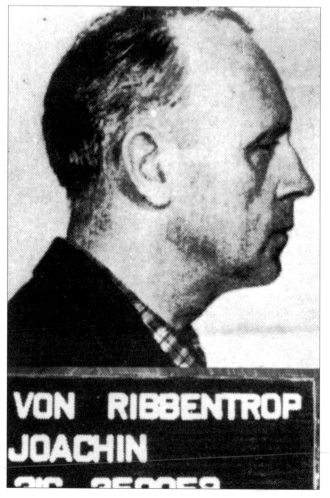

### Patrick Sarsfield, Earl of Lucan
*Irish soldier, died fighting for France at the battle of Landen 1693.*

Would to God this was shed for Ireland.

### Robert Falcon Scott
*Antarctic explorer, killed 1912.*
*Scott's last note to the public...*

Had we lived, I should have had a tale to tell of the hardihood, endurance and courage of my companions which would have stirred the heart of every Englishman. These rough notes and our dead bodies tell the tale.

### Stefan Stambouloff
*Bulgarian politician, died 1895.*

God preserve Bulgaria!

### Count Klaus von Stauffenberg
*German officer who plotted against Hitler, hanged with piano wire 1944.*

God save our sacred Germany!

### Sun-Yat-Sen
*Republican President of China, died 1925.*

Peace, struggle, save China.

### Getulio Vargas
*Brazilian President , committed suicide in 1954.*
*Once acclaimed for his reforms as 'Father of the Poor', his second administration was undermined by scandal and rather than face investigation he killed himself. A note read...*

I fought against the looting of the people. I have fought bare-breasted. The hatred, infamy and calumny did not beat down my spirit. I gave you my life! Now I offer my death. Nothing remains. Serenely I take the first step on the road to eternity and I leave life to enter history.

### Noah Webster
*American lexicographer, died 1843.*

I have struggled with many difficulties. Some I have been able to overcome and by some I have been overcome. I have made many mistakes but I love my country and have laboured for the youth of my country, and I trust no precept of mine has taught any dear youth to sin.

### William Windom
*American politician, died 1891.*
*His last speech...*

Give us direct and ample transportation facilities under the American flag, and controlled by American citizens. A currency sound in quality and adequate in quantity. An international bank to facilitate exchanges and a system of reciprocity carefully adjusted within the lines of protection and not only will our foreign commerce again invade every sea, but every American industry will be quickened and our whole people feel the impulse of a new and enduring prosperity.

### Arthur Wolfe
*Lord Chief Justice of Ireland, killed 1803.*
*Possibly mistaken for another judge near Dublin on the night of a nationalist riot, his coach was stopped rebels and he was killed.*

Murder must be punished, but let no man suffer for my death but by the laws of my country.

### Paul Ziegfried
*German citizen, committed suicide 1917.*
*A German national living in London, he was ordered to return to Germany as a hostile alien; rather than do so he took poison...*

Being forced to choose between going to Germany and death, I choose the latter.

### John Ziska
*Czechoslovak national hero, died 1424.*
*Apart from defeating the German armies under Sigismund, he was the first commander ever to deploy mobile artillery, a tactic that would not be taken up again for two centuries...*

Make my skin into drumheads for the Bohemian cause!

*The warehouse in Berlin where Klaus von Stauffenberg and the others who plotted to bomb Hitler were hanged in 1944 . Their execution was filmed for Hitler's later entertainment.*

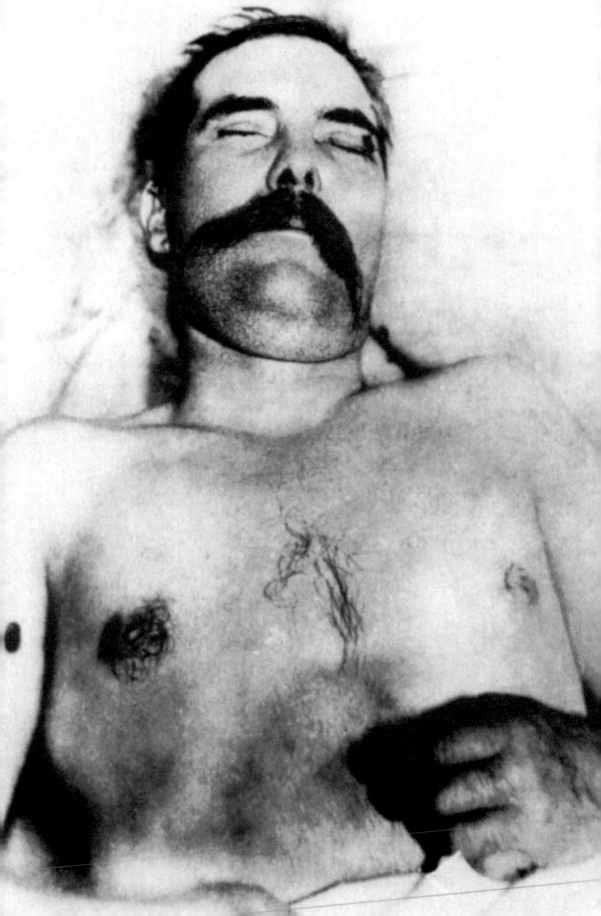

# THE TOUGH GET GOING

*Live fast, die young, and leave a good-looking corpse.*

### Louis Agassiz
*French naturalist, died 1910.*
The play is finished.

### Sir Andrew Agnew
*Scotish soldier, died 1771.*
Did the doctors really say I was not to get up? If they said so I won't get up, but I feel well. No. I will keep the pillows as the doctors left them.

### Rabbi Akiba
*Jewish patriot, flayed alive 32 AD.*
Killed in the Bar Kochba rebellion, he died adamant in his belief in a single God...
One!

### Ethan Allen
*American Revolutionary General, died 1789.*
When he was told 'I fear the angels are waiting for you'...
Waiting are they, waiting are they? Well let 'em wait!

### Anonymous Mexican sheep thief
*Hanged 1882.*
Replying to Judge Roy Bean, who had just condemned him to be hanged. The notoriously venal and racist Bean's sentence had ended 'It's the order of this court that you be took to the nearest tree and hanged by the neck until you're dead, dead, dead, you olive-coloured, chilli-eatin', sheep-stealin' sonofabitch'...

I admit I'm a thief, but so eager was this court to add another to its already long list of slaughtered victims that you remind me more of a lot of buzzards hovering over a carcass than men supposed to dispense justice. You half-starved hyena, you've sat through this trial with devilish glee written all over your hellish face. You talk about Spring with its sweet smelling blossoms and Fall with its yellow moon, you damned offspring of a diseased whore. You say that I'm to be hanged and as I gaze into your bloated, whisky-soaked face, I'm not surprised at the pretended gravity and the evil sarcasm with which you send me to my death. You haven't even the grace to call down the mercy of God on my soul, you dirty-nosed, pot-bellied, dung-eating descendant of an outhouse maggot. I despise you to the end. You can hang me by the neck until I'm dead, dead, dead, and you can also kiss my ass until it's red, red, red, and God damn your foul old soul.

### Mark Antony
*Roman general, commited suicide 30 BC.*
You must not pity me in this last turn of fate. You should rather be happy in the remembrance of our love and in the recollection that of all men I was once the most powerful and how at the end not dishonourable – a Roman by a Roman vanquished.

### Archimedes
*Greek mathematician, killed 212 BC.*
To the invading soldiers who killed him...
Stand away, fellow, from my diagram!

### Arria
*Wife of Paetus Caecina, committed suicide 42 AD.*
Killed herself to give her husband the courage to obey the Emperor's command to do the same...
It is not painful, Paetus.

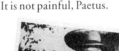

### Arizona 'Ma' Baker
*American bank robber, killed 1935.*
To her sons, ordering the start of their fatal shootout with the FBI...
All right! Go ahead!

*Facing page: John Wesley Hardin 'was a friend to the poor'.*

### Charles de Bedoyère
*French Count, shot for treachery 1815.*
*Facing execution by a firing squad he pointed to his breast...*
This is what you must not miss.

### Billy the Kid (William Bonney)
*American outlaw, killed 1881.*
*To his killer, Pat Garratt...*
Quien es? [Who's is it?]

### Comte Hippolite de Bocarme
*Belgian aristocrat, guillotined for murder 1851.*
I trust the blade is sharp.

### Jules Joseph Bonnot
*French criminal, killed 1913.*
*The 'anarchist motor bandit' was killed in a gunfight with the police.*
Bastards!
*Also a note written in his own blood...*
I am famous now. My fame has spread throughout the world. For my part I could have lived without this kind of glory. I have tried to live my own life and I have a right to live.

### John Bradshaw
*Puritan regicide of Charles I, executed 1659.*
If the king were to be tried and condemned again, I would be the first man that would do it.

### Gustavus Vaughn Brooke
*Irish actor, drowned in a shipwreck 1866.*
*Refusing to enter the lifeboat...*
No, no! Goodbye. Should you survive, give my last farewell to the people of Melbourne.

### Giordano Bruno
*Italian heretic, burnt to death 1600.*
*To his judge...*
You are more afraid to pronounce my sentence than I am to receive it. I die a martyr and willingly. My soul shall mount up with the smoke to Paradise.

### Robert O'Hara Burke
*Australian explorer, died from starvation 1861.*
*Died while attempting the first European crossing of Australia, leaving this last note...*
I hope we shall be done justice to. We have fulfilled our task but we have been abandoned. We have not been followed up as we expected. And the depot party abandoned their post. King behaved nobly. He stayed with me to the last and placed the pistol in my hand, leaving me lying on the surface as I wished.

### Lord George Byron
*English poet, died 1824.*
The damned doctors have drenched me so that I can scarcely stand. I want to sleep now. Shall I sue for mercy? Come, come, no weakness. Let me be a man to the last.

### Kit Carson
*American Western trapper, died 1868.*
Adios, compadre!

### Marcus Tullius Cicero
*Roman orator, politician and author, killed 43 BC.*
*To the soldier who killed him...*
Here veteran – if you think it right, strike.

### Ike Clanton
*American rancher, shot 1881.*
*Killed by the Earp Brothers during the gunfight at the OK Corral...*
God, God, won't somebody give me some more cartridges for a last shot...

### William F. Cody ('Buffalo Bill')
*Buffalo hunter, US Army scout and Indian fighter; his Wild West Show toured the world; died 1917.*
Well let's forget about it and play High Five. I wish Johnny would come.

### Joel Collins
*American outlaw and member of the Sam Bass gang, killed 1871.*
I'm going down with my six-guns.

### Captain Arthur Connolly
*British agent, executed on the orders of the Shah of Bokhara 1842*
Do your work!

### John Coppin (or Copping)
*British religious dissident, hanged 1583. A follower of the heretical Robert Browne, his works were burnt at the stake. His last recorded words were to the judge who condemned him...*
My lord, your face we fear not, and for your threats we care not, and to come to your service we dare not.

### Bernard Coy
*American murderer, killed 1946. While attempting to escape from Alcatraz – seconds before guards gunned him down...*
It don't matter, I figure I licked the Rock anyway.

### Francis 'Two Gun' Crowley
*American murderer and bank robber, died in the electric chair 1931. Captured after 'The Siege of W.90th St.' and sentenced to death by electrocution...*
You sons of bitches. Give my love to Mother.

### Bob Dalton
*American outlaw, killed in the Dalton Gang's disastrous raid on Coffeyville 1892. To his brother Emmett, sole survivor of the attack...*
Don't mind me boy. I'm done for. Don't surrender. Die game!

### The Decembrists
*Russian Revolutionaries, massacred 1825. Before they were mown down by a cannon in St. Petersburg...*
Yes we shall die, but it will be a fine death.

### General E. Delgado
*Executed in Honduras by firing squad 1886.*
We are ready. Soldiers fire!

### Vincent 'The Schemer' Drucci
*American gangster, killed 1927. To the policeman who shot him in a struggle...*
You take your gun off me or I'll kick hell out of you! I'll take you and your tool! I'll fix you!

### Simon Dubov
*Jewish historian, killed by the Nazis in a raid on the Riga ghetto 1941.*
Schreibt und farschreibt! (Write and record!)

### Edgar Edwards
*British killer, hanged 1902.*
I've been looking forward to this.

M. EVANS  BOB DALTON  GROT DALTON  DICK BROADW

*Above: Bob Dalton and the gang, 1892.*

### Raymond Fernandez
*American murderer, electrocuted 1951.*

I am going to die. That is all right. As you know, that's something I've been prepared for since 1949. So tonight I'll die like a man.

### Francisco Ferrer
*Spanish revolutionary and educator, killed 1909.*
To the soldiers...

I desire to be shot standing, without a bandage over my eyes.
To the schoolchildren...

Look well, my children, it is not your fault I am innocent. Long live the School.

### Adolf Fischer
*American radical and one of the Haymarket rioters, hanged 1881.*

This is the happiest moment of my life!

### Charles 'Pretty Boy' Floyd
*American bankrobber, killed 1934.*
Trapped by the FBI in an Ohio field...

Who the hell tipped you off? I'm Floyd all right. You got me this time.

### Jack 'Three Fingered' Garcia
*Mexican bandit.*

I will throw up my hands for no gringo dog.

UNITED STATES BUREAU OF INVESTIGATION
DEPARTMENT OF JUSTICE
**WANTED**
CHARLES ARTHUR FLOYD, aliases
FRANK MITCHELL, PRETTY BOY SMITH
WASHINGTON, D. C.

CRIMINAL RECORD

As Charles Arthur Floyd, No. 229 arrested police department, St. Louis, Missouri, September 16 1925, charge, highway robbery. As Charles Floyd, No. 29078, received S.F., Jefferson City, Missouri, December 18, 1925 from St. ...

37

### Antonio 'The Gentleman' Genna

*American gangster, died 1926.*
*He broke the underworld code of 'omerta', whispering on his deathbed to his girlfriend, daughter of a Baptist minister...*

The cavalier [Antonio Spano] got me.

### Mike Genna

*American gangster, killed during a Chicago gang war 1925.*
*He had just kicked a stretcher-bearer in the face...*

Take that, you dirty son of a bitch!

### Johnny Gilbert

*Australian bushranger, died holding off the police while his friend John Dunn escaped 1865.*

Save yourself, Jack. I'll fight them off.

### Gary Gilmore

*American murderer, shot 1977.*
*Gilmore asked for death by a firing squad thus paving the way for the possible restoration of the death penalty in American states.*

Let's do it.

### Lord George Gordon

*British revolutionary. The inspiration of the Gordon Riots, died 1789.*
*Quoting a French revolutionary chant...*

Ça ira!

### Frank Gusenberg

*American gangster, shot 1929.*
*Hit by fourteen bullets during Chicago gangland's St. Valentine's Day Massacre, he was asked 'Who shot you?'...*

Nobody shot me...It's getting dark, Sarge. So long.

### John Wesley Hardin

*American outlaw, most notorious killer of the Texas frontier, killed in a bar 1895.*
*Shot while playing dice in El Paso...*

Four sixes to beat!

### William Micajah 'Big' Harpe

*American desperado, lynched 1799.*
*The giant bandit wreaked havoc along the frontier until he fell, blown off his horse by a troop of frontiersmen. Mortally wounded, he lived for a while as they sawed at his neck with their long knives...*

You are a God-damned rough butcher, but cut on and be damned!

### The wife of Carthaginian general Hasdrubal

*Her husband had fled, but she burnt herself and her children at the temple in Carthage. As the flames mounted, she addressed the Roman General Scipio...*

You, oh Roman, are only acting according to the laws of open war, but may the gods of Carthage, and those in concert with them, punish the false wretch who, by such a base desertion, has betrayed his

*'Doc' Holliday: gunfighter and dentist.*

country, his gods, his wife, his children. Let him adorn thy gay triumph; let him suffer in the sight of all Rome those indignities and tortures he so justly merits.

### Marion Hedgepeth

*US trainrobber and bandit.*
*Cornered by the police, he was asked to surrender...*

Never!

### James Butler 'Wild Bill' Hickok

*American frontiersman, army scout, marksman and gambler, killed 1876.*

Agnes darling, if such should be we should never meet again, while firing my last shot I will gently breathe the name of my wife – Agnes – and with wishes even for my enemies, I will make the plunge and try to swim to the other shore.

### Andreas Hofer

*Tyrolean patriot, killed 1810.*
*Refusing to kneel before the firing squad...*

I stand in the presence of my Creator and standing I will render back my account to God who gave it. Fire!

### John Henry 'Doc' Holliday

*American gambler, gunfighter and occasional dentist, died 1885.*
*When someone took his boots off...*

Dammit! Put them back on. This is funny.

### William Hotman

*Hero of the American Revolution, killed 1781.*
*The British were about to blow up a Revolutionary fort and all within it. Hotman put out the fuse with his dying wounds...*

We will endeavour to crawl to this line, we will completely wet the powder with our blood; thus will we, with the life that remains in us, save the fort and the magazine and perhaps a few of our comrades who are only wounded.

### Paul Howe

*American teenage desperado; shot by police in 1979.*
*Only 50 per cent of his last request was granted...*

I want to go out in a puff of smoke ...and take a few policeman.

### Solyman Illeppy

*Turkish assassin of General Kleber, impaled 1800.*

That is good.

### Isaiah

*Prophet, sawed to death 660 BC.*

Go ye to the country of Tyre and Sidon for the Lord has mixed the cup for me alone.

### George Jackson

*American Black Power campaigner, author of Soledad Brother, killed 1972.*
*His last letter to his editor at Bantam Books, two months before being killed in Soledad prison...*

To paraphrase Castro, on trial after Moncada: I warn you gentlemen, I have only just begun!

### Jesse James

*American train robber and outlaw, shot 1882.*
*Trying to remain hidden...*

If anybody passes, they'll see me.

### John Jenkins

*Australian bushranger, hanged 1839.*
*He told a terrified fellow-victim...*

Come my lad, none of that crying. We'll both be right in a couple of minutes.

### William Jones

*American gambler, died 1877.*
*The traditional gambler's eulogy, recited at his funeral...*

O when I die, just bury me
In a box-back coat and hat.
Put a twenty-dollar gold piece on
my watch chain
To let the Lord know I'm
standing pat.

## Black Jack Ketchum
*American bankrobber, hanged 1901.*
I'll be in hell before you're
finished breakfast, boys...
Let her rip!

## Frank Kierdorf
*American contract arsonist and Teamsters'
Union agent, died in hospital 1958.*
He had fatally injured himself at a fire he had
set. He whispered to an attendant Michigan
policeman who had asked him to repeat
himself...
I said, go fuck yourself!

## Sir George Lisle
*English Royalist, executed 1648.*
I should have thought myself a
happy person, if I could live to
have a larger time of repentance,
and to see the king, my master,
on his throne again. I was
confident my own innocence in
this action would have rendered
me very clear from any such
punishment. Oh how many do I
see here about me, whose lives I
have shed in hot blood: and now
must mine be taken away in cold
blood most barbarously! Sure the
like was never heard of among
the Goths and Vandals, or the
veriest barbarians in the world in
any age. But what dare not those
rebels and traitors do, that have
imprisoned, and could willingly
cut the throat of their King? for
whose deliverance from his
enemies and peace to this
distracted kingdom, these my
last prayers shall be presented.
Now then rebels and traitors, do
your worst to me...Jesus.

## Harvey Logan ('Kid Curry')
*American outlaw, killed 1903.*
The toughest of the legendary Wild Bunch
was already mortally wounded by lawmen
when he shot himself. Asked by a fellow
outlaw, 'Are you hit?' he replied...
Yes. And I'm going to end it here.

## Sir Charles Lucas
*English Royalist, shot with Sir George Lisle
1648.*
I am no traitor, but a true subject
to my king and the laws of the
kingdom... I do plead before you
all the laws of this kingdom. I
have fought with a commission
from those that were my
sovereigns, and from that
commission I must justify my
action. Soldiers – fire!

## Salvatore 'Lucky' Luciano
*American gangster, died of a heart attack
1962.*
Marty...

## The seven Maccabaeus brothers
*Jewish patriots, tortured to death by the
Greek tyrant Antiochus 160 BC.*
These accounts come from the Rev. H.
Southwell's story of the Brothers, quoting
himself from Foxe's Book of Martyrs...
'Maccabaeus, the eldest, was accordingly
stripped, stretched on the rack, and
severely beaten. He was next fastened to a
wheel, and weights hung to his feet until his
sinews cracked. Afterwards his tormentor
threw him into a fire till he was dreadfully
scorched; then they drew him out, cut out
his tongue, and put him into a frying-pan,
with a slow fire under it, till he died. As long
as he had life and power of expression,
under these exquisite torments, he fervently
called upon God, and exhorted his brothers
to a similar perseverance'...
If our time be come, let us die
manfully for our brethren, and
let us not stain our honour.

'After the second son had his hands
fastened with chains, with which he was
hung up, his skin was flayed off from the
crown of his head to his knees. He was then
cast to a leopard, but the beast refusing to
touch him, he was suffered to languish till he
expired with the excruciating pain, and loss
of blood.'...
How welcome is death in any
form, when we suffer for our
religion and laws!

'Machir, the third son, was bound to a globe
till his bones were all dislocated; his head
and face were then flayed, his tongue cut
out, and being cast into a pan he was fried to
death.'...
Are you ignorant that I am the
son of the same father and
mother as those that went before
me? Shall I then at this awful
moment renounce the honour of
that alliance? The same
institutions were taught us all;
and I will abide by them while I
breathe.

'Judas, the fourth son, after having his
tongue cut out, was beat with ropes, and
then racked upon a wheel.'...
Your fire has not heat enough in
it to make me renounce my
opinion. I solemnly vow I will
not renounce the truth.

Antiochus, on hearing these words, was so
excessively enraged, that he gave
immediate orders to have Judas' tongue cut
out: whereupon the intrepid youth thus
proceeded...
You may deprive me of the
instrument of utterance; but
that God who seeth the heart
knows the inward sensations of
the silent. Here is the member;
you cannot by this act deprive
me of reason. O, that I could lose
my life by inches to support the
cause of religion. Though you
take away the tongue which
chants the praises of God,
remember that His high hand
will very soon let its vengeance
fall down on your guilty head.

'Achas, the fifth son, was pounded in a large
brazen mortar.'...
Prepare your torments! I am here
ready to suffer the worst you can
inflict. I come voluntarily to die
in the cause of virtue; what have I
done, wherein have I
transgressed, to deserve this
merciless treatment? Do we not
worship the universal Parent of
nature according to His own
decrees? Do we not act in
conformity to the institution of
His most holy law? These are
truths, that ought to meet with
reward instead of punishment.

'Areth, the sixth son, was fastened to a pillar
with his head downwards, slowly roasted by
a fire kindled at some distance; his tongue
was then cut out, and he was lastly fried in a
pan.'...
Indeed, I am younger than my
brothers: but my mind is as firm
as theirs. We had all of us the
same parents, the same
instructions; and it is but
necessary that we should die
alike for them: therefore if you
are determined to put me
torment on my refusal to eat
[pork], torment me at once!
In the midst of these torments he
exclaimed...
O glorious conflict, in which so
many brethren have engaged so
victoriously the sake of their
religion. I will accompany my
brothers: and relying on my God
as my defence, cheerfully submit
to death.

'Jacob, the seventh and youngest son, had
his arms cut off, his tongue plucked out and
was then fried to death.'...
Tyrant! Have you no fears nor
apprehensions in your mind
having received at the hands of
the Almighty the kingdom and
riches you enjoy, than to put to
death his servants, and torment
his worshippers? Is your
conscience touched with no

scruples, thus to deprive of their tongues those who share alike the same nature and passions with you? My brothers have undergone a glorious death, and shown how much their piety and uprightness were for the honour of the true religion. For this reason I will suffer death, and in my last pangs discover how much my desire was to follow the brave example of my brothers. I beg and entreat the God of my fathers, that He would be merciful to our nation.

*Desperado Joaquin Murrieta.*

'Salamona, the mother, after beholding the martyrdom of her children, was, by the tyrant's order, stripped naked, severely scourged, her breasts were cut off, and her body fried till she expired.'

### James Mclain
*American political activist, killed by police as he tried to shoot his way to freedom during his trial 1970.*
Take lots of pictures. We are the revolutionaries!

### Maréchal de Mailly
*French aristocrat and Marshal of France, murdered by a revolutionary mob 1789. He had refused to place a revolutionary cockade in his hat and was told were he not to do so he would be killed...*
Good people, you seem to know but little of the character of a soldier, or you would not attempt to move by terror a man whom profession has taught to look death in the face with calmness, and despise every danger that might threaten his life. I have often braved death in the career of glory, and I will not stoop so low as to purchase by a base compliance with a requisition supported by menace, the few days or months of life that may yet remain to an old man of fourscore. It is now too late in the day for me to think of changing my principles.

### Solomon Molcho
*Self-proclaimed Jewish Messiah, burnt to death for heresy 1535. Turning down a last offer of freedom in return for conversion...*
I repent only of one thing: that I was ever of your religion. That I spent my youth as a Catholic.

### Thomas B. Moran
*American pickpocket, died 1971.*
I've never forgiven that smart-alecky reporter who named me 'Butterfingers' – to me it's not funny.

### Harry 'Breaker' Morant
*Australian soldier, executed 1900.*
Shoot straight you bastards. Don't make a mess of it.

### Clifford Mortimer
*British barrister and father of the playwright John Mortimer.*
I'm always angry when I'm dying.

### Joaquin Murrieta
*Californian desperado, killed 1853.*
It is enough. Shoot no more. The job is finished. I am dead.

### Scipio Nasica
*Roman general, committed suicide at Thapsus 46 BC.*
All is well with the general.

### Neptune
*A Black slave in Surinam, sentenced to be broken alive on the rack for murdering an overseer.*
After his left hand had been chopped off and the bones smashed, he asked a soldier who was standing sentinal and eating a piece of dry bread...
How does came to pass that you, a white man, should have no meat to eat along with your bread?
'Because I am not so rich,' answered the soldier...
Then I will make you a present, Sir. First pick my hand that was chopped off clean to the bones; next begin to devour my body till you are glutted; when you will have both bread and meat, as best becomes you.

### Captain Lawrence Oates
*English explorer, a member of Scott's last expedition to the Antarctic, killed 1912. Although some have claimed that Oates' trip was rather more prosaic, the official line stands...*
I am just going outside and I may be some time.

### Bonnie Parker
*American bank robber, the female half of Bonnie and Clyde, killed 1934. The last verse of her final poem, 'The Story of Suicide Sal'...*
Some day they will go down together,
And they will bury them side by side,
To a few it means grief,
To the law it's relief,
But it's death to Bonnie and Clyde.

### Charles Peace
*British thief and murderer, hanged 1879.*
What is the scaffold? A short cut to heaven.

### Ravachol
*French anarchist, guillotined 1892.*
Long live anarchy!

### Arnold Rothstein
*American gangster and financial genius, killed 1928.*
*When asked who shot him...*
Me mudder did it!

### San Quentin Prison, Death Row
*Traditional joke...*
I'd like a little bicarb, Warden, because I'm gonna have some gas.

### Baron of Scanaw
*Bohemian aristocrat, died 16th century. He cut out his own tongue rather than risk confessing on the rack, where he duly died. He left a note...*
I did this extraordinary action because I would not, by means of any tortures, be brought to accuse myself, or others, as I might, through the excruciating tortures of the rack, be impelled to utter falsehoods.

### Edward 'Death Valley Scotty' Scott
*American recluse, died 1954.*
I got four things to live by: don't say nothin' that will hurt anybody; don't give advice – nobody will take it anyway; don't complain; don't explain.

### Captain E. J. Smith
*Captain of the Titanic, drowned 1912. Declining to be helped into a lifeboat to which he had just swum with a child...*
Let me go.
*An alternative witness offered...*
Be British, boys, be British!

### Richard Snell
*US murderer, executed by injection 1995. The far-right fanatic had killed a black policeman and a pawnbroker, whom he assumed to be Jewish...*
Hell has victories. I am at peace.

## Mrs. Isaac Straus
*Passenger on the Titanic, drowned 1912.*
*Refusing to take a lifeboat which would have parted her from her husband...*
We've been together for forty years, and will not separate now.

## Theoxena
*Grecian wife, died fourth century BC.*
*Pursued by the emissaries of Philip of Macedon, who had already executed her husband, she took to the sea. On deck she offered both poison and a dagger to her companions, who took her advice. She then jumped overboard to her death...*
Death is now our only remedy and means of vengeance; let each take the method that best pleases himself of avoiding the tyrant's pride, cruelty and lust. Come on, my brave companions and family, seize the sword or drink of the cup, as you prefer an instantaneous or gradual death.

## Frank R. Thompson
*Chicago gangland armourer, shot 1930.*
*Talking to sheriff Harry Baldwin from his hospital bed...*
Listen Harry, I've seen everything, done everything and got everything. And you're smart enough to know I won't talk. Go to hell.

## Johnny Torrio
*American gangster, shot 1924.*
*The killer was possibly Torrio's lieutenant Al Capone...*
Bullets tipped with garlic.

## Placido Valdes
*Cuban slave rebellion leader, shot 1844.*
Here, fire here!

## John 'Rocky' Whelan
*Tasmanian bushranger, hanged 1855.*
*Referring on the gallows to the man whose evidence had seen him condemned...*
My only regret is that I didn't put a bullet through his head.

## Robert 'Bob' Younger
*American outlaw, a member of the James/Younger gang, died of tuberculosis in jail 1889.*
*To his attendant sister...*
Don't weep for me.

*Bonnie Parker and her partner Clyde Barrow star on a wanted poster.*

WANTED FOR MURDER
JOPLIN, MISSOURI

F.P.C. 29 - MO. 9
26 U 00 6

CLYDE CHAMPION BARROW, age 24, 5'7", 130#, hair dark brown and wavy, eyes hazel, light complexion, home West Dallas, Texas. This man killed Detective Harry McGinnis and Constable J.W. Harryman in this city, April 13, 1933.

BONNIE PARKER  CLYDE BARROW          CLYDE BARROW

This man is dangerous and is known to have committed the following murders: Howard Hall, Sherman, Texas; J.N. Bucher, Hillsboro, Texas; a deputy sheriff at Atoka, Okla; deputy sheriff at West Dallas, Texas; also a man at Belden, Texas.
        The above photos are kodaks taken by Barrow and his companions in various poses, and we believe they are better for identification than regular police pictures.
        Wire or write any information to the

Police Department.

# VICTIMS OF CIRCUMSTANCE

*Nobody expects the Spanish Inquisition…let alone the Grim Reaper.*

### Vittoria Accoramboni
*Duchess of Bracciano, stabbed to death on the orders of her late husband's relations 1585.*
The dramas of her life provided the basis for John Webster's play *The White Devil* and Ludwig Tieck's novel *Vittoria Accoramboni.*
Jesus! I pardon you.

### Albert Anastasia
*American gangster and one-time boss of Murder Incorporated, killed 1957.*
Shot while he sat in a barber's chair…
Haircut!

### Anaxarchus
*Greek philosopher, pounded to death with pestles 4th century BC.*
Pound, pound the pouch containing Anaxarchus. You pound not Anaxarchus.

### Anonymous airline pilot
*Killed 1967.*
His 727 had collided with a light Cessna; a last radio message ran…
I love you Mary, love you so much…this is goodbye.

### Pilot of PSA Flight 182
*Killed 1978.*
He collided with a small plane over San Diego; the last radio message…
It's bad…we're hit man, we are hit. Tower, we're going down, this is PSA, this is it baby! Ma! I love you…

### Anonymous Scottish football fan
Dying on a stretcher after the Ibrox stadium disaster in which 78 people were crushed to death when the sides drew level at 1-1 in the 90th minute. Calling from the stretcher…
Who scored?

### Martha Beck
*American murderess, electrocuted 1951.*
What does it matter who is to blame? My story is a love story, but only those tortured with love can understand what I mean. I was pictured as a fat, unfeeling woman. True, I am fat, but if that is a crime, how many of my sex are guilty? I am not unfeeling, stupid or moronic. The prison and the death house have only strengthened my feeling for Raymond [Fernandez, her partner in crime] and in the history of the world how many crimes have been attributed to love? My last words and my last thoughts will be: Let him who is without sin cast the first stone.

### Saint Thomas à Becket
*English archbishop and martyr, assassinated 1170.*
The 'turbulent priest' was killed in his own church, Canterbury Cathedral, to satisfy his master King Henry II's anger.
I am prepared to die for Christ and His Church. I charge you in the name of the Almighty not to hurt any other person here, for none of them has been concerned in the late transactions. In vain you menace me. If all the swords in England were brandishing over my head, your terrors did not move me.

### Count Folke Bernadotte
*Swedish diplomat, pioneer of the United Nations, assassinated 1948.*
Acknowledging wishes of 'Good luck'…
I'll need it!

### Ambrose Bierce
*American writer, author of The Devil's Dictionary, vanished, presumed dead 1913.*
His last letter prior to his disappearance…
To be a gringo in Mexico. Ah, that is euthanasia.

### Rev. John Bewgill
*English clergyman, drowned.*
Oh dear, dear, dear me. We are dead.

### Donald Campbell
*British motorboat and automobile driver who emulated his father, Sir Malcolm Campbell, in setting world speed records on land and on water, died 1967.*
Campbell died on Coniston Water when his jet-propelled boat was wrecked and he was killed. This recording of his last run was not released until 1997…
Roger, Paul. I am starting return run now. Nose's up. Pitching a bit down here as I drive over my own wash…Tramping like mad, full power, tramping like hell here. I can't see much. The water's very dark…green… I can't see anything…Hello, the bow's up. I have gone…

### Gaspard de Coligny
*French Huguenot leader, killed 1572.*
He was the first victim of the St. Bartholomew's Day Massacre, in which 3,000 fellow-Protestants were killed by Parisian Catholics.
Young man, you ought to consider my age and infirmity, but you will not make my life any shorter.

*Facing page: Black Muslim Malcolm X, shot in 1966.*

### Michael Collins

*Irish patriot and hero of the Irish struggle for independence, killed 1921.*
His comment on signing the Irish Treaty, 1921; as he prophesied, he was assassinated soon after...

I am signing my death warrant.

### A. P. Dostie

*American anti-slavery campaigner, killed by a mob.*

I am dying. I die for the cause of liberty. Let the good work go on.

### Daniel Draper

*American Methodist minister, drowned in a shipwreck.*

We may all make the port of Heaven. Oh God, may those that are not converted be converted now, hundreds of them. In a few moments we must all appear before Our Great Judge. Let us prepare to meet Him. Rock of ages cleft for me...

### Anthony Joseph Drexel III

*American banker and philanthropist, shot himself 1893.*
He was demonstrating a new pistol...

Here's one you've never seen before...

### Jean E. Duranti

*President of the Toulouse Parliament during the reign of King Henri III, killed by a mob 1589.*
To his wife...

Adieu, my beloved; what God has granted me: life, goods, honours, I am presently to be stripped of. Death is the end, but not the punishment of life; innocent of the charges imputed me, my soul is to appear at the tribunal of the sovereign Judge. Trust in Him; He will always help you.

and to the mob...

Yes, here I am. But what crime have I committed, what wrong, O people, am I guilty of in your eyes? Lord God, receive my soul. Do not blame them for this wrong, for they know not what they do.

### Elizabeth

*Empress of Austria, stabbed 1898.*

Why, what has happened?

### Charles Frohman

*American theatrical manager, killed 1915.*
He was drowned when the S S *Lusitania* was torpedoed by a German submarine...

Why fear death? It is the most beautiful adventure in life.

### Margaret Fuller

*American critic, teacher and woman of letters, drowned in a shipwreck 1850.*
Her last words reflected her transcendentalist faith...

I see nothing but death before me; I shall never reach the shore.

### Evariste Galois

*French mathematician, a specialist in the 'higher algebra', killed in a duel 1832.*

Don't cry, I need all my courage to die at 20.

### James Garfield

*American President, assassinated 1881.*

The people my trust.

### Alexander Hamilton

*American politician, killed in a duel with fellow politician Aaron Burr 1804.*

Remember, my Eliza, you are a Christian.

### Prince Hirobumi Ito

*Japanese statesman who played a crucial role in the building of modern Japan, assassinated by a member of the Korean independence movement 1909.*
Told the identity of his assailant Ito regretted that he had killed the one Japanese leader who might have backed his aims...

The fellow is a fool.

### Elbert Hubbard

*American editor, publisher and author, drowned 1915.*
Going down on the S S *Lusitania*, torpedoed by a German submarine...

Well, Jack, they have got us. They are a damned sight worse than I thought they were.

### Anonymous sailor on S S *Jenny*

*Lost at sea 1823.*
On September 22, 1860 the whaling schooner Hope discovered the *Jenny*, trapped in the Antarctic ice. All the crew were dead, and preserved in the ice. Her last port of call had been Lima, Peru on January 17, 1823. The last entry in her log read...

May 4, 1823. No food for 71 days. I am the only one left alive.

### Pope John Paul I

*Italian pontiff, died 1978.*
The Pope died on the 34th day of his papacy; his last comment referred to news of the latest assassination by the radical Red Brigades; according to *Time*...

They kill each other, even the young people.

According to *Newsweek*...

Are those young people shooting each other again? Really, it is terrible.

### David Johnson

*American volcano expert, died 1980.*
Standing on the slopes of the exploding Mt. St. Helens, Washington...

Vancouver, Vancouver, this is it!

### Terry Kath

*Rock musician with the band Chicago, killed 1978.*
He was playing Russian roulette with a loaded pistol...

Don't worry, it's not loaded

### John Fitzgerald Kennedy

*American President, assassinated 1963.*
On insisting on visiting Dallas...

If someone is going to kill me, they will kill me.

### Jean Baptiste Kléber

*Napoleon's commander in Egypt, stabbed 1800.*

I have been assassinated.

### Leo X

*Italian pontiff, poisoned 1521.*
One of the most extravagant of the Renaissance popes, he raised the papacy to significant political power in Europe.

I have been murdered. No remedy can prevent my speedy death.

### Richard A. Loeb
*American child murderer, killed in prison 1936.*
Loeb, who with fellow rich boy Nathan Leopold had killed 14-year-old Robert Franks for an 'intellectual thrill', was slashed 56 times with a razor in the Joliet Prison shower by a fellow inmate whom he had tried to seduce...

I think I'm going to make it...

### Huey P. Long
*Governor of Louisiana, assassinated 1935.*

I wonder why he shot me.

### William McKinley
*American President, assassinated 1901.*

We are all going, we are all going, we are all going...oh dear!

### Malcolm X (Malcolm Little)
*Black Muslim leader, killed 1966.*
He was shot dead by three rival Muslims, who were attending one of his meetings at a Harlem ballroom.

Let's cool it brothers...

### John Marsh
*American explorer, killed 1868.*
To Mexican robbers...

Do you want to kill me?

### Father Basil Maturin
*Drowned 1915.*
He was lost on the S S Lusitania after handing over a little child as the last boat was lowered...

Find its mother.

### Paul Merritt
*British playwright, died 19th century.*
Visiting a murder scene he slipped on an orange peel and died, shortly after asking a policeman...

Constable, could you indicate the site on which the poor woman fell?

### Thomas Moleneux
*Constable of Chester, killed 14th century.*
Caught by his enemies refreshing himself in a river; his request was not granted...

Suffer me to come up and let me fight either with thee or some other, and die like a man.

### Nadir Shah
*Iranian ruler who created an empire that stretched from the Indus River to the Caucasus Mountains, assassinated 1747.*

Thou dog!

### Spencer Perceval
*British Prime Minister, assassinated 1812.*
Murder!

### David Graham Phillips
*American novelist and social reformer, shot by a paranoiac 1911.*

I could have won against two bullets but not against six.

### Francisco Pizarro
*Spanish explorer, the conqueror of Peru, assassinated 1541.*

Jesu!

### Virginia Rappe
*Hollywood starlet, killed 1921.*
A 'good time girl', she tangled fatally with Hollywood comic Fatty Arbuckle. His career languished, but her life ended.

I'm dying, I'm dying; he hurt me!

### Ernst Roehm
*Head of the Nazi S.A., killed 1934.*
Roehm and all the other S.A. leaders were killed on Hitler's orders in a mass purge.

If I am to be killed, let Adolf do it himself.

### Alexander Ruthven
*Lord Ruthven and Earl Gowrie, conspirator against James VI of Scotland, stabbed 1600.*

Alas! I had na wyte (blame) of it!

### Marie François Sadi-Carnot
*President of France, assassinated 1894.*
To those who were trying to save him...

I am very touched by your presence and I thank you for what you are doing for me.

### Louis Michel Lepelletier de Saint-Fargeau
*French politician, assassinated on the eve of the execution of Louis XVI...*

I am cold.

### Egon Schiele
*Austrian artist, died of Spanish influenza in the last days of World War I, 1918.*

The war is over and I must go.

### Galeazzo Sforza, Duke of Milan
*Assassinated 1476.*

Oh God!

### Joseph Smith
*Founder of the Mormon church, killed alongside his brother by a mob 1844.*

That's right brother Taylor, parry them off as well as you can.

### Carl 'Alfalfa' Switzer
*American actor, star of the 'Our Gang' film series, shot 1959.*
His stardom far behind him, he was drunk in a bar; so was the man who shot him...

I want that fifty bucks you owe me and I want it now!

Leon Trotsky: killed with an ice-axe in Mexico, 1940.

### Leon Trotsky
*Exiled leader of the Russian Revolution, assassinated 1940.*
On the way to hospital...

I feel here that this time they have succeeded.

### George Villiers, Duke of Buckingham
*English statesman and favourite of King James I of England, assassinated 1628.*

God's wounds, the villain has killed me!

### Cornelius de Witt
*Dutch official and brother of Johan de Witt, killed by a mob 1672.*
To the angry mob...

What do you want me to do? Where do you want me to go?

### Johan de Witt
*Ruler of the Netherlands and one of the leading European statesmen of his era, killed by a mob 1672.*
To the angry mob...

What are you doing? This is not what you wanted.

# GALLOWS HUMOUR

*Dying isn't the problem: what counts is the way you do it.*

## Agesistrata
*Mother of Agis of Sparta, hanged third century BC.*

I trust it may redound to the good of Sparta.

## John André
*British army officer who negotiated with the American general Benedict Arnold, executed as a spy 1780.*

I am reconciled to my death; but I detest the mode. It will be but a momentary pang. I pray you to bear witness that I met my fate like a brave man.

## Archibald Campbell, eighth Earl of Argyll
*Scottish political leader, beheaded for heresy 1661.*
*He was beheaded with the maiden (an early guillotine) at the cross of Edinburgh...*

I die not only a Protestant, but with a heart-hatred of Popery, Prelacy and all superstitions whatsoever. I am free from any accession by knowledge, contriving, counsel, or any other way to His late Majesty's death.

## Archibald Campbell, ninth Earl of Argyll
*Scottish royalist, beheaded for treason 1685.*
*His head was placed on a high pin of iron on the west end of the Tolbooth, Edinburgh...*

Lord Jesus, receive me into Thy glory.

## Major Henry Rowse Armstrong
*British solicitor and murderer, hanged 1922.*
*Armstrong was condemned for the murder of his wife, Katherine...*

I am coming Katie!

## Benedict Arnold
*A former American patriot who turned traitor and joined the British army, shot for treason 1801.*

Let me die in the old uniform in which I fought my battles for freedom. May God forgive me for putting on any other.

## Tom Austin
*British murderer, hanged.*

Nothing to say. Only there's a woman yonder with some curds and whey and I wish I could have a pennyworth before I am hanged, because I don't know when I'll see any again.

## Anthony Babington
*English leader of a Roman Catholic conspiracy against Queen Elizabeth I, beheaded 1586.*
*Babington had attempted to assassinate the Queen...*

The murder of the Queen has been represented to me as a deed lawful and meritorious. I die a firm Catholic.

## Jean Sylvain Bailly
*French astronomer and politician, first Mayor of Revolutionary Paris, guillotined 1793.*
*A bystander remarked that Bailly was trembling as he awaited his death on the scaffold.*

Only from cold, my friend.

## James Bainham
*British martyr, burnt 1532.*

Oh ye papists! Behold, ye look for miracles – here now ye may see a miracle. For in this fire I feel no more pain than if I were in a bed of down, but it is to me as a bed of roses.

## Vasco Nunez de Balboa
*Spanish explorer and conqueror of the Indies, beheaded 1519.*

This is false. I have always served my king loyally and sought to add to his domains.

*Facing page: Mata Hari, erotic dancer and spy, executed 1917.*

### Lienhardt Bardtmann

*German thief, hanged at Nuremberg 1586.*

I have been called 'the horseman' for a long time, but now I shall really learn how to ride. I fear, however, that I shall remain hanging with my head in the stirrup.

### Chevalier de la Barre

*French aristocrat, beheaded.*
*He died for mutilating a crucifix...*

I did not think they would put a young gentleman to death for such a trifle.

### Jeroboam Beauchamp

*British suicide, hanged after failed suicide attempt 1826.*
*Beauchamp and his wife were both due to die but she alone succeeded in their suicide pact. He went to the gallows clutching her dead body...*

Farewell, child of sorrow! For you have I lived, and for you I die!

### John 'Any Bird' Bell

*British murderer, hanged, aged 14, 1831.*
*The last under-16 to be executed in the UK. A five-thousand-strong crowd watched.*

All you people be warned by me.

### John Bellingham

*The assassin of Prime Minister Spencer Perceval, hanged 1812.*

I thank God for having enabled me to meet my fate with so much fortitude and resignation.

### Zulfikar Ali Bhutto

*Former President and Prime Minister of Pakistan, hanged 1979*

A poet and a revolutionary that is what I have been all these years. And that is how I shall remain until the last breath is gone from my body.

### Duc de Lanzon de Biron

*Former military commander with the French forces in the American Revolution, he backed its French successor but was guillotined during 'the Terror' of 1793.*
*Telling the executioner to wait...*

I beg a thousand pardons, my friend, but permit me to finish this last dozen of oysters.

*On the scaffold...*

I have been false to my God, my order and my King. I die full of faith and repentance.

### William Boyd, fourth Earl of Kilmarnock

*Jacobite supporter, beheaded on Tower Hill 1746.*
*Prior to making his last prayers, to the executioner.*

In two minutes I shall give the signal. [By dropping a handkerchief.]

### John Bradford

*British Protestant dissenter, burnt 1555.*

Be of good comfort, brother, for we shall have a merry supper with the Lord tonight. If there be any way to heaven on horseback or fiery chariots, thus is it. Strait is the way and narrow is the gate that leadeth to salvation, and few there be that find it.

### Elizabeth Branch and her daughter Mary

*British murderesses, executed for murder at Ivelchester, Somerset, 1740.*
*The pair murdered one Jane Buttwerworth, a servant girl, who they claimed had taken too long to fulfil an errand. A troop of soldiers kept the mob from lynching them...*

*Elizabeth:* You who are masters and mistresses of families, to you I speak in a more particular manner. Let me advise you never to harbour cruel, base and mean thoughts of your servants, as that they are your slaves and drudges, and that any sort of usage, be it ever so bad, is good enough for them. These, and such like, were the thoughts that made me use my servants as slaves, vagabonds and thieves; it was these that made me spurn at and despise them, and led me on from one degree of cruelty to another. Keep your passions within due bounds; let them not get the mastery over you, lest they bring you to this ignoble end. I am fully punished for all my severities; and it is true I did strike my maid, but not with a design to kill her, and so far I think the sentence about to be executed upon me is unjust; but the Lord forgive my prosecutors, and all those who have maliciously and falsely sworn against me. Another caution I would give to you who are parents; namely, to suppress in your children the first appearance of cruelty and barbarity. Nothing grieves me so much, under this shock, as that I have, by my example, and by my commands, made my daughter guilty with me of the same follies, cruelties and barbarities, and thereby have involved her in the same punishment with myself. I declare I had no design of killing the deceased, as the Lord is my judge, and before whom I must shortly appear. I beg of you to pray for me unto God that my sins may be forgiven me, and that I may be received to mercy.

*Mary:* Good people, pity my unhappy case, who, while young, was trained up in the paths of cruelty and barbarity; and let all present take warning by my unhappy end, so as to avoid the like crimes. You see I am cut off in the prime of life, in the midst of my days. Good people, pray for me!

### William Brereton

*British aristocrat, beheaded 1536.*
*He was executed with Henry VIII's second wife Anne Boleyn...*

I have deserved to die if it were one thousand deaths. But the cause wherefore I die, judge it not. But if you judge, judge the best.

### Matthias Brinsden

*An unemployed cloth-drawer, executed for murdering his wife 1722.*
*He read the following speech from the gallows.*

I was born of kind parents, who gave me learning: I went apprentice to a fine-drawer. I had often jars, which might increase a natural waspishness in my temper. I fell in love with Hannah, my last wife, and after much difficulty won her, she having five suitors courting her at the same time. We had ten children (half of them dead), and I believe we loved each other dearly; but often quarrelled and fought. Pray, good people, mind, I had no malice against her, nor thought to kill her two minutes before the deed; but I designed only to make her obey me thoroughly, which the Scripture says all wives should do. This I thought I had done when I cut her skull on Monday, but she was the same again by Tuesday. Good people, I request you to observe, that the world has spitefully given out, that I carnally and incestuously lay with my eldest daughter. I here solemnly declare, as I am entering into the presence of God, I never knew whether she was a man or a woman since she was a babe. I have often taken her in my arms, often kissed her, sometimes given her a cake or a pie, when she did any particular service beyond what came to her share; but never lay with her, or carnally knew her, much less had a child by her. But when a man is in calamities, and is hated like me, the women will make surmises be certainties. Good Christians, pray for me! I deserve death: I am willing to die; for, though my sins are great, God's mercies are greater.

## John Brown
*American abolitionist, the inspiration of the song 'John Brown's Body', hanged 1859.*
To his executioner...
Don't keep me waiting longer than necessary.

## James Caldclough
*British highwayman, hanged 1739.*
His gallows speech...
I humbly beg that all you young men whom I leave behind me would take warning in time, and avoid bad houses as well as bad company. Remember my dying words, lest some of you come to the same end, which I pray God you never may. What I am now going to suffer is the just punishment for my crimes; for, although I did not commit murder, yet I look upon myself as equally guilty, as the poor gentleman must have died had he not met with assistance. Were I able to make satisfaction to those whom I have wronged, I would do it; but, alas! I cannot, and therefore I pray that they will forgive me. I hope my life will be at least some satisfaction, as I have nothing besides to give: and, as I die in charity with all mankind, may the Lord Jesus receive my soul.

## Dr. Archibald Cameron
*Scottish Jacobite rebel, hanged, drawn and quartered 1753.*
Cameron had helped conceal Bonnie Prince Charlie (Charles Stuart) after the defeat at Culloden and was executed for high treason. He showed considerable courage throughout his ordeal. On arriving at Tyburn he greeted the clergyman, offering him help in mounting the gallows (despite having his own hands tied), saying...
So, are you come? This is a glorious day to me 'tis my new birth-day!...there are more witnesses at this birth than at my first. The clergyman then asked 'how he felt himself.' Thank God, I am very well, but a little fatigued with my journey; but, blessed be God! I am now come to the end of it. [He continued...] Sir, you see a fellow-subject just going to pay his token for doing my duty, according to my conscience. I freely forgive all my enemies, and those who have been instrumental in taking away my life. I thank God I die in charity with all men. As to my religion, I die a steadfast, though unworthy, member of that Church in which I have always lived, the Church of England; in whose communion I hope, through the merits of my blessed Saviour for forgiveness of my sins, for which I am heartily sorry. The custom of delivering something in writing, on such occasions as this, I should willingly have complied with, had it not been put out of my power, being denied the use of pen, ink and paper, except in the presence of some of my keepers. But what I intend my country should be informed of, with regard to my dying sentiments, I have, by means of a blunt pencil, endeavoured to set down on some slips of paper, as I came by them, in as legible characters as I was able; and these I have left in the hands of my wife, charging her, on her duty to her dying husband, to transmit, with all convenient speed, a faithful transcript of them to you; and I am confident she will faithfully discharge the trust. I have now done with this world, and am ready to leave it.
As the divine was going down from the cart he had nearly missed the steps and Cameron called out...
Take care how you go: I think you don't know this way as well as I do.

## Bart Caritativo
*American criminal, gassed 1958.*
A houseboy in California, he murdered his employers for their money...
God bless you all, God bless you all.

## Thomas Cartwright
*The head and most learned of that sect of dissenters then called Puritans, died 1603.*
After recanting his Puritanism he declared...
I wish I could begin life again so as to testify to the world the dislike I have of my former ways.

## Beatrice Cenci
*Italian noblewoman, beheaded for the assassination of her sadistic father 1599.*
Beatrice received widespread public sympathy; her story inspired poems, dramas and novels, including *The Cenci* by Percy Bysshe Shelley.
Jesus! Mary!

## Henri de Talleyrand, Comte de Chalais
*Conspirator against Louis XIII, beheaded 1626.*
To his executioner...
Do not keep me in suspense.

## Gerald Chapman
*British swindler, conman and murderer, hanged 1926.*
Chapman was a real-life Raffles until he blundered and killed a policeman...
Death itself isn't dreadful, but hanging seems an awkward way of entering the adventure.

## André Chénier
*French poet and political journalist, guillotined 1794.*
Considered the greatest French poet of his era, he was still composing verses on the scaffold...
Le sommeil du tombeau pressera ma paupière. [The sleep of the tomb will press on my eyelid.]

## Cherokee Bill
*American outlaw, hanged 1896.*
The quicker this thing's over the better.
Asked if he had anything to say...
No. I came here to die. Not make a speech.

## Jacques Clement
*French agitator, executed for treason 1589.*
Clement, who attempted the murder of Henri III of France, was asked 'Dare you look an angry King in the face?'.
Yes, yes, yes! And kill him too!

## 'Anacharsis' Clootz (Jean-Baptiste du Val de Grace, Baron de Clootz, 'Orator of the Human Race')
*French revolutionary, guillotined 1794.*
In the name of the earth, in the name of humanity, do not confuse me with your memory of these common fellows. No patched up peace!

*Cherokee Bill, hanged in 1896.*

### William Collingbourn

*Hanged, drawn and quartered for libelling King Richard III, fifteenth century.*
Collingbourn allegedly muttered this complaint as the executioner tore out his heart and entrails; the whole execution took an hour…

Lord Jesus, yet more trouble.

### Miles Corbet

*British lawyer and regicide, executed 1662.*
He was one of those who signed the death warrant of Charles I.

When I was first called to serve in parliament I had an estate; I spent it in the service of the parliament. I never bought any king's or bishop's lands; I thought I had enough, at least I was content with it; that I might serve God and my country was that I aimed at….For this for which we are to die I was no contriver of it; when the business was motioned I spoke against it, but being passed in parliament I thought it my duty to obey. I never did sit in that which was called the high court of justice but once.

### Charlotte Corday

*French assassin of Marat, guillotined 1793. Gazing at the guillotine…*

I have a right to be curious, I have never seen one before. It is the toilette of death, but it leads to immortality.

### William Corder

*British murderer, hanged 1828.*
Corder had killed Maria Marten, a murder that fascinated all of England.

I am justly sentenced and may God forgive me.

### Benjamin Courvoisier

*French servant, hanged for murder 1810.*
Valet to Lord William Russell, he killed his master. He revealed his technique on the gallows.

I actually committed the crime in the nude. Afterwards I had only to wash myself at the sink.

### Thomas Cranmer

*Archbishop of Canterbury and one of the architects of the English Reformation, burnt 1556.*
Cranmer recanted his Protestant views, then repudiated his statement. At the stake he tortured himself physically and mentally with this moment of weakness, plunging his right hand deep into the flames…

This hand having sinned in signing the writing must be the first to suffer punishment. This hand hath offended.

### Neil Cream

*British murderer, hanged 1929.*
Did Cream try to confess to the 'Jack the Ripper' killings?…

I'm Jack…

### Hawley Harvey Crippen

*American dentist who poisoned his wife in London, hanged 1910.*

In this farewell letter to the world, written as I face eternity, I say that Ethel le Neve loved me as few women love men and that her innocence of any crime, save that of yielding to the dictates of her heart, is absolute. My last prayer will be that God will protect her and keep her safe from harm and allow her to join me in eternity.

### Thomas Cromwell, Earl of Essex

*Secretary to Henry VIII, beheaded 1540.*
He was executed after falling out with his master.

The devil is ready to seduce us and I have been seduced, but bear me witness that I die in the Catholic faith of the Holy Church and I heartily desire you to pray for the King's grace, that he may long live with you in health and prosperity, and after him that his son Edward, that goodly imp, may long reign over you, and once again I desire you to pray for me, that as long as life remaineth in this flesh I wander nothing in my faith.

### Bood Crumpton

*American outlaw, hanged 1875.*

Men, the next time you lift a glass of whisky, I want you to look into the bottom of the glass and see if there isn't a hangman's noose in it, like the one here.

### Georges Danton

*Leading figure in the French Revolution, guillotined 1794.*

Show my head to the people…it is worth it.

### Colonel Edward Marcus Despard

*British army officer, hanged and beheaded for treason and conspiracy 1803.*
He delivered a long address on the scaffold in front of the gaol, which was loudly cheered…

Fellow citizens, I come here as you see after having served my country faithfully, honourably and usefully for thirty years and upwards to suffer death upon a scaffold for a crime of which I protest I am not guilty. His Majesty's ministers avail themselves of a legal pretext to destroy a man because he has been a friend to truth, to liberty and to justice, because he has been a friend to the poor and oppressed…I have little more to add except to wish you all health, happiness and freedom which I

have endeavoured, as far as was in my power, to procure for you and mankind in general.

### Robert Devereux, second Earl of Essex

*English soldier and courtier, beheaded 1601.*

In humility and obedience to Thy commandment, in obedience to Thy ordinance and to Thy good pleasure, Oh God, I prostrate myself to my deserved punishment. Lord be merciful to Thy prostrate servant. Lord, into Thy hands I commend my spirit.

### Sir Everard Digby

*British nobleman, hanged drawn and quartered 1605.*
As the executioner exposed Digby's heart with the cry of 'Here is the heart of a traitor', his victim replied…

Thou liest!

### Rev. William Dodd

*British forger, hanged 1777.*
Dodd persuaded the executioner to drag on his legs to speed up the process of strangulation…

Come to me.

### Etienne Dolet

*French heretic, burnt 1546.*

This is not doleful for Dolet, but it means dole [sorrow] for the people.

### James Douglas, fourth Earl of Morton

*Scottish aristocrat, died 1581.*
Supposedly involved in the plot to murder Mary Queen of Scots' husband, Lord Darnley, he was executed on the maiden, the prototype guillotine that he had imported into Scotland from its original town of use, Halifax.

I am sure the king shall lose a good servant this day.

### Jean-François Ducos

*French aristocrat, guillotined 1793.*
To the executioner who was cutting off his hair…

I hope that the edge of your guillotine is sharper than your scissors.

### John Dudley, Duke of Northumberland

*Beheaded for treason 1553.*
He had sponsored Lady Jane Grey as Queen in an attempt to usurp power from Mary, the proper successor to Edward VI.

I have deserved one thousand deaths.

### Theo Durrant

*American sex killer, hanged 1898.*
An ostentatiously pious Sunday school superintendent and church librarian, Durrant's firmest faith was in the joy of necrophilia...

Don't put that rope on, boy, till I talk.

### Arthur Elphinstone, sixth Baron Balmerino

*Jacobite, executed on Tower Hill 1746.*

O Lord! reward my friends, forgive my foes, bless King James and receive my soul!

### Robert Emmett

*Irish patriot, hanged 1803.*

Not...

### George Engel

*American radical and one of the Haymarket Rioters in Chicago, hanged 1881.*

Hurray for Anarchy!

### Laurence, Earl Ferrers

*British aristocrat and murderer, hanged 1760.*
Ferrers, an aristocratic psychopath, who should have been confined and not killed, was the only nobleman to suffer hanging rather than the usual beheading. He did, however, demand and receive a silken rope.

I freely forgive you as I do all mankind and hope myself to be forgiven.

### Albert Fish

*American child molester, murderer and cannibal, electrocuted 1936.*
Fish butchered scores of youngsters. He fixed his own electrodes in the death cell.

What a thrill that will be if I have to die in the electric chair. It will be the supreme thrill. The only one I haven't tried.

### George Robert Fitzgerald

*Irish rake, hanged for murder 1786.*
The rope broke for the first time; later with a new rope and a new hangman it worked.

You see, I am once more among you unexpectedly!

### Subrius Flavus

*Conspirator against Emperor Nero, beheaded 67 AD.*
Told to offer his neck resolutely...

I wish that your stroke may be as resolute.

### Francis Fonton

*British forger, hanged.*
Declared on the scaffold that it was best for God to lead him home...

By a way I know not.

### Sam Fooy

*American murderer, hanged 1875.*
Fooy told the assembled press of a dream he had on the night before his execution.

When the drop came I felt no pain. I just fell asleep and woke up in the beautiful garden. It had running waters and stars were dancing on the waves.

### Hans Forstner

*German horse thief, hanged 1598.*
To the assistant executioner...

There's a pair of shoes for you and five florins besides, if you'll exchange with me.

### Henry Garnett

*British revolutionary, executed for his part in the 1605 Gunpowder Plot, 1606.*
Wonderful accounts were circulated about a miraculous straw on which a drop of Garnett's blood had fallen...on one of the husks a portrait of him surrounded with rays of glory had apparently been formed. Hundreds, it was alleged, were converted to Catholicism by the mere sight of Garnett's straw.

Imprint the cross on my heart Mary, mother of grace.

### Sir John Gates

*Beheaded for treason 1553.*
He had been part of Northumberland's plot to put Lady Jane Grey on the throne instead of Queen Mary. To his executioner...

I forgive thee with all my heart. I will see how meet the block is for my neck. I pray thee strike not yet, for I have a few prayers to say, and that done, strike on God's name, good leave have thou.

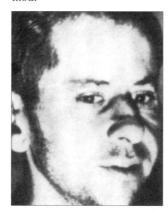

### Harvey Glatman

*American rapist and murderer, gassed 1959.*
Glatman was a rope fetishist who tied up his victims first.

It's better this way. I knew this is the way it would be.

### Barbara Graham

*American murderess, gassed 1955.*
Graham killed for money; she asked for a blindfold at San Quentin to avoid looking at the obligatory witnesses.

I don't want to have to look at people.

### Urbain Grandier

*French witchfinder-general, executed for causing religious mania in Loudun, burnt 1634.*

My God, by the light I wait for you My God, forgive my enemies.

### Judd Gray

*American murderer, electrocuted 1928.*
Gray had helped his lover Ruth Snyder do away with her husband...

I am ready to go. I have nothing to fear.

### Lady Jane Grey

*Queen of England for ten days, beheaded for treason 1554.*

I die in peace with all people. God save the Queen.

### Charles Julius Guiteau

*Assassin of US President Garfield, hanged 1882.*

Glory Hallelujah! I'm going to the lordy!

### James Hackman

*British murderer; he killed Martha Ray, mistress of Lord Sandwich, because she refused to marry him, hanged 1779.*
This note was scribbled to a friend...

Farewell for ever in this world. I die a sincere Christian and penitent, and everything I hope that you can wish me. Would it prevent my example's having any bad effect if the world should know how I abhor my former ideas of suicide. My crime... will be the best judge. Of her fame I charge you to be careful. My poor sister will...

### John Hadfield ('The Keswick Imposter')

*British criminal, hanged 1803.*
Was his reference to the gallows, or the heavens beyond?

Oh happy sight! I see it with pleasure!

### Gordon Faucet Hamby (aka John H. Allen)

*American criminal, executed in Sing Sing 1920.*
Following a meal of lobster salad...

I want to thank you for the wonderful treatment I have

*Albert Fish: do-it-yourself electrocution.*

*Barbara Graham: gassed in 1955 at St. Quentin.*

received here. You have all been very kind. Nobody ever died in front of John H. Allen's guns unless he had a chance. I don't wish to appear in the light of a moralist, but you can tell all young men from me not to start ever doing wrong for once you start a career of crime you can never stop.

## Jacob S. Harden
*Minister who murdered his wife, hanged.*

God have mercy upon me! Lord Jesus save me in heaven.

## General Thomas Harrison
*British regicide, hanged, drawn and quartered following the Restoration of Charles II, 1660.*

He hath covered my head many times in the day of battle. By God I have leaped over a wall, by God I have run through a troop, and by my God I will go through this death and He will make it easy for me. Now into Thy hands, Oh Lord Jesus, I commit my spirit.

## Neville Heath
*British murderer, hanged 1946.*
*Asking for a last whisky...*

Ah… you might make that a double.

## Richard Eugene Hickok
*American murderer, hanged 1965.*
*One of the two youths who killed the Mid-West Clutter family for their non-existent fortune. His exploits were immortalized by Truman Capote's book In Cold Blood...*

I just want to say I hold no hard feelings. You people are sending me to a better world than this ever was.

## John Holloway
*British murderer, hanged 1807.*
*Forty thousand Londoners flocked to Holloway's execution, dozens died in the stampede...*

I am innocent, innocent by God! Innocent, innocent, innocent! Gentlemen, no verdict, no verdict, no verdict! Gentlemen! Innocent, innocent, innocent!

## John Hooper
*Bishop of Gloucester and Worcester, burnt for heresy 1555.*

If you love my soul, away with it!

## Father John Houghton
*Prior of the London Charterhouse, hanged, drawn and quartered 1535.*
*Houghton refused to accept Henry VIII's rejection of Catholicism and died for his beliefs. As the executioner prepared to tear out his heart...*

Good Jesu, what will you do with my heart?

## William Howard, Viscount Stafford
*British Catholic nobleman, beheaded 1680.*
*He was convicted for his role in the Titus Oates conspiracy. To the executioner...*

I do forgive you. This block will be my pillow and I shall repose there without pain, grief or fear.

## Rev. Thomas Hunter
*British clergyman, executed for murder 1700.*

There is no God. I do not believe there is any. Or if there is, I hold him in defiance.

## John Huss
*German Protestant reformer, burnt 1415.*
*Watching a peasant add more fuel to the fire...*

Oh sancta simplicitas!
(O blessed simplicity!)

## Amy Hutchinson
*British murderess, strangled then burnt to death for killing her violent husband 1750. She had given him arsenic and ran off with a lover (who had in fact jilted her earlier and led her to make her unhappy marriage to a wife-beater). She died at the same time as a wife-murderer, John Vicars, who was hanged. He asked to watch her go, which he was allowed, then helped the executioner fix the knot around his neck and leapt voluntarily from the cart.*

All the good I can now do, after my repentance and abhorrence of my abominable crime, and prayers to God is, First, To warn all young women to acquaint their friends when any addresses are made to them; and, above all, if any base or immodest man dare to insult you with any thing shocking to chaste ears. Secondly, That they should never leave the person they are engaged to in a pet, nor wed another, to whom they are indifferent, in spite; for, if they come together without affection, the smallest matter will separate them. Thirdly, That, being married, all persons should mutually love, forgive, and forbear: and afford no room for busy meddlers to raise and foment jealousy between two who should be one.

## James Ings
*Member of the Cato Street Conspiracy to assassinate all the members of the British Cabinet, hanged 1820.*
*Ings addressed a fellow prisoner, William Davidson...*

Come, give us your hand, good-bye. Come, my old cock o' wax, keep up your spirits. It will all be over soon. Oh give me death or give me liberty!
[To which fellow prisoner John Thomas Brunt responded…]
Ay, to be sure. It is better to die free than live like slaves.
*Ings then added...*

Mind, I die an enemy to all tyrants. Mind, and put that down. [Looking at coffins] I will turn my back on death. These coffins are for us, I suppose.
*Then, to the executioner, as he put on the blindfold...*

Mind you do it well. Pull; it tidy.
*Finally, to the regular Tyburn vicar, Rev. Mr Cotton...*

I hope you'll give me a good character, won't you, Mr Cotton.

## Kaliayev
*Russian anarchist revolutionary, hanged 1905.*
*He refused a crucifix on the scaffold...*

I already told you that I am finished with life and am prepared for death. I consider my death as the supreme protest against a world of blood and tears.

## Hermann von Katte
*German revolutionary, executed 1730.*
*Von Katte was charged with conspiracy with Frederick the Great when the Emperor was still the Crown Prince...*

Death is sweet for a Prince I love so well.

## Ned Kelly
*The best-known of Australia's bushrangers, hanged 1880.*

Such is life.

## Hans Kolbein
*German killer and thief, broken on the wheel at Nuremberg 1598.*
*To the ministering priest...*

Be silent. I have heard it all before. I don't want to hear it all now. It gives me a headache.

## Kusakabe
*Japanese revolutionary, executed.*
*He repeated this Chinese verse on his way to execution...*

It is better to be a crystal and be broken,
Than to remain perfect like a tile upon the housetop.

## John Lambert (John Nicholson)
*British martyr, burnt 1538.*
*Lambert debated for five hours with five bishops and the King. Exhausted, his defence finally petered out.*

None but Christ, none but Christ.

## Henri Landru
*The French 'Bluebeard', guillotined 1922.*
*Landru had done away with a number of hapless 'wives'...*

Ah well, it is not the first time that an innocent man has been condemned.

*Facing page: Armour worn by Ned Kelly.*

Tho: Moor L. ªChancelour.

*Thomas More, beheaded by Henry VIII in 1535.*

### Hugh Latimer
*Protestant martyr, burnt 1555.*
He comforted his fellow-sufferers, Cranmer and Ridley...
Be of good comfort, Master Ridley, and play the man. We shall this day light such a candle, by God's grace, in England, as I trust shall never be put out.

### William Laud
*Archbishop of Canterbury and supporter of King Charles I, beheaded 1645.*
Lord, receive my soul.

### John Doyle Lee
*'Official assassin' of the Mormon Church, shot 1857.*
Lee and a gang of other renegades used their membership of the Church to prey on wagon trains. He was killed for massacring the 123 adults in one such train, sparing only their seventeen children. A last letter prior to his execution...
I hope to meet the bullets with manly courage. I declare my innocence. I have done nothing wrong. I have a reward in heaven and my conscience does not accuse me. This to me is a consolation. I place more value upon it than I would upon an eulogy without merit. If my work be finished on earth, I ask God in heaven, in the name of his son Jesus Christ, to receive my spirit and to allow me to meet my loved ones who have gone beyond the veil...with whom I parted in sorrow but shall meet in joy. I bid you farewell. Be true to each other. Live faithful before God that we may meet in the mansion God has prepared for his servants. Remember the last words of your most true friend on earth, and let them sink into your aching hearts. I leave my blessing with you. Farewell.

### Captain Lightfoot (Michael Martin)
*American highwayman, hanged 1822.*
To the hangman, asking the executioner when he wanted to give the order for the horses to pull the cart from beneath him...
When shall I drop the handkerchief?
Whenever you're ready.

### William P. Longley
*American gunfighter and killer, hanged 1871.*
Longley was obsessed with the mythical Old South. He killed in the name of the defunct Confederacy...
I deserve this fate. It is a debt I owe for a wild and reckless life. So long, everybody!

### Alvaro de Luna
*Favourite of King John II of Castile, beheaded 1453.*
After being shown the post and hook which would display his remains.
It does not matter what they do with my body and head after my death.

### Maccail
*Scottish covenanter, tortured to death 1668.*
Farewell moon and stars, farewell world and time, farewell weak and frail body. Welcome eternity, welcome angels and saints, welcome saviour of the world, welcome God, the judge of all.

### James Macpherson ('The Banff freebooter')
*Scottish criminal, hanged 1700.*
Macpherson composed his own funeral oration which he sang accompanying himself on the violin. He offered the instrument as a keepsake to any one in the crowd who would think well of him, and, receiving no offers, broke it and threw it into the open grave awaiting him.
I've spent my time in rioting
Debauched my health and strength.
I squandered fast as pillage came,
And fell to shame at length.
But dauntingly and wantonly and rantingly I'll go
I'll play the tune and dance it round
Beneath the gallows tree.

### Marc, Chevalier de Montréal
*French aristocrat, beheaded.*
He reached up to make sure that the executioner would put the axe through the right part of his neck...
You are not putting it in the right place.

### Marcus of Arethusa
*Marcus was covered in honey, hoisted up in a basket and stung to death by bees.*
How I am advanced, despising you that are upon the earth.

### Mata Hari (Margarete Zelle)
*Dutch dancer and spy, shot 1917.*
The quintessential glamorous spy, Mata Hari went smiling to her death.
Thank you, monsieur.

### Richard Mills
*British smuggler, hanged for murder with six fellow gang members, including his own son,1749.*
A small man, Mills had to stand on tiptoes to get his head through the noose...
I hope I shall not die by inches.

## James Scott, Duke of Monmouth

*British aristocrat, beheaded for treason 1685.*

Prithee, let me feel the axe. I fear it is not sharp enough. Do not hack me as you did my Lord Russell.

## Duc Henri II de Montmorency

*French nobleman, beheaded 1632. Cardinal Richelieu had the Duke killed for rebellion against him...*

Give a good stroke. Sweet Saviour, receive my soul.

## James Graham, Earl of Montrose

*Supporter of Charles I, hanged 1650.*

May God have mercy upon this afflicted Kingdom.

## Sir Thomas More

*British statesman, beheaded 1535. More refused to sacrifice his beliefs, despite Henry VIII's laws...*

Pluck up thy spirits man, and do not be afraid to do thine office. My neck is very short, take heed therefore, do not strike awry, for saving of thine honesty.

## Fra Moriale

*Italian adventurer, hanged. He shouted to the crowds...*

I die for your poverty and my wealth!

## Herman Mudgett

*America's most prolific nineteenth-century murderer, hanged 1896. Mudgett was executed for the killings of at least two hundred women. He lured them to their deaths by promising marriage and then obtaining their insurance payments. He pleaded innocence until the end.*

As God is my witness I was responsible for the death of only two women. I didn't kill Minnie Williams. Minnie killed her...!

## Musquito

*Australian bushranger, known as 'The Black Napoleon'. Hanged 1825.*

Hanging no good for Blackfellow. All right for Whitefellow, they used to it.

## Benito Mussolini

*Duce of Italy, shot by partisans 1945.*

But, but, Mr. Colonel...

## Earle Nelson

*American mass murderer, hanged 1927. A sex killer with a Bible in his hand, Nelson oozed sanctimonious religiosity as he raped and strangled his way across America...*

I am innocent. I stand innocent before God and man. I forgive those who have wronged me and I ask forgiveness of those whom I have injured. God have mercy!

## Marshal Ney

*French soldier, shot 1815.*

Don't you know, sir, that a soldier does not fear death? I protest against my condemnation. My honour...

## John Noyes

*British Protestant martyr, burnt 1555.*

We shall not lose our lives in this fire, but change them for a better. And for coals have pearls.

## Girolamo Olgiatti

*Assassin of Galeazzo Sforza, ruler of Milan, executed 1476.*

My death is untimely, my fame eternal, the memory of the deed will last for aye.

## Duc d'Orléans

*French aristocrat, executed 1793. The executioner tried to take off the Duke's boots...*

You can do that more easily to my dead body. Come – be quick!

## Johann Philipp Palm

*German book dealer, shot 1806. Palm issued a pamphlet attacking Napoleon. The Emperor had him shot. He wrote to his family.*

To you, my dear wife, I say a thousand thanks for your love. Trust in God and do not forget me. I have nothing in the world to say but farewell, you and the children. God bless you and them. My regards to Mr. and Mrs. Schwagerin and all my friends, whom I thank for their goodness and love. Once more, farewell. Yonder, we shall meet again. Your husband and children's father, Johann Palm. Braunau, in prison, August 26, 1806, a half-hour before my death.

## William Palmer ('The Rugeley poisoner')

*British murderer, hanged 1856. Stepping onto the gallows...*

Are you sure it's safe?

## Carl Panzram

*American mass murderer, hanged 1930. In a letter to the Society for the Abolition of Capital Punishment, who were campaigning to save him from death...*

I do not believe that being hanged by the neck until dead is a barbaric or inhuman punishment. I look forward to that as a real pleasure and a big relief to me...when my last hour comes I will dance out of my dungeon and onto the scaffold with a smile on my face and happiness in my heart... the only thanks that you and your kind will ever get from me for your efforts is that I wish you all had one neck and I had my hands on it.

*Asked on the gallows if he had anything to say, Panzram, who admitted to his killings and resolutely refused any form of repentance, replied...*

Yes. Hurry it up, you Hoosier bastard! I could hang a dozen men while you're fooling around.

## Albert Parsons

*American radical and one of the Haymarket Rioters in Chicago, hanged 1881.*

Let the voice of the people be heard!

## Charles Peace

*British criminal, executed for murder 1879. He wrote his own memorial card...*

In memory of Charles Peace who was executed in Armley Prison February 25, 1879. Aged 47. For what I done but never intended.

*To a clergyman on the scaffold...*

*Robespierre, architect of 'the Terror', guillotined in 1794.*

My greatest mistake, sir, is this. In all my career I have used ball cartridge. I ought to have used blank.

### Anthony Peerson
*British martyr, burnt 1555.*
He pulled the straw around his legs and put a bundle of it on his head...

This is God's hat. Now I am dressed like a true soldier of Christ, by whose merits only I trust to enter into His joy.

### Colonel John Penruodock
*Supporter of Charles I, beheaded 1655.*
Kissing the axe...

I am like to have a sharp passage of it, but my Saviour hath sweetened it unto me. If I would have been so unworthy as others have been, I suppose I might by a lie have saved my life, which I scorn to purchase at such a rate. I defy temptations and them that gave them me. Glory be to God on high, on earth peace, good will towards men, and the Lord have mercy upon my poor soul. Amen.

### Pavel Ivanovich Pestel
*Russian military officer and a main leader of the Decembrist revolutionaries, hanged 1826.*
The first attempt to hang him broke the rope.

Stupid country, where they do not even know how to hang.

### Hugh Peters
*British regicide, hanged, drawn and quartered in 1660 for aiding in the execution of Charles I.*
The executioner was mocking him as he waited by the scaffold.

Friend, you do not well to trample on a dying man.

### Thomas Phipps
*British forger, executed 1789.*
The father, aged 48, died alongside his son, aged 20.

Tommy, thou hast brought me to this shameful end, but I freely forgive thee.
Then, at the bottom of the gallows ladder...
You have brought me hither, do you lead the way?
His son then went up the steps first.

### Phocion
*Athenian statesman, executed 117 BC.*
No resentment.

### John Plackett
*British criminal, hanged for murder 1762.*
The first robbery I committed was on a young woman on the long causeway, Islington, about sixteen years ago; the second was on a man in Jenning's Field, in the same town; the next was stealing a copper from Mr. Beazley, in St. John's Street, for which I was transported for seven years; but I staid in the plantations fourteen. After my return to England I stole a silver watch and a gown from my uncle's house; and the last was the fatal robbery of the Danish young gentleman [his hanging offence, actually one Fayne, a Norwegian merchant], for which I most deservedly suffer. All the above robberies I committed by myself, and no person was ever concerned with me. This I solemnly declare, as I expect mercy from God, before whom I am now going to appear.

### General Alfredo Quijano
*Mexican revolutionary, shot 1927. Asking the firing squad to move closer...*
Still a little closer.
Goodbye, goodbye.

### Sir Walter Ralegh
*Elizabethan adventurer, beheaded 1618.*
As he laid his head on the block someone objected that it ought to be towards the east. He replied...
What matter how the head lie, so the heart be right?
Then added...
'Tis a sharp remedy, but a sure one for all ills.

### François Ravaillac
*Assassin of Henri IV of France, tortured to death 1510.*
Ravaillac swore, despite the tortures, that he was the sole assassin, thus entitling himself to the solace of religion, in the name of which he was subjected to the rack, the pincers, boiling oil and being torn asunder by four horses.

I am a sinner, I know no more than I have declared, by the oath I have taken, and by the truth I owe to God and the court: all I have said was to the little Franciscan, which I have already declared I never mentioned my design in confession or in any other way: I never spoke of it to the visitor of Angoulême, nor revealed it in confession in this city. I beseech the court not to drive my soul to despair. My God, receive this penance as an expiation for the greater crimes I have committed in this world: Oh God! accept these torments in satisfaction for my sins. By the faith I owe to God, I know no more than what I have declared. Oh! do not drive my soul to despair.

### Nicholas Ridley
*British Protestant martyr, burnt for heresy 1555.*
The wood piled around him was too green to burn well...
Let the fire come unto me! I cannot burn! Lord have mercy upon me!

### Maximilien de Robespierre
*French revolutionary leader and architect of 'the Terror', guillotined 1794.*
Thank you, sir.

### James W. Rodgers
*American criminal, shot 1960.*
Asked whether he had a final request...
Why yes – a bulletproof vest!

### Rev. John Rogers
*Burnt for heresy 1555.*
He was the first Protestant martyr to suffer under Queen Mary's pro-Catholic purge.
Lord, receive my soul.

### Jeanne-Marie Roland de la Platière
*French Jacobin leader, guillotined 1793.*
To an old man, waiting with her on the scaffold and terrified of his own death...
Go first. At least I can spare you the pain of seeing my blood flow.

### Ethel Rosenberg
*American housewife, convicted of spying with her husband Julius Rosenberg, and executed in the gas chamber in 1953.*
We are the first victims of American fascism.

### Julius Rosenberg
*American electrical engineer, executed in the gas chamber as a spy, 1953.*
In his petition to President Eisenhower...
We are innocent. That is the whole truth. To forsake this truth is to pay too high a price even for the priceless gift of life. For life thus purchased we could not live out in dignity.

## Bartolomeo Sacco
*American radical, hanged for alleged anarchism 1927.*

If it had not been for these things I might live out my life talking at street corners to scorning men. I might have died unmarked, a failure, unknown. Now we are not failures. This is our career and our triumph. Never in our full life could we hope to do such work for tolerance, for justice and for man, and for man's understanding of man.

## Caserio Santo-Ironimo
*Assassin of French Prime Minister Sadi-Carnot, guillotined 1894.*

Courage comrades! Long live anarchy!

## Girolamo Savonarola
*Florentine administrator, hanged and burnt 1498.*
The great censor and scourge of artistic heresy in others was himself hanged and burnt for heresy.

The Lord hath suffered so much for me.

## Lieutenant Schmidt
*Shot as a spy.*

My death will consummate everything and my cause, crowned by my death, will emerge irreproachable and perfect.

## Michael Servetus
*Spanish theologian and physician, burnt as a heretic 1553.*
The green wood burnt too slowly...

Jesus, son of the eternal God have mercy on me.

## Jack Sheppard
*British thief and adventurer, hanged 1724.*

Of two virtues have I ever cherished an honest pride. Never have I stooped to friendship with Jonathan Wild or with any of his detestable thief-takers, and though an undutiful son, I never damned my mother's eyes.

## Christopher Slaughterwood
*British murderer, executed 1700.*
He handed this letter to the witnessing sheriff...

Being brought here to die, according to the sentence passed upon me at the Queen's bench bar, for a crime of which I am wholly innocent, I thought myself obliged to let the world know, that...I know nothing of the death of Jane Young, nor how she came by her death, directly or indirectly, though some have been pleased to cast reflections on my aunt. However, I freely forgive all my enemies, and pray to God to give them a due sense of their errors, and in his due time to bring the truth to light. In the mean time, I beg every one to forbear reflecting on my dear mother, or any of my relations, for my unjust and unhappy fall, since what I have here set down is truth, and nothing but the truth, as I expect salvation at the hands of Almighty God; but I am heartily sorry that I should be the cause of persuading her to leave her dame, which is all that troubles me.

## Perry Edward Smith
*American murderer, hanged 1965.*
With Eugene Hickok, Smith killed the mid-Western Clutter family for no apparent reason other than their not having the cache of money he had been informed they did...

I think it's a hell of a thing to take a life in this manner. I don't believe in capital punishment, morally or legally. Maybe I had something to contribute, something...It would be meaningless to apologize for what I did – But I do. I apologize.

## William Snow (aka 'Skitch')
*British criminal, executed 1789.*
The rope broke the first time...

Good people, be not hurried. I can wait a little.

## Ruth Snyder
*American murderess, electrocuted 1928.*
Snyder's crime was a simple enough 'eternal triangle' situation, but she gained special notoriety when a New York *Daily News* cameraman snapped her death agony with a hidden camera...

Oh Father forgive them for they know not what they do... Father, forgive me! Oh Father, forgive me! Father, forgive them, Father forgive them...

## Henry Beaufort, Duke of Somerset
*Executed at the battle of Hexham, 1464.*

Lord Jesus save me.

## Henry Spencer
*British murderer, hanged 1914.*
Spencer, who killed a rich spinster, claimed to have repented and found God but he cracked on the scaffold...

What I got to say is that I'm innocent of the murder of Allison Rexroat. I never killed her! It's a lie! You're all dirty bastards! You got no right! I never touched her! So help me God, I never harmed a hair on her head! So help me God!

## August Spies
*American radical and one of the Haymarket Rioters in Chicago, hanged 1881.*

There will come a time when our silence will be more powerful than the voices you strangle today.

## Charlie Starkweather
*American mass murderer, electrocuted 1959.*
Asked if he would donate his eyes to medicine.

Hell no! No-one ever did anything for me. Why in hell should I do anything for anyone else?

## Thomas Wentworth, first Earl of Strafford
*Supporter of Charles I, beheaded 1641.*

I do as cheerfully put off my doublet at this time as ever I did when I went to bed.

## Jack Straw
*British leader of the Peasants' Revolt, hanged 1381.*
He confessed on the gallows...

Against that same day that Wat Tyler was killed, we proposed that evening, because the poor people of London seemed to favour us, to set fire in four corners of the city and so to have burnt it, and to have divided the riches at our pleasures amongst us.

## Julius Streicher
*Nazi war criminal, hanged 1946.*

Heil Hitler!

## Fritz Suckel
*Nazi war criminal, hanged 1946.*

I pay my respects to American officers and American soldiers, but not to American justice.

*Following page: The New York* Daily News *photograph of the actual moment Ruth Snyder died in the electric chair.*

### Mary Surratt
*American conspirator to assassinate President Lincoln, hanged 1865.*
Please don't let me fall.

### Rev. Rowland Taylor
*British martyr, burnt 1555.*
Pointing out that he would be burnt rather than buried...
I shall this day deceive the worms in Hadley churchyard.

### Martin George Thorn
*American murderer electrocuted 1897.*
Thorn killed his landlady's ex-lover. She was jailed for twenty years and he was executed...
I have no fear. I am not afraid. I am positive God will forgive me.

### Roger 'The Terrible' Touhy
*American bootlegger, shot dead 1959.*
Touhy fell foul of the Chicago mobs, and was killed after serving a seventeen-year jail sentence...
I've been expecting it. The bastards never forget.

### William Tyndale
*British Protestant martyr strangled at the stake 1536.*
Lord, open the King of England's eyes!

### Wilbur Underhill
*'The Tri-State Terror', American bankrobber shot by police 1934.*
Tell the boys I'm coming home.

### Niccolo Vanzetti
*Amercian radical, hanged with Bartolomeo Sacco for alleged anarchy 1927.*
I am so convinced to be right that if you execute me two times, and if I could be reborn those other two times, I would live again to do what I have already.

### Paul Vergniaud
*French Jacobin politician, guillotined 1794.*
Death before dishonour.

### Waltheof
*Earl of Northumberland, executed 1076.*
He began reciting the Lord's prayer and reached...
Lead us not into temptation...

His voice then choked with tears. The headsman would wait no longer; he drew his sword, and with one blow cut off the earl's head. But bystanders declared that they heard the severed head clearly pronounce the last words of the prayer...
But deliver us from evil, Amen.

### Mendy Weiss
*American gangland murderer, electrocuted 1944.*
All I want to say is I'm innocent. I'm here on a framed up case. Give my love to my family and everything.

### Charles Whitman
*American mass murderer, shot by police 1966.*
Whitman took over the tower of Texas University campus and shot 46 people, sixteen of whom died. He left a note...
Life is not worth living.

### Russell Whittemore
*American murderer, hanged 1926*
All I've got to say is goodbye. That's the best I could say to anyone.

### Captain Henry Wirz
*American soldier, commander of the notoriously barbaric Andersonville prison camp for Union prisoners, hanged 1866.*
This is too tight, loosen it a little. I am innocent. I will have to die sometime. I will die like a man. My hopes are in the future.

### George Wishart
*Martyr burnt for heresy, 1546.*
Wishart was convicted of heresy, and burnt on March 1, 1546 at St.Andrews castle. His last words given by Knox were spoken to the executioner, to whose prayer for forgiveness Wishart answered...
Come hither to me, and when he was come kissed his cheek, and said, Lo, here is a token that I forgive thee. My harte, do thine office. I shall suffer this with a glad heart. Behold and consider my visage. You shall not see me change colour. I fear not this fire.

### Sir Thomas Wyatt
*British nobleman and leader of a Protestant rebellion against Queen Mary, beheaded 1554.*
Referring to a confession he had made under duress...
That which I said then, I said. But that which I say now is true.

### Joseph Zangara
*American working man; he attempted to assassinate US President Franklin D. Roosevelt, electrocuted 1933.*
Zangara fired at Roosevelt as a protest against the Depression; he killed Mayor Cermak of Chicago instead...
Goodbye. Adios to the world.

### Emiliano Zapata
*Mexican freedom fighter, killed 1919.*
Better fighting death than a slave's life!

*Martin Thorn: died in the chair, 1897.*

# WHAT? ME WORRY?

*The strangest things happen when one least expects them.*

### Jim Averill
*American brothel-keeper, lynched 1888.*
To the enraged cowboys who had strung a rope around his neck...
Stop your fooling, fellows!

### Mr Barton
*A citizen of Invercargill, New Zealand, killed by his wife on April Fool's Day 1977.*
She stabbed him 36 times in the heart... her mother had done the same to her father 33 years before.
You can't kill an Invercargill man.

### Catherine Beecheil
*American feminist, died 1878.*
An unwittingly final telegram...
I hope to be in Phil' in about ten days. I am stronger than for years, but take no new responsibilities.

### Ludwig van Beethoven
*German composer, died 1827.*
I shall hear in heaven!

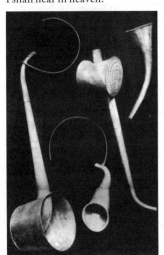

### Aneurin Bevan
*British socialist politician, died 1960.*
To a friend on his plans for the future...
I want to live because there are one or two things I want to do.

### Thomas Blood
*British adventurer and one-time thief of the Crown Jewels, died 1680.*
I do not fear death.

### Léon Blum
*French politician, died 1950.*
My belief is rooted in hope.

### David Bogue
*British missionary, died 1825.*
Told that a visitor had just arrived...
Is he?

### Nicolas Boileau
*French critic and poet, died 1711.*
It is a great consolation to a dying poet to have never written anything against morality.
To a playwright who was offering him his latest work...
Do you wish to hasten my last hour?

### Horatio Bottomley
*British super-patriot and charlatan, died 1933.*
Despite his successes during the Great War, Bottomley died in poverty...
Goodbye and God bless you. I'll see you again tomorrow.

### Chevalier de Boufflers
*French poet, died 1815.*
My friend, I believe that I sleep.

### Clara Bow
*American film star and the original 'It Girl', died 1965.*
For all her early success, Clara Bow's contract lapsed without renewal by her company, Paramount. Her 'trip' was in fact to the mental home where she died...
I've been working hard for years and I need a rest. So I'm figuring on going to Europe for a year or more when my contract expires.

### Brasidas
*Spartan general, killed in the battle of Amphipolis, 422 BC.*
These men do not mean to face us. See how their heads and spears are shaking. Such behaviour always shows that an army is going to run away. Open the gates as I ordered and let us attack them boldly at once.

### Bertolt Brecht
*German playwright, died 1956.*
Commenting on his 58th birthday, a few months before his death...
At least one knows that death will be easy. A slight knock at the windowpane, then...

### George 'Beau' Brummel
*British social arbiter and dandy, died 1840.*
Told that he should pray...
I do try.

*Facing page: Clara Bow, The 'It' Girl.*

*Left: Beethoven's deaf aids, designed for him by the inventor of the metronome.*

### George Buchanan
*Scottish scholar, died 1582.*
*Showing how little he cared for the fate of his mortal remains...*

It matters little to me, for if I am once dead, they may bury me or not bury me as they please. They may leave my corpse to rot where I die if they wish.

### Benjamin Butler
*American Attorney General, died 1858.*

I have peace, perfect peace.

### Joseph Butler
*British bishop, moral philosopher, preacher in the royal court, and influential author, died 1752.*
*The prelate was referring to John vi 37...*

I have often read and thought of that scripture, but never till this moment did I feel its full power, and now I die happy.

### Donn Byrne
*American novelist, killed 1928.*
*Byrne failed to return from his drive...*

I think I'll go for a drive before dinner. Anyone come along?

### Saint Frances Xavier Cabrini ('Mother Cabrini')
*Founder of the Missionary Sisters of the Sacred Heart and first American citizen to be cannonised, died 1917.*
*She was asked what she wanted for lunch...*

Bring me anything you like. If I don't take it I may take something else.

### Caligula
*Emperor of Rome, killed 41 AD.*

I am still alive!

### Sir Henry Campbell-Bannerman
*British Prime Minister, died 1908.*

This is not the end of me.

### Giovanni Giacomo Casanova, Chevalier de Seingalt
*Italian lover and adventurer, died 1798.*

I have lived as a philosopher. I die as a Christian.

*Noel Coward: died at his Jamaican home in 1976.*

### Marcus Porcius Cato The Younger
*Roman republican leader, committed suicide 46 BC.*

Now I am master of myself.

### Robert Chambers
*Scottish publisher, died 1871.*
*Asked how he felt...*

Quite comfortable, quite happy, nothing more.

### Chuang Tzu
*Chinese philosopher, died 4th century BC.*

Above ground I shall be food for the kites. Below I shall be food for mole-crickets and ants. Why rob one to feed the other?

### Emily 'Annie' Chapman
*The fourth victim of Jack the Ripper, murdered 1888.*
*Leaving her regular pub, she remarked...*

I'll soon be back again. I'll soon get the money for my doss.

### Chrysippus
*Greek philosopher, died 207 BC.*
*After an ass had eaten his store of figs...*

Now give the ass a drink of pure wine to wash down the figs.

### Elizabeth Chudleigh
*Countess of Bristol and society beauty, died 1796.*
*Bursting a blood-vessel on news of a failed lawsuit, she refused to acknowledge that it would shortly cause her death. Seeing her ill a servant urged to her to stay in bed.*

I am not very well, but I will rise. At your peril disobey me: I will get up and walk about the room; ring for the secretary to assist me. [She duly rose and demanded breakfast] I could drink a glass of my fine Madeira, and eat a slice of toasted bread. I shall be quite well afterwards; but let it be a large glass of wine.
*She ate and drank and declared...*

I am perfectly recovered; I knew the Madeira would do me good. My heart feels oddly. I will have another glass.
*She drank it, then spoke for the last time...*

I will lie down on the couch; I can sleep, and after that I shall be entirely recovered.

### Joseph Conrad (Jözef Konrad Korzeniowski)
*Polish-born British writer, author of* Heart of Darkness *died 1924.*

You, Jess. I am better this morning. I can always get a rise out of you.

### Benjamin Constant
*French philosopher, novelist and orator, died 1830.*
*Taking a break from correcting proofs...*

The rest tomorrow.

### Noel Coward
*British dramatist, died 1976.*
*To Cole Lesley, his lifelong companion...*

Goodnight my darlings, I'll see you tomorrow.

### Pearl Craigie
*American novelist, died 1906.*
*She sent a final telegram...*

Excellent journey. Crowded train. Reached here by nine. Fondest love Pearl.

### James Croll
*Scottish scientist, died 1890.*
*Teetotal all his life, Croll asked for spirits on his deathbed...*

I'll take a wee drop of that. I don't think there's much fear of me learning to drink now.

### Bing Crosby
*American singer, died 1977.*

That was a great game of golf, fellers.

### William Cullen
*British physician, died 1790.*

I wish I had the power of writing for then I would describe to you how pleasant a thing it is to die.

### e. e. cummings
*American poet, died 1962.*
*His wife told him to stop chopping wood on such a hot day...*

I'm going to stop now, but I'm going to sharpen the axe before I put it up, dear.

### Charles Darwin
*English scientist and discoverer of 'natural selection', died 1882.*

I am not in the least afraid to die.

### Thomas Davis
*Irish poet, died 1845.*
In four days I hope to be able to look at light business for a short time.

### Mary Delany
*British literary hostess and letter-writer, died 1788.*
*She was reluctant to accept the use of a remedy that, rightly, she suspected...*
I have always had a presentiment that if bark were to be given it would be my death; you know I have at times a great defluxion on my lungs…it will stop that, and my lungs with it. Oh, I was never reckoned obstinate and I will not die so.

### Demonax
*Greek philosopher, died 150.*
Draw the curtain, the farce is over.
*Then, asked whether he cared that his corpse might be exposed to wild animals...*
I can see nothing out of the way in it if even in death I am going to be of service to living things.

### Jack 'Legs' Diamond
*American gangster, shot 1931.*
*His perennial, delusory boast...*
The bullet hasn't been made that can kill me.

### Benjamin Disraeli
*British Prime Minister, died 1881.*
I had rather live, but I am not afraid to die.

### Alfred L. Dupont
*American millionaire, died 1902.*
Thank you doctors, thank you nurses. I'll be all right in a few days.

### Jeanne Eagels
*American actress, died 1929.*
I'm going to Dr. Caldwell's for one of my regular treatments.

### Joseph B. Eastman
*American bureaucrat, died 1944.*
I am glad to say that I seem to be making good progress, and from all prognostications I shall be back in circulation again before too long.

### Mary Edmondson
*British murderess, hanged 1759.*
*She had cut her aunt's throat...*
It is now too late to trifle either with God or man. I solemnly declare that I am innocent of the crime laid to my charge. I am very easy in my mind, as I suffer with as much pleasure as if I was going to sleep. I freely forgive my prosecutors, and earnestly beg your prayers for my departing soul.

### John Scott, Lord Eldon
*Lord Chancellor of England, died 1838.*
*Told that the weather was fine...*
It matters not to me, where I am going, whether the weather here is hot or cold.

### Aly Mahmoud Elefesh
*Egyptian 20th-century soccer player.*
*He had just scored and gone on a celebratory run round the pitch, but after shouting he collapsed and died...*
Goal! Goal!

### Havelock Ellis
*English essayist, physician and pioneer sexologist, died 1939.*
You must go to bed, you are so tired and I feel better. Perhaps I may sleep a little. I shall ring if I need you.

### Eugene, Prince of Savoy
*Austrian general, died 1736.*
*Postponing a conference till the next day...*
That is enough for today. We will reserve the rest for tomorrow…if I live that long.

### Edward Everett
*British orator, died 1865.*
*In a letter to his daughter...*
I have turned the corner and as soon as I can get a little appetite, shake off my carking cough, and get the kidneys to resume their action, and subdue the numbness of my limbs, and get the better of my neuralgic pain

### Alfred L. Dupont
in the left shoulder, I hope to do nicely.

### Douglas Fairbanks Sr.
*American film star, died 1939.*
I've never felt better.

### Leo Ferrera
*Belgian anthropologist.*
*Reassuring those who were concerned for him...*
It is nothing. A little dizziness.

### Reginald Fessenden
*British electrical engineer, died 1932.*
That was a nice little party. I am sure this summer is helping me with all this rest and sunshine and the sunshine lamps. I ought to be able to find out something that will be helpful not only to me, but to others.

### Johann Fichte
*German philosopher, died 1814.*
Never mind that I need no more medicine. I feel that I am cured.

### Millard Fillmore
*American President, died 1874.*
The nourishment is palatable.

### F. Scott Fitzgerald
*American novelist, author of* The Great Gatsby, *died 1940.*
*When his companion Sheila Graham asked him if he wanted Hershey Bars from Schwab's drugstore in Hollywood...*
Good enough, they'll be fine.

### John Flavel
*British nonconformist clergyman, died 1691.*
I know that it will be well with me.

### Charlier de Gerson 'The Most Christian Doctor'
*French theologian and Christian mystic, died 1429.*
Now God dost thou let thy servant depart in peace. The soul that is accompanied to divinity by the prayers of three hundred children may advance with humble hope into the presence of their Father and their God.

### James Gibbons

*Second Roman Catholic cardinal of North America, died 1921.*

I have had a good day.

### Sir William Schwenck Gilbert

*British librettist...the 'Gilbert' of 'Gilbert and Sullivan', died 1911.*
He suffered a heart attack when he tried to rescue a girl from drowning on his estate...

Put your hands on my shoulders and don't struggle.

### Earl Godwin

*Earl of the West-Saxons, died 1053.*
Edward the Confessor accused him of murdering his brother. Godwin choked on the testing piece of bread...

So might I safely swallow this morsel of bread, as I am guiltless of the deed.

*Facing page: Allen Ginsberg, London, 1974.*

### Allen Ginsberg

*American poet and radical, died 1997.*

I am quite happy. Unaccountably happy.

### Robert Grimston

*British sportsman, died 1884.*

I don't think I shall join you at dinner, but I will punish your dinner for you. I will have a bit of your fish.

*Right: Gustav Holst, composer.*

### François Guizot

*French historian, died 1874.*
To his daughter who said 'We shall meet again, my father'...

No one is more convinced of that than I am.

### Douglas Haig

*British general, commander-in-chief of British forces in World War I, died 1928.*
His final appointment...

I hope to see you on Tuesday at 10.30 am

### Edward Everett Hale

*American priest and author, died 1909.*
The last entry in his journal...

It was a lovely day and I spent all the time on the deck from 10.30 till 5.00. Had a very good night.

### John Hancock

*American Revolutionary leader and first signer of the American Declaration of Independence, died 1793.*
His name has been immortalized in the slang 'John Hancock', meaning a signature.

I shall look forward to a pleasant time.

### Franz Joseph Haydn

*Austrian composer, died 1809.*

Cheer up children, I'm all right.

### Rutherford B. Hayes

*American President, died 1893.*
Welcoming the chance to see his late wife again...

I know that I'm going where Lucy is.

### Heinrich Heine

*German poet, died 1856.*

God will pardon me...it is His profession.

### Myron T. Herrick

*American ambassador to France, died 1929.*
After doctors said he would be 'all right'...

Do you really think so? Well, I will do my best.

### Richard Hillary

*English fighter pilot and writer on flying, killed in a crash 1943.*
Asked over the intercom 'Are you happy'...

Moderately, I am continuing to orbit.

### Paul von Hindenburg

*German Chancellor, died 1934.*
'Friend Heim' was the German poet Claudius Matthias' pet name for death.

It is all right Sauerbruch; now tell Friend Heim that he can come in.

### Gustav Holst

*English composer, best known for 'The Planets', died 1934.*
A last note...

And I wish myself the joy of your Fellowship at Whitsuntide.

### Harry Hopkins

*American statesman, died 1946.*
Writing to Winston Churchill...

Do give my love to Clemmie and Sarah [Churchill's wife and daughter], all of whom I shall hope to see before you go back, but I want to have a good talk with you over the state of world affairs, to say nothing of our private lives.

### John Henry Hopkins

*Episcopal Bishop of Vermont, died 1868.*

I feel easier.

### Rev. Samuel Hopkins

*British divine, died 1837.*

My anchor is well cast and my ship, though weatherbeaten, will outride the storm.

### John Hough

*Bishop of Worcester, died 1743.*

We part to meet again, I hope in endless joys.

### Joe Howard

*A minor US gangster, shot (possibly by Al Capone) for foolishly hijacking a lorry belonging to gang boss Johnny Torrio.*
He put out his hand to greet his assassin ...

Hi, Al...

Indochina War
Statistics
1965-1973

DEAD:
1,993,807
WOUNDED:
1,737,642
REFUGEES:
12,900,000
BOMBS:
6,130,074 TONS
COST:
135,974,000,000

### John Howard
*British Quaker leader, died 1790.*

Suffer no pomp at my funeral, nor monumental inscription where I am laid. Lay me quietly in the earth and put a sundial over my grave and let me be forgotten.

### William Hutton
*Geologist, died 1815.*
*Asked if he sat comfortably?...*

Oh yes.

### Thomas Huxley
*British scientist and philosopher, died 1895.*

At present I don't feel like sending in my cheques! And without being over-sanguine, I rather incline to think that my natural toughness will get the best of it. Albuminuria or otherwise. Ever your faithful friend…

### Robert Ingersoll
*American militant atheist, died 1899.*
*Asked how he felt...*

Oh, better.

### Rev. Sylvester Judd
*Unitarian and author, died 1853.*

Cover me up warm. Keep my utterance clear. I'm doing well.

### Anne Judson
*Wife of the American missionary Adironam Judson, died 1826.*

I feel quite well. Only very weak.

### George S. Kaufman
*American dramatist and wit, died 1961.*

I'm not afraid any more.

### John Philip Kemble
*British actor, died 1823.*
*Reassuring his wife...*

Don't be alarmed my dear, I have had a slight attack of apoplexy.

### Colonel J. Howard Kitching
*American officer in the Army of the Potomac.*
*To his sister, just before an operation...*

It will be over in a few minutes, darling, and we will have such a nice talk about it afterward.

### Richard Knibb
*British missionary, died 1845.*
*To his congregation in Jamaica.*

The service is over, you may go. All is well.

### Henry Labouchère
*British politician, died 1869.*
*As a lamp flared at his bedside...*

Flames? Not yet, I think.

### Marquis de Lafayette
*French aristocrat who played a leading role in both the American and French Revolutions, died 1834.*
*Commenting on the inevitability of death...*

What do you expect? Life is like the flame of a lamp … when there is no more oil…zest! It goes out and all is over.

### Kenesaw Mountain Landis
*American judge and baseball Commissioner, died 1944.*
*He asked his nurse to give out an optimistic message to callers...*

The Judge is doing all right.

### Abraham Lincoln
*American President, assassinated 1865.*
*Replying to his wife who asked whether the theatre audience would laugh at their holding hands in their box...*

They won't think anything about it

### T. E. Lawrence ('Lawrence of Arabia')
*English soldier and writer, killed 1935.*
*'Shaw' was serving with the army in Dorset; he had just posted this telegram about a meeting to discuss a visit to Hitler, when his motorcycle mysteriously crashed...*

Lunch Tuesday wet fine cottage one mile Bovington Camp Shaw.

### Jake Lingle
*Chicago newspaperman, killed 1930.*
*Lingle, an intimate of many gangsters, paid dearly for this boast. It was presumed Al Capone had him executed...*

I fix the price of beer in this town.

### Henry Cabot Lodge
*American diplomat, died 1924.*
*In a letter to President Coolidge...*

The doctors promise prompt recovery. I shall be back in Washington well and strong and I trust that I shall be able to be of some service to you when I get there.

### Jack London (John Griffith Chaney)
*American writer, author of* Call of the Wild *and* White Fang, *died 1916.*
*He sent what proved to be a final telegram...*

I leave California Wednesday following. Daddy.

### Thomas Babington Macaulay, first Baron Macaulay
*British historian, died 1859.*

I shall retire early. I am very tired.

### General George B. McClellan
*American soldier, died 1885.*
*He sent word to his wife...*

Tell her I am better now.

### General Francis Marion
*American soldier, died 1795.*

Thank God I can lay my hand upon my heart and say that since I came to man's estate I have never intentionally done wrong to anyone.

### Harriet Martineau
*British writer and reformer, died 1876.*

I have had a noble share of life and I do not ask for any other life. I see no reason why the existence of Harriet Martineau should be perpetuated.

### Meher Baba
*Indian guru, died 1969.*
*The Baba's last words in 1925 preceded 44 years of silence before his actual death...*

Don't worry, be happy.

### Michelangelo Buonarroti
*Florentine sculptor and painter, died 1564.*

My soul I resign to God, my body to the earth, my worldly goods to my next of kin.

## Mary Russell Mitford
*British novelist, died 1855.*
*Her last letter...*
Today I am better, but if you wish for another cheerful evening with your old friend, there is no time to be lost.

*Jean Baptiste Poquelin de Molière.*

## Molière (Jean-Baptiste Poquelin)
*French dramatist, author of* Tartuffe *and* Le Malade Imaginaire, *died 1673.*
There is no need to be frightened. You have seen me spit more blood than that and to spare. Nevertheless, go and ask my wife to come up to me.

## H. H. Munro ('Saki')
*British author, killed 1916.*
*In trying to save a fellow-soldier's life, he lost his own...*
Put that bloody cigarette out!

## Hugo Munsterberg
*American psychologist, died 1916.*
By spring we shall have peace.

## Jack Mytton
*British eccentric, died 1834.*
*Mytton died after he had set his shirt on fire in order to banish his hiccups. Although he duly burnt himself to death, he was able to remark...*
Well, the hiccup is gone, by God!

## Ramón Maria Narvez
*Spanish patriot, died 1868.*
*To his confessor...*
I do not have to forgive my enemies, because I killed them all.

## Kenneth Neu
*American psychotic double-killer, hanged 1933.*
*He composed his own farewell song which he delivered on the gallows...*
I'm fit as a fiddle and ready to hang!

## Sir William Robertson Nicholl
*British writer, died 1923.*
I believe everything I have written about immortality.

## Dion O'Banion
*American gangster, killed 1923.*
*Innocent of his fate, he was referring to an upcoming gangland funeral when he asked a couple of men entering his florist's shop...*
Hello boys, you from Mike Merlo's?

## William O'Brien
*Irish nationalist, died 1864.*
Well, the night is so long and dreary, I think I will wait up a little longer.

## Wilfred Owen
*British poet, killed 1918.*
*To one of the troops under his command...*
Well done, you are doing that very well, my boy.

## Viscount Palmerston
*British Prime Minister, died 1865.*
*Told by his doctor he was dying...*
Die, my dear doctor...that's the last thing I shall do!

## President Park of Korea
*Assassinated 1979.*
*He was asked 'Are you all right?'*
I'm all right.

## Gram Parsons
*American rock musician, killed 1972.*
*Told that his habitual drug use could prove fatal...*
Death is a warm cloak, and old friend. I regard death as something that comes up on a roulette wheel every once in a while.

## Boris Pasternak
*Russian poet and novelist, author of* Dr Zhivago, *died 1959.*
Goodbye...why am I haemorrhaging?

## Anna Pavlova
*British prima ballerina, died 1931.*
Get my 'Swan' costume ready.

## Sir Robert Peel
*British Prime Minister, killed 1850.*
*Saying goodbye to his wife as he set out for a ride which proved fatal...*
You are not going without wishing me goodbye, or saying those sweet words 'God bless you'.

## Philoxenes of Cythera
*Greek philosopher.*
*Told that the delicious fish he was enjoying eating would kill him through indigestion...*
Be it so. But before I go, allow me to finish the remainder.

## Max Plowman
*British poet, died 1941.*
*A last letter to one of his magazine editors...*
Good wishes to you very sincerely. Do come and see us here some day...even tho' we are bunged up at the moment. And let me know if the enclosed needs revision. Yours ever, Max.

## Preston B. Plumb
*American politician, died 1891.*
*A letter to his former secretary...*
Dear Frank, Please come to my room tomorrow about ten o'clock. Yours truly, P. B. P.

## Henry Plummer
*The crooked sheriff of Bannock, Washington, lynched for corruption by the townspeople 1864.*
You wouldn't hang your own sheriff, would you?

## Beatrix Potter
*Author and illustrator of children's books, creator of Peter Rabbit, Mrs.Tiggywinkle and many others, died 1943.*
*Her last letter was to a neighbour...*
Dear Joe Moscrop, Still some strength in me. I write a line to shake you by the hand...our friendship has been entirely pleasant. I am very ill with bronchitis. With best wishes for the New Year...

## Frederick Remington
*American painter, died 1909.*
*Before an operation on his appendix from which he did not recover...*
Cut her loose, doc!

## Pierre-Auguste Renoir
*French artist, died 1919.*
I am still progressing.

## Stephen Reynolds
*British essayist.*
*In a telegram...*
Reference my letter of last night. Have got influenza myself now. Stop. Pretty sure unable to come to London next week.

## Sarah Ribicoff
*American girl, shot by a mugger.*
*To her companion...*
This has been a wonderful night.

## Comte Henri de Saint-Simon
*French social theorist, a pioneer of Christian socialism, died 1825.*
The future belongs to us. In order to do great things one must be enthusiastic.

### Moritz von Schwind
*German artist, died 1871*
Asked how he felt...
Excellent!

### Sir Walter Scott
*British novelist, author of* Ivanhoe,
*died 1832.*
I have written nothing which on my deathbed I should wish blotted. God bless you all, I feel myself again.

### George Smalridge
*British clergyman, Bishop of Bristol, died 1719.*
God be thanked I have had a very good night.

### John Sutter
*American pioneer, died 1880.*
Next year, next year they will surely…

### Sofia Soymanov Svetchine
*Russian writer, died 1857*
It will soon be time for Mass. They must raise me.

### Sir Rigby Swift
*British judge, died 1937.*
A final letter...
My dear Chief, Your most kind and sympathetic letter has been a wonderful tonic and already I feel much better. Yours very faithfully, Rigby Swift.

### Charles Maurice de Talleyrand-Périgord
*French statesman and diplomat, died 1838.*
Hearing that the Archbishop of Paris had offered his own life rather than see Talleyrand die...
He can find a better use for it.

### Vassili Tarakin
*Russian conscientious objector, shot by a firing squad for refusing to join up 1919.*
Know it brethren, and always remember that by shooting my body you are killing your own soul. My body shall perish but my spirit will live, because I die for love and brotherhood.

### Edward Thring
*British schoolmaster, died 1887.*
Last entry in his diary...
And now to bed. Sermon finished and a blessed feeling of Sunday coming.

### SS Titanic
*The 'unsinkable' jewel of the White Star Line, sunk on her maiden voyage 1912. A last SOS....*
Have struck iceberg. Badly damaged. Rush aid.

### Rudolph Valentino
*American film star, died 1926.*
Don't pull down the blinds. I feel fine. I want the sunlight to greet me!

### Eva Maria Veigel (Mrs. David Garrick)
*Viennese opera dancer and wife of the actor, died 1822.*
Offered a cup of tea by a maid...
Put it down, hussy! Do you think I cannot help myself.

### Richard Wagner
*German composer, best-known for 'The Ring' Cycle, died 1883.*
I am fond of them, of the inferior beings of the abyss, of those who are full of longing.

### Archbishop Warham
*British clergyman, died 1532.*
On being told that he still had some £30 in cash...
That is enough to last until I get to heaven.

### Charles Warner
*American author, died 1900.*
To his hosts at the house in which he was staying...
I am not well and should like to lie down. Will you call me in ten minutes. Thank you, you are very kind. In ten minutes, remember.

### Mary Webb
*British rural author, died 1927.*
Told that everyone would gather for tea in the afternoon...
That will be nice.

### Daniel Webster
*American politician, died 1852.*
I still live.

### Arthur Wellesley, Duke of Wellington
*British soldier, hero of Waterloo, died 1852.*
Do you know where the apothecary lives? Then send and let him know that I should like to see him. I don't feel quite well and I will lie still till he comes.

### H. G. Wells
*British novelist and reformer, best-known for* The Time Machine *and* War of the Worlds, *died 1946.*
To his nurse...
Go away: I'm all right.

### Henry Kirke White
*British poet, died 1806.*
A letter to his brother from Cambridge, where White died of overwork...
Our lectures begin on Friday, but I do not attend them until I am better. I have not written to my mother, nor shall I while I remain unwell. You will tell her, as a reason, that our lectures begin on Friday. I know she will be uneasy, if she do not hear from me, and still more so if I tell her I am ill. I cannot write any more at present, than that I am your truly affectionate broth.

### Jack B. Yeats
*Irish painter and brother of William Butler Yeats, died 1957.*
To a friend...
Remember, you have promised me a sitting in the morning.

### William Butler Yeats
*Irish poet, died 1939.*
His last letter...
In two or three weeks…I am now idle that I may rest after writing much verse…I will begin to write my most fundamental thoughts and the arrangement of thought which I am convinced will complete my studies. I am happy and I think full of an energy I had despaired of. It seems to me that I have found what I wanted. When I try to put all into a phrase I say 'Man can embody truth, but he cannot know it'. I must embody it in the completion of my life. The abstract is not life and everywhere drags out its contradictions. You can refute Hegel, but not the Saint or the Song of Sixpence.

### Emile Zola
*French novelist and activist, celebrated for his defence of Alfred Dreyfus, 'J'accuse', died 1902.*
I feel sick. My head is splitting. No, don't you see the dog is sick too? We are both ill. It must be something we have eaten. It will pass away. Let's not bother them.

### Ulrich Zwingli
*Swiss Protestant divine, killed 1531.*
What does it matter? They may kill the body, but they cannot kill the soul.

*The Duke of Wellington, after the portrait by Goya, sometimes to be found in London's National Gallery.*

# ON TOP OF THE WORLD

*Die? That's the very last thing I intend to do.*

## Pietro Aretino
*Italian satirical dramatist, known as 'The Scourge of Princes', died 1556.*
*After receiving Extreme Unction...*
Keep the rats away now that I'm all greased up.

## John J. Audubon
*American ornithologist, died 1851.*
I have enjoyed a world which, though wicked enough in all conscience, is perhaps as good as worlds unknown.

## Francis Bacon
*British lawyer, statesman, philosopher and master of the English tongue, died 1626.*
My name and memory I leave to man's charitable speeches, to foreign nations and to the next age.

## Major Norman Baesell
*American Air Force pilot, killed 1944.*
*Baesell flew bandleader Glenn Miller to France on the flight that vanished over the Channel...*
What's the matter Miller, do you want to live forever?

## Walter Bagehot
*British banker, economist and constitutional historian, died 1877.*
Let me have my own fidgets.

## John Barrymore
*American actor, died 1942.*
*Interviewed during his final illness...*
Die? I should say not, dear fellow. No Barrymore would allow such a conventional thing to happen to him.

## Lionel Barrymore
*American actor, died 1954.*
*Invited to contribute his own epitaph to a fanzine...*
Well, I've played everything but a harp.

## Henry Ward Beecher
*American religious author and orator, died 1887.*
*Asked by his doctor whether he could raise his arm...*
Well, high enough to hit you, Doctor!

## Lyman Beecher
*American divine, died 1863.*
I have fought a good fight. I have finished my course. I have kept the faith, henceforth there is laid up for me a crown which God the righteous judge will give me at that day. That is my testimony. Write it down. That is my testimony.

## Dominique Bouhours
*French grammarian, died 1702.*
I am about to, or, I am going to die. Either expression is used.

## Robert Williams Buchanan
*British poet and novelist, died 1901.*
I should like to have a good spin down Regent Street.

## Don Rodrigo Calderón
*Spanish courtier, executed 1621.*
*His death gave rise to the Spanish proverb 'to be haughtier than Don Rodrigo on the scaffold'.*
All my life I have carried myself gracefully.

## Julia Margaret Cameron
*American photographer, died 1875.*
*Cameron and her husband were on a trip to Ceylon, and, fearing their deaths, had taken their own coffins, just in case such items might not be available.*
Beautiful.

*Facing page: Radclyffe Hall, celebrated lesbian writer.*

71

### Sir Winston Churchill
*British Prime Minister, perhaps the most important British leader of the twentieth century, died 1965.*
*Interviewed on his 75th birthday, Churchill's sentiments were probably unchanged at his death...*

I am ready to meet my Maker. Whether my Maker is prepared for the ordeal of meeting me is another matter.

### John Singleton Copley the Elder
*American artist, died 1815.*

Happy, happy, supremely happy.

### George Crabbe
*British poet, died 1832.*

All is well at last. You must make an entertainment. God bless you, God bless you!

### Bruce Cummings
*British diarist and biologist, died 1919.*

My horizon has cleared. My thoughts are tinged with sweetness and I am content.

### Baron Georges Cuvier
*French zoologist and statesman, founder of comparative anatomy and paleontology, died 1832.*
*To his nurse who was applying leeches...*

Nurse, it was I who discovered that leeches have red blood.
*To his daughter, who was drinking a glass of lemonade he had refused...*

It is delightful to see those whom I love still able to swallow.

### Archbishop Elector Karl von Dalberg
*German clergyman, died 1817.*

Love! Life! God's will!

### Father Damien (Joseph de Veuster)
*Belgian priest who devoted his life to missionary work among Hawaiian lepers, died 1889.*

Well, well. God's will be done and He knows best. My work, with all its faults and failures, is in His hands. Before Easter I shall see my Saviour.

### René Descartes
*French mathematician and philosopher, died 1650.*

My soul, thou hast long been held captive. The hour has now come for thee to quit thy prison, to leave the trammels of this body. Then to this separation with joy and courage!

### John Donne
*British poet, died 1631.*

I were miserable if I might not die. Thy Kingdom come, Thy Will be done.

### Norman Douglas
*British author, died 1952.*

Love, love, love!

### Samuel Drew
*British metaphysician, died 1833.*
*Told 'Today you will be with Christ'...*

Yes, my good sir, I trust that I will.

### Theodore Frelinghuysen
*American politician and educator, died 1862.*

All peace, more than ever before.

### Charles James Fox
*British politician, died 1806.*

I die happy.

### Joseph Duncan
*American educator and politician, died 1844.*

Ever precious, ever precious.

### General William Eaton
*American soldier, died 1811.*

Asked if he wanted his head raised to see the sunrise… Yes sir, I thank you.

### John Eliot
*'The Indian Apostle', American missionary, died 1690.*

Welcome joy.

### Rev. Nathaniel Emmons
*American divine, died 1840.*

I am ready.

### John Ericsson
*American naval engineer and inventor, builder of the first armoured-turret warship and developer of the screw propeller, died 1889.*

I am resting. This rest is more magnificent, more beautiful than words can tell.

### Ralph Erskine
*Scottish poet, died 1752.*

I shall be for ever a debtor to free grace. Victory, victory, victory!

### William Etty
*British artist, died 1849.*

Wonderful, wonderful this death.

### Marshal Ferdinand Foch
*French soldier, died 1929.*

Let us go!

### Bernard de Fontenelle
*French scholar, died 1757.*
*Aged one hundred, de Fontenelle's words are an understatement...*

I feel nothing except a certain difficulty in continuing to exist.

### Georg Forster
*Polish naturalist, explorer and scientist, died 1794.*

This is a beautiful world.

### Stephen F. Foster
*Texan patriot, died 1836.*

Texas recognised! Archer told me so. Did you see it in the papers?

### Thomas Gainsborough
*British artist, died 1788.*

We are all going to heaven and Van Dyck is of the party.

### Sir Samuel Garth
*British doctor and poet, died 1719.*
*To his doctors...*

Dear gentlemen, let me die a natural death.
*After receiving the Last Rites...*

I am going on a long journey, they have greased my boots already.

### Henry George
*American land reformer and economist, died 1897.*

Yes, yes, yes!

### André Gide
*French novelist, died 1951.*

C'est bien.

### George Gissing
*British novelist, author of New Grub Street, died 1903.*

Patience, patience, God's will be done.

### Sir Edmund Gosse
*British biographer and critic, died 1928.*
*Gosse died on the operating table, this is his last letter...*

You will think of me in this hour with sympathy and hope. There seems good reason to think I will survive the shock. In any case I am perfectly calm, and able to enjoy the love which has accompanied me through such long years and surrounds me still.

### Henry Grattan
*Irish statesman, died 1820.*
I am perfectly resigned. I am surrounded by my family. I have served my country. I have reliance upon God and I am not afraid of the Devil.

### Robert Gray
*Bishop of Cape Town, died 1872.*
*Told that to take Holy Communion 'tomorrow' would be too late...*
Well, dear fellow, I am ready when you like.

### James Alexander Haldane
*First Congregational minister in Scotland, died 1851.*
*Told by his wife 'You are going to Jesus, how happy you will be soon'...*
Oh, yes.

### Radclyffe Hall
*British writer, author of* The Well of Loneliness, *the notorious, much censored lesbian novel, died 1963.*
What a life, but such as it is, I offer it to God.

### Jean François la Harpe
*French dramatist, died 1803.*
I am grateful to divine mercy for having left me sufficient recollection to feel how consoling these prayers are for the dying.

### William H. Harvey
*British botanist, died 1866.*
Yes, it has been a pleasant world to me.

### William Hazlitt
*British critic and essayist, 1830.*
Well, I have had a happy life.

### Sidney Herbert, Lord Herbert of Lea
*British statesman, died 1861.*
Well, this is the end. I have had a life of great happiness. A short one, perhaps, but an active one. I have not done all I wished, but I have tried to do my best.

### Alexander Henderson
*Moderator of the Glasgow Assembly, died 1646.*
*His written declaration that he was...*
...most of all obliged to the grace and goodness of God, for calling me to believe the promises of the Gospel, and for exalting me to be a preacher of them to others, and

to be a willing, though weak instrument in this great and wonderful work of Reformation, which I beseech the Lord to bring to a happy conclusion.

### Thomas Hendricks
*American Vice President, died 1885*
At rest at last. Now I am free from pain.

### Matthew Henry
*British theologian and translator, died 1714.*
A life spent in the service of God and in communion with Him is the most comfortable and pleasant life anyone can live in the world.

### Eugene A. Hoffman
*American theologian, died 1902.*
*Saying goodbye to his favourite retreat...*
Goodbye, Matapedia.

### Richard Hooker
*British theologian, died 1600.*
My days are past as a shadow that returns not.

### Thomas Hooker
*American founding father and minister at Hartford, Connecticut, died 1647.*
*Told 'You are going to receive the reward of all your labours...'*
Brother, I am going to receive mercy.

### Gerard Manley Hopkins
*British poet, died 1889*
I am so happy, so happy.

### Patrick Henry
*American patriot, died 1799.*
Be thankful for the kind God who allows me to go this painlessly.

### George Herbert
*British composer of hymns, died 1633.*
I am now ready to die. Lord, forsake me not, now for my strength faileth me, but grant me mercy for the merits of Jesus. And now Lord, receive my soul.

### Ureli Corelli Hill
*Founder of the New York Philharmonic Orchestra, committed suicide 1875.*
Haha! I go, the sooner the better!

### Leigh Hunt
*British essayist and critic, died 1859.*
Deep dream of peace.

### Selina Hastings, Countess of Huntingdon
*British philanthropist, died 1791.*
My work is done. I have nothing to do but go to my Father.

### Alexander Humboldt
*German naturalist and geographer, died 1859.*
How grand is the sunlight. It seems to beckon earth to heaven.

*Above:*
*Patrick Henry.*

### Colonel John Hutchinson
*British Puritan leader, died 1664.*

'Tis as I would have it, 'tis where I would have it.

### Alexander Ilitchewski
*Russian writer.*
*His life's quest was for a perfect love...*
*On finding it he seems to have died of joy...*

I have found at last the object of my love!

### Henry James Sr.
*American philosopher, died 1882.*

I stick by Almighty God. He alone is. All else is death. Don't call this dying I am just entering on life.

### William James
*American philosopher, died 1910.*

It's so good to get home.

### Rev. James J. Janeway
*British nonconformist divine, died 1674.*

I am tired of eating, I want to go home!

### Tom L. Johnson
*American politician, died 1911.*

It's all right. I'm so happy.

### Henry A. Jones
*British dramatist, died 1929.*
*Told that 'Gertie' would be back...*

I'm so glad.

### John Jortin
*British ecclesiastic and historian, died 1770.*
*Refusing some food ...*

No thank you, I have had enough of everything.

### Immanuel Kant
*German philosopher, died 1804.*

It is enough.

### Angelica Kauffmann
*Swiss artist, died 1807.*
*Stopping her cousin who had begun to read her a hymn for the dying...*

No, Johann, I will not hear that. Read me the 'Hymn for the Sick' on page 128.

### John Stuart Mill
*British philosopher and economist, died 1873.*

My work is done.

### Michael C. Kerr
*American politician, died 1876.*

I stand upon my record.

### Reginald de Koven
*American composer, conductor and critic, died 1920.*
*His final telegram...*

House sold out for Friday night, box office Vox Dei hurrah!

### Robert M. la Follette
*American politician, died 1925.*

I am at peace with all the world, but there is still a lot of work I could do. I don't know how the people will feel towards me, but I shall take to the grave my love for them which has sustained me through life.

### Lucy Larcom
*American author and educator, died 1893.*

Freedom!

### Ninon de Lenclos
*French wit, beauty and literary hostess, died 1705.*

Let no vain hope…at the core, I'm ripe for death…business here…

### Sinclair Lewis
*American novelist, died 1951.*

I am happy. God bless you all.

### Theophilus Lindsey
*British Unitarian divine, died 1808.*
*Asked if he lived by the maxim 'Whatever is, is right'?...*

No. Whatever is, is best

### Hamilton W. Mabie
*American editor and essayist, died 1916.*

I have had a quiet but very happy Christmas.

### Niccolò Machiavelli
*Florentine political theorist, author of The Prince, died 1530.*

I desire to go to hell and not to heaven. In the former place I shall enjoy the company of Popes, Kings and Princes, while in the latter are only beggars, monks and apostles.

### Sir James Mackintosh
*Scottish historian and essayist, died 1832.*

Happy, happy!

### A. T. Mahan
*British writer on seapower, died 1914.*
*Looking out of his window at the garden...*

If a few more quiet years were granted me, I might see and enjoy these things, but God is just and I am content.

### Louis Mandrin
*French brigand, executed 1755.*

Ah, what a moment, great God! And one I ought to have foreseen.

### Andrew Marvell Sr.
*British clergyman, drowned 1641.*
*Marvell, father of the poet, stepped on board a ferry with this comment. The boat promptly sank...*

Ho for heaven!

### Cotton Mather
*American Puritan divine, died 1728.*

Is this dying, is this all? Is this what I feared when I prayed against a hard death? Oh, I can bear this, I can bear it!

### Increase Mather
*American Puritan clergyman, died 1723.*
*Asked how he felt...*

Far from well, yet better than my iniquities deserve.

### Philipp Melanchthon
*German humanist, died 1560.*
*Asked what he needed...*

Nothing else but heaven.

### Alice Meynell
*British poet and essayist, died 1922.*

This is not tragic. I am happy.

### Lady Mary Wortley Montagu
*British essayist and the most outstanding Englishwoman of her era, died 1762.*

It has all been very interesting.

## Hannah More
*English poet, died 1833.*
Joy!

## Jean Victor Moreau
*French general, died 1813.*
*Dying in exile, Moreau sent his last words to Napoleon...*
Say to the Emperor that I go to the tomb with the same feelings of veneration, respect and devotion that he inspired in me the first time I saw him. I have nothing to reproach myself with.

## Samuel Morse
*American inventor, pioneer of telegraphy, died 1872.*
*Being told 'This is the way we doctors telegraph' to allay his fears of the instruments...*
Very good.

## Arthur Murphy
*British dramatist, died 1805.*
Taught half by reason, half by mere dismay. To welcome death and calmly pass away.

## Richard Newton
*British divine, died 1753.*
I am going, going to glory. Farewell sir, farewell death. Praise the Lord.

## Torlogh O'Carolan
*Irish bard, died 1738.*
*Calling for a last tot of whisky...*
It would be hard if such friends should part at least without kissing.

## Charlotte Elizabeth, Duchesse d'Orlèans
*French noblewoman, died early 18th century.*
*Her last letter...*
Thank God, I am prepared to die, and I only pray for strength to die bravely. It is not bad weather although today a fine rain is setting ill But I do not think any weather will help me. Many complain of coughs and colds, but my malady lies deeper. Should I recover you will find me the same friend as ever. Should this be the end, I die with full faith in my Redeemer.

## William Oughtred
*British mathematician, died 1660.*
*Hearing that King Charles II had been restored...*
And are you sure he is restored? Then give a glass of sack to drink his Sacred Majesty's health.

## Robert Owen
*British socialist and philanthropist, died 1858.*
Relief has come!

## Silvio Pellico
*Italian poet, died 1854.*
Oh Paradise, Paradise! At last comes to me the grand consolation. My prisons disappear, the great of earth pass away, all before is rest.

## Pablo Picasso
*Spanish artist, died 1973.*
Drink to me.

## Albert Pike
*American poet, died 1891.*
*His last words were written in Hebrew...*
Peace, peace, peace.

## Sir Isaac Pitman
*British graphologist, the inventor of shorthand, died 1897.*
To those who ask how Isaac Pitman passed away, say peacefully and with no more concern than passing from one room into another to take up some further employment.

RAPHAELIS SANCTII VRBINATIS
PICTORIS EMINENTISS·EFFICIEM·IVLIVS·BONASONIVS·BONONIEN
EXEMPLARI·SVMPTAM·CAELO·EXPRESSIT·

## Raphael
*Italian artist, died 1520.*
Happy.

## Julie de Récamier, 'Madame Récamier'
*French literary hostess and beauty, died 1849.*
We shall meet again.

## Ernest Renan
*French writer, philologist and historian, died 1892.*
I have done my work. It is the most natural thing in the world to die. Let us accept the laws of the Universe. The heavens and the earth remain.

## Sir Joshua Reynolds
*British artist, died 1792.*
I have been fortunate in long good health and constant success and I ought not to complain. I know that all things on earth must have an end and now I am come to mine.

## Christina Rossetti
*British poet, died 1894.*
I love everybody. If ever I had an enemy I should hope to meet and welcome that enemy in heaven.

## Dante Gabriel Rossetti
*British poet and painter, died 1882.*
Then you really think I'm dying? At last you think so. But I was right from the first.

## Robert Sanderson
*British clergyman, Bishop of Lincoln, died 1663.*
My heart is fixed, oh God. My heart is fixed where true joy is to be found.

## Maurice, Comte de Saxe
*German-born French general and military theorist, died 1750.*
I have had a beautiful dream.

## Paul Scarron
*French dramatist, died 1660.*
I would never have thought it was so easy to laugh at the approach of death.

## Carl Schurz
*American politician, died 1906.*
It is so simple to die.

## Junipero Serra
*Spanish Franciscan priest whose missionary work in North America earned him the title of 'Apostle of California', died 1784.*
Now I shall rest.

## William Henry Seward
*American statesman, died 1872.*
*His daughters asked if he had any last messages for them...*
Nothing. Only 'Love another'.

### Algernon Sidney
*British plotter, executed 1683.*
*Condemned for his role in the 'Rye House*
*Plot' against Charles II, the executioner*
*asked 'Will you rise again?'...*
Not until the general
Resurrection.

### Rev. Edward Smedley
*British poet, died 1836.*
Be always thankful.

### Arthur Stanley
*British clergyman, Dean of Westminster,*
*died 1881.*
I am perfectly happy,
perfectly satisfied.
I have no misgivings.

### Henry Starr
*American bankrobber, fatally wounded*
*during his last raid.*
*He had robbed up to 48 banks in a*
*30-year career.*
I have robbed more banks than
any man in America.

### Sir John Stewart
*Scottish poet and soldier, died 1752.*
*His last words established his son*
*as his legal heir...*
Lady Jane Douglas, my lawful
spouse, did, in the year 1748,
bring to the world my two sons,
Archibald and Sholto and I
firmly believe the children
were mine, as I am sure they were
hers. Of the two sons, Archibald
is the only one in life now.
I make this declaration as
stepping into eternity before the
witnesses afore-mentioned.
Jo. Stewart.

### Emmanuel Swedenborg
*Swedish philosopher, scientist and mystic,*
*died 1772.*
It is well. I thank you.
God bless you.

### John Taylor
### 'The Water Poet'
*British poet, died 1653.*
How sweet it is to rest.

### Ellen Terry
*British actress, died 1928.*
*Scribbled in the dust on her bedside table...*
Happy.

### William S. Thayer
*American doctor, died 1932.*
This is the end and I am not
sorry.

### William 'Big Bill' Thompson
*Mayor of Chicago, died 1944.*
*Reassuring his aides that his affairs*
*were all in order...*
Everything is all set, Jim…
that's right, that's right.

*Facing page:*
*George Washington*
*as depicted on*
*the American one*
*dollar bill.*

### John Toland
*British deist, died 1722.*
*Asked whether he wanted anything...*
I want nothing but Death.

### Sir Harry Vane
*British Puritan leader, executed for*
*treason 1662.*
Why should we shrink from
death? I find it rather shrinks
from me than I from it.

### Eugene Vidocq
*French thief turned detective and the*
*inspiration for Balzac's fictional figure*
*Vautrin, died 1857.*
How great is the forgiveness
for such a life.

### General Lew Wallace
*American religious author, died 1905.*
*The author of Ben Hur told his wife...*
We shall meet in heaven.

### George Washington
*American President, died 1799.*
Doctor, I die hard, but I am not
afraid to go.

### Ethel Waters
*American blues singer, died 1977.*
*Interviewed shortly before her death...*
I'm not afraid to die, honey.
In fact I'm kind of looking
forward to it. I know that the
Lord has his arms wrapped
around this big, fat sparrow.

### Thomas E. Watson
*American politician, died 1922.*
I am not afraid, I am not afraid
to die.

### Isaac Watts
*British nonconformist schoolmaster and*
*composer of hymns, died 1748.*
It is a great mercy to me that
I have no manner of fear or
dread of death. I could,
if God please, lay my head
back and die without terror
this afternoon.

### William Webster
*British divine, died 1758.*
Peace.

### Charles Wesley
*British Methodist leader (brother of John)*
*and hymn composer, died 1788.*
I shall be satisfied with thy
likeness satisfied.

### John Wesley
*British Methodist leader, preacher and*
*lexicographer, died 1791.*
The best of all is that God is
with us.

### William Whitaker
*British divine, died 1595.*
Life or death is welcome to me
and I desire not to live but so far
as I may be serviceable to God
and His church.

### Philip Wicksteed
*British economist and literary critic,*
*died 1927.*
Hurrah, hurrah!

### William Wilberforce
*British anti-slavery campaigner, died 1833.*
Heaven!

### John Sharp Williams
*American politician, died 1932.*
I've done things that seemed
at the time worth doing.
I think that if a man can
get to my age and, looking
back, believe a majority
of things he did were
worth the effort, he has
nothing to regret.

### Thomas Woolston
*British theologian, died 1733.*
This is a struggle which all men
go through and which I bear not
only with patience but with
willingness.

### Sir Henry Wooton
*Diplomatist and poet, died 1639.*
I now draw near to the
harbour of death, that
harbour that will rescue
me from all the future
storms and waves of this
restless world. I praise God
and am willing to leave it.
I expect a better, that world
where dwelleth righteousness,
and I long for it.

### Eugene Ysaye
*Belgian violinist, died 1929.*
*He had his own Fourth Sonata played for*
*his enjoyment...*
Splendid, the finale just a
little too fast.

# THE BARNUM AND BAILEY

P. T. BARNUM.

J. A. BAILEY.

# GREATEST SHOW ON EARTH

# THE SHOW MUST GO ON

*Living well may be the best revenge, but how about death.*

**Jane Addams**
*American temperance campaigner, died 1935.*
Offered spirits as a restorative...
Always, always water for me!

**Anonymous French Aristocrat**
*Guillotined 1794.*
Refusing a glass of rum...
I lose all sense of direction when I am drunk.

**Anonymous Reporter for the New York *World***
*Killed in a train crash, 1915.*
Call up the New York *World* right away and tell them there is a wreck here, a big story. Also tell them that I'm sorry I won't be able to work the story because I'm all smashed up. Call my mother too.

**Hugo Astley**
*British man-about-town and bon viveur, died c. 1895.*
Bear in mind that three things, not two, are absolute certainties. Death and Quarter day are common parables, but it's not generally known that it's a million to one on crab against lobster sauce with a turbot. God bless you. Goodbye!!

**Honoré de Balzac**
*French novelist, best-known for his greatest creation La Comédie Humaine, some 90 interlinked novels and short stories providing a fictional history of post-Revolutionary France, died 1850.*
Summoning one of his own fictional creations, 'Dr. Horace Bianchon'...
Send for Bianchon!

**Henri Barbusse**
*French novelist, died 1935.*
He wrote on military themes and died urging the escalation of worldwide conflicts...

Telephone and say they must still enlarge it. Always larger, broader, more universal. It is the only way of saving the world.

**Phineas T. Barnum**
*America's supreme showman, died 1901.*
How were the circus receipts tonight at Madison Square Garden?

**Clarence Barron**
*American publisher, founder of The Wall Street Journal, died 1928.*
What's the news?

**Johann Basedow**
*German educational reformer, died 1790.*
I want an autopsy made for the benefit of my fellow men.

**Warner Baxter**
*American film star, died 1951*
Invited to make up his own epitaph for a fanzine...
Did you hear about my operation?

**George M. Beard**
*American surgeon, died 1883.*
Tell the doctors it is impossible for me to record the thoughts of a dying man. It would be interesting to do so, but I cannot. My time has come. I hope others will carry on my work.

**Robert Benchley**
*American humorist, died 1945.*
Benchley had been reading a book called *Am I Thinking?* during his final illness. His comment adorned the title page.
No. And supposing you were?

**Constance Bennett**
*American film star, died 1965.*
Invited to contribute her own epitaph to a fanzine...
Do not disturb.

**Josh Billings (H. W. Shaw)**
*American humorist, died 1885.*
His final public lecture...
My doctors East ordered a rest of brain, but you see I do not have to work my brain for a simple lecture. It comes spontaneously.

**Jess Bishop**
*American murderer, executed 1979.*
His was the first involuntary execution (Gary Gilmore volunteered) in America since the 1960s. It took him ten minutes to die in the Nevada gas chamber...
This is just one more step down the road of life.

**Franz Boas**
*German-born American anthropologist, died 1942.*
It isn't necessary to wear oneself out repeating that racism is either a monstrous error or a shameless lie. The Nazis themselves have recently had to appreciate the accuracy of the facts that I have brought together on the European immigrants of America.

*Honoré de Balzac, died in 1850.*

*Facing page: P. T. Barnum of Barnum and Bailey, died 1901.*

79

### Humphrey Bogart
*American film star, died 1956.*
*Popularly attributed last words…*
I should never have switched from Scotch to Martinis.

### Baron Christian Bunsen
*Prussian diplomat and scholar, died 1860.*
*Died as he greeted guests…*
Very kind, very glad…

### Thomas Campbell
*British poet, died 1844.*
*Campbell's friends were not sure whether the poet was dead or merely silent. In the hope of a response they asked who was the real author of one of his poems. The poet proved himself still (if temporarily) alive when he heard another's name suggested…*
No. It was one Tom Campbell.

### Alonzo Cano ('The Spanish Michelangelo')
*Spanish painter, sculptor and architect, died 1677.*
*The sculptor refused the ornate crucifix his confessor was offering…*
Vex me not with this thing, but give me a simple cross that I may adore it both as it is in itself and as I can figure it in my mind.

*Daniel Defoe, creator of Crusoe, died 1731.*

### Antoine Carème
*French master chef, died 1833.*
*The culinary maestro was fittingly tasting food in his kitchen…*
The quenelles are good, only they were prepared too hastily; you must shake the saucepan lightly.

### Isaac Casaubon
*Huguenot theologian, died 1614.*
*Asked on his deathbed which religion, Protestant or Catholic, he finally believed…*
Then you think, my Lord, that I have all along been a dissembler in a matter of the greatest moment?

### Cato the Censor
*Roman legislator, committed suicide 149 BC.*
Shut the door.

### René de Chateaubriand
*Pioneer of the French Romantic movement, died 1848.*
*Hearing of the outbreak of fighting in Paris…*
I want to go there.

### Anton Pavlovich Chekhov
*Russian dramatist, author of* Uncle Vanya *and* The Seagull, *died 1904.*
*Calling for a last drink…*
I am dying. I haven't drunk champagne for a long time.

### Hannah Chickering
*American prison reformer.*
Say only that I was at peace. More than this, if repeated, might indicate a deeper spiritual experience than I ever had.

*Right: Aleister Crowley, 'The Great Beast' died 1947.*

### David Chytraus
*Historian, died 1600.*
*Chytraus had finished his final manuscript…*
I have concluded the history of this century and put the finishing touches to it and not another word will I write.

### George Coghill
*British naturalist, died 1941.*
*Taking a peppermint water from the nurse…*
Why, that's what we used to give to babies.

### Harry Cohn
*Hollywood magnate, died 1958.*
*Cohn's last words were not recorded but comic Red Skelton provided what many would have found to be an apt epitaph as he surveyed the crowds at Cohn's funeral…*
It proves what they say: give the public what they want to see and they'll come out for it.

### Spencer Cole
*British divine.*
I should like to finish my exposition of the Twenty-Second of Revelation.

### Arthur Bernard Cook
*British classical scholar and archaeologist, died 1952.*
*Perfectionist to the last, he commented on the opening verses of the 121st psalm which were being read to him…*
That is a mistranslation.

### Jean-Baptiste Corot
*French artist, died 1875.*
In spite of myself, I go on hoping with all my heart that there will be painting in heaven.

### Lou Costello
*American comic film star, died 1959.*
That was the best ice-cream soda I ever tasted.

### Aleister Crowley
*British mystic, the self-proclaimed 'Great Beast' and black magician, died 1947.*
*The final paragraph of his* Confessions…
What may befall, I know not, and I have almost ceased to care. It is enough that I should press towards the mark of my high calling, secure in the magical virtue of my oath: 'I shall endure unto the End'.

### Lady Emerald Cunard
*British socialite, died 1948.*
*Turning down a teaspoon of champagne her maid was offering…*
No. Open a bottle for the nurse and yourself.

### Daniel Defoe
*British novelist, author of* Robinson Crusoe, *died 1731.*
I do not know which is more difficult in a Christian life…to live well or to die well.

### John Dubos
*Died 1742.*

Death is a law and not a punishment. Three things ought to console us for giving up life…the friends we lost, the few persons worthy of being loved whom we leave behind us, finally the memory of our stupidities and the assurance that they are now going to stop.

### Henri Dunant
*Swiss founder of the YMCA and of the Red Cross, winner of the first ever Nobel Peace Prize, died 1910.*
*A follower of the faith of the earliest Christians, he rejected the rites of the later faith…*

I wish to be carried to my grave like a dog without a single one of your ceremonies which I do not recognise. I trust to your goodness faithfully to respect my last earthly request. I count upon your friendship that it shall be so. Amen. I am a disciple of Christ as in the First Century and nothing more.

### Isadora Duncan
*American interpretative dancer, died in 1927, strangled when her long scarf caught in the wheel of her open car.*

Adieu my friends, I go on to glory!

### Joseph Duveen
*British international art dealer, died 1939.*
*Referring to his living beyond all medical prognoses, not his ability to sell art…*

Well, I fooled them for five years.

*Isadora Duncan, dance revolutionary, killed in 1927.*

### Amelia Earhardt
*American aviation pioneer, killed 1937.*

*Her last letter to her husband…*
Please know that I am quite aware of the hazards. I want to do it because I want to do it. Women must try to do things as men have tried. When they fail, their failure must be but a challenge to others.

### Nelson Eddy
*American bandleader, died 1967.*
*He was working on stage in a Miami hotel…*
Play 'Dardanella', and perhaps I'll remember the words.

### Epicurus
*Greek philosopher, died 271 BC.*
Farewell, and remember my teachings.

### Charles d'Everuard
*French gourmet, died 1703.*
*Asked if he'd be reconciled with Christ…*
With all my heart I would be fain reconciled with my stomach which no longer performs its usual functions.

### Andrea 'Whips' Feldman
*An Andy Warhol 'superstar', suicide 1972.*

*Jumping out of a window…*
I'm going for the big time: Heaven.

### François Fénelon
*French divine and religious theorist, died 1715.*
Lord, if I am still necessary to Thy people, I refuse not to labour for the rest of my days. Thy will be done!

### Kathleen Ferrier
*British opera singer, died 1953.*
Now I'll have eine kleine pause.

### W.C. Fields
*American film comic, died 1946.*
*Referring to his lifelong bête noire among cities, the great performer chose this epitaph…*
On the whole, I'd rather be in Philadelphia.

### Mme de Fontaine-Martel
*French literary hostess.*
*Asking what time it was, then reminding herself.*
God be blessed! Whatever the hour there is always a rendezvous going on.

### Benjamin Franklin

*American diplomat and writer, possibly the most famous American of his era, died 1790.*
*Aged 25, Franklin composed this possible epitaph for himself.*

The body of Ben Franklin, Printer (like the cover of an old book, its contents torn out and stripped of its lettering and gilding) lies here, food for worms. But the work shall not be lost, for it will (as he believed) appear in a new and more elegant edition, revised and corrected by the Author.

### Clark Gable

*American film star, died 1960.*
*Gable died while shooting 'The Misfits' with Marilyn Monroe. The last words he spoke on camera were suitably symbolic...*

*Marilyn Monroe:* How do you find the way back in the dark?
*Clark Gable:* Just head for the big star straight on. The highways under it take us right home.

### Galileo Galilei

*Italian astronomer, died 1642.*
*Galileo was forced to recant his new and accurate theories, that the Earth moves around the Sun and not, as the Church claimed, vice versa. But he remained privately defiant...*

Yet it still moves.

### John Garfield

*American film star, died 1952.*
*Garfield died in bed, but not alone. A Hollywood wit suggested this epitaph...*

Died in the saddle.

### George Gipp

*American football star, died 1920.*
*Gipp died of pneumonia after the 1920 college season. He left this last request with Notre Dame's legendary coach Knute Rockne (or so Rockne always claimed)...*

One day, when the going is tough and a big game is hanging in the balance, ask the team to win one for the Gipper. I don't know where I'll be, Rock, but I'll know about it and I'll be happy.

### William Godwin

*British political philosopher, died 1836.*
*Last entry in his diary...*

Cough, snow.

### George Washington Goethals

*American engineer, builder of the Panama Canal, died 1928.*
*Dying in New York City...*

Let me stay here. If I stay here, I'll be much nearer to West Point.

### Cary Grant (Archibald Leach)

*British-born American film star, died 1986.*
*Invited to write his own epitaph for a fanzine...*

He was lucky, and he knew it.

### Joseph Green

*British surgeon, died 1863.*
*Green checked his own pulse...*

Congestion…stopped.

### Rufus W. Griswold

*Edgar Allen Poe's executor, died 1857.*

Sir, I may not have been always a Christian, but I am very sure that I have been a gentleman.

### George Gunn

*19th century British cricketer*

Batsmen take too great a heed of bowlers.

### William Haines

*American silent movie star, died 1973.*
*Invited to write his epitaph for a fanzine...*

Here's something I want to get off my chest.

### Alexander Hamilton Douglas, tenth Duke of Hamilton

*Eccentric British aristocrat, died 1852.*
*Ordering his servants to ensure, by whatever means, that his body would fit into the ornate Egyptian sarcophagus costing £11,000 which he had purchased for his remains. He was duly buried in it and it was placed in a colossal mausoleum erected near Hamilton Palace.*

Double me up! Double me up!

### Mark Hanna

*American politician, died 1904.*
*Asked if he wanted a handkerchief, joked back...*

Yes, I would like one, but I suppose I cannot have it. My wife takes them all.

### John Pritt Harley

*British actor and singer, died 1858.*
*He suffered a stroke on stage and was rushed to his home where he died. His last words were a quotation from A Midsummer Night's Dream...*

I have an exposition of sleep come upon me.

### Calvin S. Harrington

*American classical scholar.*

As it was in the beginning, is now, and ever shall be, world without end, Amen.

### Joel Chandler Harris

*American humorous author, creator of Br'er Rabbit, died 1908.*

I am about the extent of a tenth of a gnat's eyebrow better.

### William Harrison

*American President, died 1841.*

I wish you to understand the true principles of government, I wish them carried out. I ask nothing more.

### Johann Herder

*German poet and critic, died 1803.*

Refresh me with a great thought.

### Theodor Herzl

*German Zionist leader, died 1904.*
To his son...

Your brethren are dispersed throughout the whole world. If you want to, you will find them. I have found them too, because I have been looking for them. Think of it and don't forget that your people need young, healthy strength and that you are heir to the name Herzl.

### Herman Hesse

*German novelist, died 1961.*
Last line of his final poem...

One more summer and another winter.

### Jacob Hiltzheimer

*American diarist.*
His last entry referred to the epidemic that killed him...

Deaths today...sixty-six.

### Adolf Hitler

*Nazi dictator, committed suicide 1945.*
Hitler's final political testament, dictated in his bunker before he and his mistress Eva Braun killed themselves...

Above all I enjoin the governments of the nation and the people to uphold the racial laws and to resist mercilessly the poisoner of all nations, international Jewry. Berlin, 29 April 1945 0400 hours. My wife and I choose to die in order to escape the shame of overthrow or capitulation. It is our wish for our bodies to be cremated immediately on the place where I have performed the greater part of my daily work, during twelve years of service to my people.

### Jimmy Hoffa

*American trade union leader, missing, presumed dead, 1975.*
His last known words came in a telephone call to his wife...

Has Tony Giacalone called?

### Henry Fox, first Baron Holland

*British aristocrat, died 1774.*
He remained sociable to the last...

If Mr. Selwyn calls again, show him up. If I am alive I shall be delighted to see him, and if I am dead he would like to see me.

### Burton Holmes

*American 19th-century lantern lecturer.*
Thinking of the ultimate show...heaven...

How I could pack them in with that one!

### Winifred Holtby

*British novelist, died 1935.*
Announcing her intention to get married...

Not an engagement...just an understanding.

*An anti-Hitler poster by the Social Democratic Party from the last free election in Germany before Hitler came to power in 1933.*

### Thomas Hood

*British editor and humorist, died 1845.*
Watching the application of a mustard plaster to his foot...

There's very little meat for the mustard.

### Howard Hughes

*American recluse, millionaire film and plane maker, died 1976.*
Hughes' last public statements came in a special telephone interview in 1972, held to disprove any claims that a fraudulent 'biography' by Clifford Irving was his true story...

I am certainly not happy about my condition. I mean I'm not in any seriously disparaging...or, that's not the word. What the hell is the word I'm looking for? I am not in any seriously derogatory...er, that's not the word either. I'm not in any seriously deficient, now there's the word! I'm not in a deficient condition...I'm not going to continue being quite as reclusive as I have been, because it has apparently attracted so much attention that I have just got to live a somewhat modified life in order not to be an oddity...for one thing I would like to see an accurate story of my life printed.

### William Hunter

*British professor of anatomy, died 1783.*
If I had the strength to hold a pen, I would write how easy and pleasant it is to die.

### William Jackson

*Irish revolutionary, died 1795.*
Jackson was on trial but before the verdict could be announced, he collapsed dead in the dock; it was assumed that his wife, with whom he had been allowed to take breakfast, had brought him poison. His last words, whispered to a confederate on his arrival in court, were those of the suicide Pierre in Otway's play *Venice Preserved*.

We have deceived the senate.

### Johann George Jacobi
*German lyric poet, died 1919.*
*After finishing on New Year's Eve a poem about New Year's Day...*

I shall not in fact see the New Year which I have just commemorated. I hope, at least, it is not apparent in the poem how elderly I am.

### John Jay
*American politician, died 1829.*

I would have my funeral decent, but not ostentatious. No scarfs, no rings. Instead, thereof, I give two hundred dollars to any one poor deserving widow or orphan of this town whom my children shall select.

### Sir William Johnson
*British agent to the Iroquois Indians, died 1774.*
*To his halfbreed son Joseph, a Mohawk chief..*

Joseph, control your people. I am going away.

### Ronald Knox
*British religious writer, died 1957.*
*Asked if he would like to hear someone read a portion of his version of the Bible...*

Awfully jolly of you to suggest it though.

### Bernard de la Ville, Comte de Lacépède
*French naturalist and writer, died 1825.*
*Called for an unfinished manuscript and told his son...*

Charles, write in large letters the word 'End' at the foot of the page.

*Martin Luther: founder of Protestantism*

### Thomas de Lagny
*French mathematician, died 1734.*
*Asked on his deathbed for the square of 12...*

One hundred and forty-four.

### Jimmy Lee Laine
*Blues pianist.*
*Died still playing the piano...*
Let it roll! Let it roll!

### Gertrude Lawrence
*British actress, died 1952.*
*Starring in 'The King And I' she remained generous to the end...*

See that Yul [Brynner] gets star billing. He has earned it.

### Anton van Leeuwenhoek
*Pioneer Dutch microscopist who was the first to observe bacteria and protozoa, died 1723.*

Hoogvliet my friend, be so good as to have those two letters on the table translated into Latin. Send them to the Royal Society in London.

### Dr. Ludwig Leichhardt
*Australian explorer, died 1848.*
*Leichhardt vanished mysteriously on a trek across the country. This was his last letter...*

The only serious accident that has happened was the loss of a spade, but we are fortunate to make it up on this station. Though the days are still very hot, the beautiful nights are cool and benumb the mosquitoes which have ceased to trouble us. Myriads of flies are the only annoyance we have. Seeing how much I have been favoured in my present progress, I am full of hopes that our Almighty Protector will allow me to bring my darling scheme to a successful termination. Your most sincere friend, Ludwig Leichhardt.

### David Livingstone
*Scottish missionary and explorer of Africa, died 1873.*
*After taking a dose of calomel, he told his personal servant, Susi, who was ministering to his illness...*
All right; you can go out now.

### Martin Luther
*German monk and the founder of Protestantism, died 1546.*
*Asked whether he still held his revolutionary beliefs...*
Yes!

### Sir Alfred Macalpine
*Irish building tycoon.*
Keep Paddy behind the big mixer.

### Stephen Mackenna
*British novelist, died 1956.*
*Letter from hospital...*

Dear Peggy, I cannot resist, tho' I mean to see no-one, never no more. But you mustn't bring me anything whatever. I abhor grapes, am worried by flowers, can't read magazines. I'm greatly touched by your goodness, Peggy. Probably you could come any hour, arranging things over the telephone with Sister, you know the ropes. But Regular Visiting Fixtures: Sunday 2-3. Tuesd. and Frid. 3-6. I wept when I got you. S.M.K. What a howling swell of an address you have acquired, God save us.

### André Maginot
*French statesman and military planner, died 1932.*
*To President Laval...*
For me, this is the end, but you continue!

### William Barclay 'Bat' Masterson
*US gunfighter and later a sports journalist for the New York Morning Telegraph.*
*Signing off his last column, 1921.*

There are many in this old world of ours who hold that things break about even for all of us. I have observed, for example, that we all get about the same amount of ice. The rich get it in summertime and the poor get it in the winter.

### Increase Mather
*American divine, died 1723.*
Be fruitful.

### W. Somerset Maugham
*British novelist and short story writer, died 1965.*

Dying is a very dull, dreary affair And my advice to you is to have nothing whatever to do with it.

### Vladimir Mayakowski
*Russian poet, committed suicide 1930. His last note urged against imitating him.*

I don't recommend it for others.

### H. L. Mencken
*American editor, critic and social commentator, died 1956.*
*'The Sage of Baltimore' stricken by paralysis, composed his own epitaph...*

If, after I depart this vale, you remember me and have some thought to please my ghost, forgive some sinner and wink your eye at some homely girl.

### Elie Metchnikoff
*Russian zoologist and microbiologist, winner of the Nobel Prize, died 1916.*

You remember your promise? You will do my post-mortem? And look at the intestines carefully, for I think there is something there now.

### Edna St. Vincent Millay
*American poet, died 1950.*
*Left a note for her maid as she went to bed...*

Dear Lena, The iron is set too high. Don't put it on where it says 'Linen' or it will scorch the linen. Try it on 'Rayon' and then perhaps on 'Woollen'. And Lena, be careful not to burn your fingers when you shift it from one heat to another. It is 5.30 and I have been working all night. I am going to bed. Good morning.

### Wilson Mizner
*Hollywood wit, died 1933.*
*To his doctor...*

Well, doc, I guess this is the main event.

Rejecting an attendant priest...

Why should I talk to you? I've just been talking to your boss.

### Duc de Montmorency
*Constable of France, killed 1567.*
*Facing death on the scaffold...*

Do you think a man who has known how to live honourably for eighty years does not know how to die for a quarter of an hour.

### William de Morgan
*Potter and novelist, died 1917.*
*De Morgan was at work on this manuscript at his death...*

Pinning her faith on this, she passed into the passage, where he ought to have been, the import of her demeanour being that her shrewder insight would at once discern the whereabouts of…

### Wolfgang Amadeus Mozart
*Austrian composer, one of the greatest figures in the history of Western music, died 1791.*
*Playing his own 'Requiem'...*

Did I not tell you I was writing this for myself?

### Margaret Noble ('Nivedita')
*Campaigner for Indian independence, died 1911.*

The ship is sinking, but I shall see the sun rise.

### John Toler, Lord Norbury
*Irish lawyer, known as 'Ireland's Judge Jeffreys' for the severity of his sentencing, died 1827.*
*He heard on his deathbed that his neighbour Lord Erne was also dying and summoned his valet...*

James, run round to Lord Erne and tell him with my compliments that it will be a dead heat between us.

### Anne Oldfield
*British actress, died 1730.*

Alexander Pope included her last words in his *Moral Essays*...

Odious! in woollen! 'twould a saint provoke, Were the last words that poor Narcissa spoke; No, let a charming chintz and Brussels lace Wrap my cold limbs and shade my lifeless face: One would not, sure, be frightful when one's dead, And Betty give this cheek a little red.

### George Orwell (Eric Blair)
*British journalist and writer, author of 1984 and Animal Farm, died 1950.*
*The final entry in his working notebook...*

At fifty, everyone has the face that he deserves.

### Thomas Paine
*British radical political theorist and pamphleteer, author of The Rights of Man, died 1809.*
*His doctor observed 'Your belly diminishes'...*

And yours augments.

### Courtlandt Palmer
*American founder of the Nineteenth Century Club.*

I want you to say that you have seen a free-thinker die without fear of the future, and without changing his opinion.

### Dorothy Parker
*American writer and wit, died 1967.*
*To her friend Beatrice Ames, a few days before her lonely death...*

I want you to tell me the truth. Did Ernest [Hemingway] really like me?

### Thomas Love Peacock
*British novelist, poet and official of the East India Company, killed 1866.*
*Peacock was burnt to death refusing to give up his efforts to save his library from the flames...*

By the immortal God, I will not move!

### George Washington Plunkitt
*American politician, boss of New York's 19th century political 'machine', Tammany Hall.*

Now, in conclusion, I want to say I don't own a dishonest dollar. If my worst enemy was given the job of writing my epitaph when I'm gone, he could do no more than write 'George W. Plunkitt He Seen His Opportunities and He Took'Em'.

### Elvis Presley
*American rock superstar, died 1977.*
*His final press conference ended...*

I hope I have not bored you.

## François Rabelais
*French satirist and doctor, author of*
Gargantua *and* Pantagruel, *died 1553.*
Ring down the curtain, the farce
is over.
*His will concluded...*
I have nothing. I owe much.
The rest I leave to the poor.

## William Chapman Ralston
*American Comstock Lode speculator,*
*died 1875.*
Keep these for me. There are
valuable papers in my pocket.

## Grantland Rice
*American sports columnist, died 1954.*
*The end of his last column, on baseball star*
*Willie Mays...*
Willie, at least, has a golden
start.

## Edward G. Robinson
*American film star, died 1973.*
*On receiving in hospital news of an*
*honorary Oscar and looking forward to*
*the ceremony...*
Do you think they'd mind if I
came in a wheelchair? I don't
think I'm gonna make it.

## Henry Crabb Robinson
*British foreign correspondent, died 1867.*
*His last diary entry approved of fellow writer*
*Matthew Arnold...*
He thinks of Germany as he
ought, and of Goethe with high
admiration. On this point I can
possibly give him assistance,
which he will gladly...but I feel
incapable to go on.

## Auguste Rodin
*French sculptor, died 1917.*
And people say that Puvis de
Chavannes is not a fine artist.

## Harold Ross
*Founder and editor of* The New Yorker,
*died 1951.*
*His last telephone conversation from his*
*hospital bed was to George S. Kaufman...*
I'm up here to end this thing and
it may end me too. But it's better
than going on this way. God
bless you, I'm half under the
anaesthetic now.

## Meyer Amschel Rothschild
*German-Jewish banker, died 1874.*
*Rothschild called his five sons together and*
*gave them instructions to be faithful to the*
*law of Moses, to remain united until the end*
*and to consult their mother on all actions.*
Observe these three points, and
you will soon be among the
richest, and the world will
belong to you.

## Richard Rumbold
*British republican member of the Rye*
*House Plot aimed at deposing Charles II,*
*executed for treason 1685.*

*On the gallows he continued to mock the*
*doctrine of the 'Divine Right of Kings'...*
I am sure there was no man born
marked of God above another;
for none comes into the world
with a saddle upon his back,
neither any booted and spurred
to ride him.

## Damon Runyon
*American writer and journalist, died 1946.*
You can keep the things of
bronze and stone and give me
one man to remember me just
once a year.

## Charles, Abbé Saint-Pierre
*French writer on social questions,*
*died 1814.*
*Told his priest that he had only gone through*
*the Last Rites for the sake of his family...*
I am only to be reproached for
this action. I do not believe a
word of all this. It was a vile
concession for the family, but I
wanted to be the confessor of
truth all my life.

## Samson
*Biblical hero, killed c.1155 BC.*
Let me die with the Philistines.

## Fra Paolo Sarpi
*Venetian patriot, scholar and state*
*theologian, died 1623.*
*His last thoughts were of Venice...*
Be thou everlasting.

## E. W. Scripps
*American journalist, died 1926.*
Too many cigars this evening,
I guess.

## Sir Henry Segrave
*British sportsman, killed while attempting*
*to break the world speedboat record 1930.*
*He survived long enough to ask...*
Did we do it?

## William Shakespeare
*British dramatist, died 1616.*
*Shakespeare left no recorded last words,*
*but the inscription on his gravestone has*
*provided his final message to the world...*
Good friend, for Jesus' sake
forbear
To dig the dust enclosed here.

## George Bernard Shaw
*Irish dramatist, journalist and Fabian,*
*died 1950.*
*To his nurse...*
Sister, you're trying to keep me
alive as an old curiosity. But I'm
done, I'm finished. I'm going
to die.

## Sisera of Harosheth-ha-goiim
*Biblical soldier.*
*To Jael, who killed him in his sleep with a*
*hammer and nail...*
Stand in the door of the tent, and
it shall be, when any man doth
come and enquire of thee and
say, 'Is there any man here?' that
thou shalt say 'No'.

## Logan Pearsall Smith
*American aphorist, died 1946.*
Thank heaven the sun has gone
in, and I don't have to go out and
enjoy it.

## Sidney Smith
*British clergyman, essayist and wit, Canon*
*of St. Paul's, died 1845.*
*His wife told him that he had mistakenly*
*drunk some ink.*
Bring me all the blotting paper
there is in the house.

## C. P. Stanton
*American explorer, killed 1847.*
*Stanton was resting by his campfire, after*
*making three arduous rescue trips through*
*the Donner Pass for avalanche victims...*
Yes, I'm coming soon.

## Elizabeth Cady Stanton
*American feminist, died 1902.*
*Still campaigning for women's rights, she*
*sent this plea to President Theodore*
*Roosevelt...*
Abraham Lincoln immortalised
himself by the emancipation of
four million Southern slaves.
Speaking for my suffrage
coadjutors, we now desire that
you, Mr. President, who are
already celebrated for so many
honourable deeds and worthy
utterances, immortalise yourself
by bringing about the complete
emancipation of thirty-six
million women.

## Alexander H. Stephens
*American statesman, died 1883.*
But I carried it individually by a
six hundred majority.

## Lewis Stone
*American film star, died 1953.*
*Invited to compose his own epitaph for a*
*fanzine...*
A gentleman farmer goes back to
the soil.

## Lucy Stone
*American suffragist, died 1893.*
Make the world better!

## Lytton Strachey
*British biographer and critic, author of
Eminent Victorians, died 1932.*

If this is dying, I don't think
much of it.

## Charles Sumner
*American politician, died 1874.*

Don't let the Civil Rights Bill fail!

## Horace Tabor
## ('The Silver King')
*American miner, died 1899.
To his wife who believed him and still died in
abject poverty thirty-six years later.*

Hang on to the Matchless
[mine]. It will make millions
again.

## Archibald Campbell Tait
*Scottish-born Anglican clergyman,
Archbishop of Canterbury, died 1882.
His last note was to Queen Victoria.*

A last memorial of twenty-six
years of devoted service, with
earnest love and affectionate
blessing on the Queen and her
family. A.C. Cantuar.

## Bayard Taylor
*American traveller and author, died 1878.*

I want…oh, you know what I
mean, the stuff of life!

## Theophrastus
*Greek philosopher, died 287 BC.
Leaving his pupils…*

Farewell, and may you be happy.
Either drop my doctrine, which
involves a world of labour, or
stand forth its worthy champion,
for you will win great glory. Life
holds more disappointment than
advantage. But, as I can no
longer discuss what we ought to
do, do you go on with the
inquiry into right conduct.

## Dylan Thomas
*Welsh poet, died 1953.*

I've had eighteen straight
whiskies, I think that's the
record. After 39 years, this is all
I've done.

## James Thurber
*American cartoonist and humorist,
died 1964.*

God bless…Goddamn…

## Ben Travers
*British playwright and farceur, died 1980.
Shortly before his death he told an
interviewer that he would like his last words,
engraved on his tombstone, to be…*

This is where the real fun starts.

## Sir Herbert
## Beerbohm Tree
*British actor-manager, died 1917.
Thinking of his forthcoming appearance…*

I shall not need to study the part
at all. I know it already.

## Harry S. Truman
*American President, died 1972.
A view of his life…*

There is an epitaph in Boot Hill
cemetery in Arizona which reads
'Here lies Jack Williams … he
done his damnedest. What more
can a person do?' Well, that's all I
could do. I did my damnedest
and that's all there is to it.

## Voltaire
## (François Marie Arouet)
*French writer and philosopher, died 1778.
To the priest hoping for a deathbed
conversion…*

In God's name, let me die in
peace!
*Then, looking at a lamp at his side…*
The flames already?

## Karl Wallenda
*High-wire virtuoso, killed 1978.
Wallenda, like so many of his tightroping
family, was killed on the job, in his case
while promoting the circus in Puerto Rico.*

The only place I feel alive is the
high wires.

## Walter White
*American Black leader, died 1954.
Asked by his daughter whether he liked her
dress, White mocked the current
McCarthyite witch hunts…*

I plead the Fifth Amendment.

## Oscar Wilde
*Irish dramatist and wit, died 1900.
Noting the turn of the century…*

It would really be more than the
English could stand if another
century began and I were still
alive. I am dying as I have
lived…beyond my means.

## Wendell Wilkie
*American diplomat, died 1944.*

I enjoyed our talk this morning
very much. Frankly I cannot
answer your ultimate question
[as to whom he would support]
because I have not yet fully
decided.

## Mary Wollstonecraft
*English pioneer feminist, died 1797.*

I know what you are thinking of;
but I have nothing to
communicate on the subject of
religion.

## Alexander Woolcott
*American journalist, broadcaster and wit,
died 1951.
To a hospital visitor when he was ill just
before his death…*

I have no need of your God-
damned sympathy. I only wish to
be entertained by some of your
grosser reminiscences.
*To helpers, who tried to save him when he
collapsed during his radio show…*

Get back in there. Never mind
me. Go back in there!

## Zip 'The What Is It?'
*Exhibited by Barnum as 'The Missing link',
actually the feeble-minded son of poor
Blacks from Brooklyn, died 1926.*

Well, we fooled them a long
time.

*Oscar Wilde: died in
Paris 1900.*

# THE END IS NIGH

*Next stop eternity, so please don't bother me now.*

### Abd-Er-Rahman
*First caliph and greatest ruler of the Umayyad Arab Muslim dynasty of Spain, died 961.*
Oh man, place not thy confidence in this present world.

### Louisa M. Alcott
*American writer, author of Little Women, died 1888.*
Is it not meningitis?

### Edward Alderson
*American judge, died 1857.*
*Asked how he felt...*
The worse, the better for me.

### Henry Alford
*British clergyman, died 1871.*
*Making the arrangements for his funeral...*
Will you tell the Archdeacon? Will you move a vote of thanks for his kindness in performing the ceremony?

### Stewart Alsop
*American journalist and political commentator, died of leukaemia 1973.*
*The final words of his autobiography Stay of Execution...*
There is a time to live, but there is also a time to die. That time has not yet come for me. But it will. It will come for all of us.

### Felix Arvers
*French poet, died 1850.*
*To his confessor...*
Ah, Coquereau, I forgot to mention one of the greatest faults of my life. I have spoken badly of Charles X.

### 'La Rivière' de Bailli
*French doctor, died 1605.*
*After disposing of all his possessions he looked around his room...*
I must hasten away since my baggage has been sent off before me.

### George Bancroft
*British historian, died 1891.*
*Turning to a friend, he admitted...*
I cannot remember your first name. [He was told 'It is George. Like yours…'] Then what is your last name?

### Johann Barneveldt
*Dutch patriot, executed 1619.*
Oh God! What then is man?

### Sir James M. Barrie
*Scottish playwright and novelist, author of Peter Pan, died 1937.*
I can't sleep.

### Clarissa Harlowe Barton ('The Angel of the Battlefield')
*Humanitarian and founder of the American Red Cross, she died in 1912.*
Let me go! Let me go!

### Thomas Lovell Beddoes
*British poet and physiologist, author of Death's Jest Book, died 1849.*
I am food for what I am good for – worms. I ought to have been among other things a good poet.

Life was too great a bore on one peg, and that a hard one. But for Dr. Elkins above mentioned, Reade's best stomach pump.

### Max Beerbohm
*British writer, broadcaster and wit, died 1956.*
*Asked whether he had slept well...*
No. Thanks for everything.

### Pierre-Joseph-Georges Pigneau de Behaine.
*French missionary in Vietnam, died 1799.*
I willingly leave this world where I have been thought happy in that I have had public admiration, been respected by the great, esteemed by Kings. I can't say that I regret these honours – it's just that they add up to vanity and trouble.

*Max Beerbohm*

### Daniel Blake
*British footman, hanged 1763.*
*Killed his fellow-servant, Lord Dacre's butler, Mr Murcott, with a poker and a knife to cut his throat.*
You seem to look at me with earnestness. You were all born; but you know not in what manner you shall die. Let my fate warn you to keep the sabbath, and honour your parents. Be careful to attend divine worship; profane not the sabbath; repent of your sins, and make a timely peace with God. Behold the consequence of my iniquities! Fear God, and honour your parents, for neglecting which I must suffer a disgraceful death.

### Ludwig Borne
*German political satirist, died 1837.*
Pull back the drapes, I'd gladly see the sun. Flowers. Music.

*Facing page:
Oliver Cromwell.*

### Anne du Bourg
*French priest and martyr, executed 1559.*

Six feet of earth for my body and the infinite heavens for my soul is what I shall soon have.

### Nathaniel Bowditch
*American mathematician, died 1838.*
*Taking a final glass of water...*

How delicious. I have swallowed a drop from Silva's brook that flowed fast by the oracle of God.

### Charles Brace
*British social campaigner, died 1890.*
*Reading about a new sanatorium...*

I wish you would send this to Mr. Potter.

### James Brindley
*British engineer, despite his illiteracy, responsible for the construction of more than 365 miles of canals, died 1772.*
*Instructing a group of canal builders whose plans consistently went wrong...*

Then puddle it, puddle it and puddle it again.

*Confucius: his time came in 479BC.*

### Emily Brontë
*British novelist, author of Wuthering Heights, died 1848.*

If you will send for a doctor I will see him now.

### General Sir Redvers Buller
*Soldier and colonial administrator, commander of the relief of Ladysmith in 1900, died 1908.*

Well, I think it is about time to go to bed now.

### Bishop Burgess
*Bishop of St. David's and Salisbury, died 1837.*

I will lie down now.

### Frances Hodgson Burnett
*British writer, author of Little Lord Fauntleroy, died 1924*

With the best that was in me I have tried to write more happiness into the world.

### Samuel Butler
*British philosophical writer, author of Erewhon, died 1902.*

Have you brought the cheque book, Alfred?

### George Gordon Byron, sixth Baron Byron
*English Romantic poet and satirist, died of fever in Greece 1824.*

Now I shall go to sleep.

### Henriette Campan
*French educator, died 1822.*
*After making a brusque demand of a servant...*

How imperious one is when one no longer has the time to be polite.

### Canius
*Roman, died 1st century AD.*

I have determined with myself to mark well whether in this short pang of death my soul shall perceive and feel that he goes out of my body. This point I intend fully to take heed of; and if I can, I will surely bring you and the rest of my fellows word, what I felt and what is the state of our souls.

### Jane Carlyle
*British literary hostess and wife of the essayist Thomas Carlyle, died 1866.*
*Her last letter to her husband, who had requested her to buy him a certain picture...*

I will go back for it, if you like, and can find a place for it on my wall.

### Thomas Carlyle
*British historian and essayist, died 1881.*

So this is death, well...

### Andrew Carnegie
*American railroad baron, died 1919.*
*Replying to his wife who had wished him a good night's rest...*

I hope so.

### Lewis Carroll (Charles Lutwidge Dodgson)
*British writer and academic, author of Alice in Wonderland, died 1898.*

Take away those pillows – I shall need them no more.

### Viscount Castlereagh
*British Foreign Secretary, committed suicide 1821.*

Oh Bankhead, it is all over!

### Neville Chamberlain
*British Prime Minister, died 1940.*

Approaching dissolution brings relief.

### William Ellery Channing
*'The Father of American Unitarianism', died 1842.*

You need not be anxious concerning tonight. It will be very quiet and peaceful with me.

### Joseph Choate
*American lawyer and diplomat, died 1917.*

I am feeling very ill. I think this is the end.

### Joseph Clare
*British poet, died 1864.*

I have lived too long. I want to go home.

### Thomas Cole
*British artist, died 1848.*

I want to be quiet.

### Samuel Colt
*American arms manufacturer, creator of the Colt .45, died 1862.*

It's all over now.

### George Combe
*British phrenologist, died 1858.*

From my present sensations I should say that I were dying and I am glad of it.

### Confucius (K'ung-fu-tzu: Master K'ung)
*Chinese philosopher, died 479 BC.*

No intelligent monarch arises. There is no-one in the kingdom that will make me his master. My time has come to die.

### Jay Cooke
*American banker, died 1905.*
*Overhearing the reading of a prayer for the dead...*

That was the right prayer.

### Oliver Cromwell
*Lord Protector of England, died 1658.*

My desire is to make what haste I may to begone.

### Marie Curie (Maria Sklodowska)
*Polish-born French physicist, discoverer of radium and twice winner of the Nobel prize, died 1893.*
*Offered an injection to ease her pain...*

I don't want it.

### John Philpot Curran
*Irish author and wit, died 1817.*
*Replying to his doctor who commented, 'You are coughing with more difficulty'...*

That is surprising, since I have been practising all night.

## Sir William Davenant

*British Poet Laureate, died 1668.*
*Putting off the conclusion of a poem on which he was working...*

I shall have to ask leave to desist, when I am interrupted by so great an experiment as dying.

## Stephen Decatur

*American naval officer in the War of 1812 and coiner of the phrase 'Our country, right or wrong', killed in a duel 1820.*

I am mortally wounded, I think.

## Madame de Staël

*French political and literary hostess, died 1817.*
*When asked if she would sleep...*

Heavily, like a big peasant woman.

## Emily Dickinson

*American poet, died 1886.*

I must go in, the fog is rising.
*Offered a glass of water...*

Oh, is that all it is?

## Diogenes the Cynic

*Greek philosopher, died c. 320 BC.*
*Waking for the last time...*

One brother anticipates the other: Sleep before Death. Everything will shortly be turned upside down.

## Philip Doddridge

*British nonconformist divine, died 1751.*

There is a hope set before me.

## Sir Howard Douglas

*British general, died 1861.*

All I have said about armoured ships will prove correct. How little do they know of the undeveloped power of artillery.

## Paul Doumer

*President of France, assassinated 1932.*
*The statesman never knew that a bullet and not a car had hit him. His aides refused to reveal the truth.*

Ah, a road accident...a road accident.

## Timothy Dwight

*American educator, theologian and poet, died 1817.*
*As he finished his last manuscript...*

There, I have done. Oh, what triumphant truth!

## Morgan Earp

*American lawman, killed 1882.*
*As he died at the O.K. Corral, Morgan finally accepted his brother Wyatt's refusal to believe in an afterlife...*

I guess you were right, Wyatt. I can't see a damn thing.

## Pablo Escobar

*Columbian cocaine baron, shot 1993.*
*On the telephone to his son, he was ambushed by armed police...*

I'm hanging-up...because something funny's going on here.

## Eugene Field

*American poet and journalist, his popular nickname 'the poet of childhood' did not please him, died 1895.*

Good night.

## George Fordyce

*Scottish physician, died 1802.*
*Dismissing his daughter who had been reading to him...*

Stop. Go out of the room. I am about to die.

## Henry Clay Frick

*American industrialist, died 1919.*

That will be all; now I think I'll go to sleep.

## Rev. Christopher P. Gadsden

*American clergyman, died 1805.*
*Raising his arms to heaven...*

I am reaching towards my inheritance.

## Rev. Thomas H. Gallaudet

*American teacher of the deaf and dumb, died 1902.*

I will go to sleep.

## Christian Fürchtegott Gellert

*German poet, whose works, at his peak, were outsold only by the Bible, died 1769.*

Now, God be praised, only one hour.

## Richard Watson Gilder

*British poet and editor, died 1909.*
*Writing about Tennyson...*

He wrote some of his sagest and loveliest things in the last days there seems to have been an otherworld light on these latest utterances. You see him standing serene in the afterglow, awaiting in tranquillity the natural end.

## William Ewart Gladstone

*British Prime Minister, died 1898.*
*His last entry in a diary that spanned seventy years...*

I do not enter any interior matters. It is so easy to write, but to write honestly is nearly impossible.

## John Gough

*American lawyer, died 1886.*
*Maintaining his pro-temperance stand until the end...*

Young man, keep your record clean.

## William Graham

*British passenger on the liner S.S. Pacific, which went down in an icefield on a trip from Liverpool to New York, 1856.*
*This message in a bottle was washed ashore in the Hebrides.*

On board the Pacific from Liverpool to NY. Ship going down. Confusion on board. Icebergs around us on every side. I know I cannot escape. I write the cause of our loss that friends may not live in suspense. The finder will please get it published.

*Pablo Escobar.*

## Henry W. Grady

*American editor and orator, died 1889.*

And the little children cried in the streets.

## Sir James Graham

*British statesman, died 1861.*
*As he rested after a heart attack...*

Ah! I thought it was over then.

## Horace Greeley

*American publisher and editor, founder of the New York Daily Tribune, died 1872.*

It is done.

## Edvard Grieg

*Norwegian composer, died 1907.*

Well, if it must be so.

## Albrecht von Haller

*German physician, died 1777.*
*He checked his own pulse...*
Now I am dying. The artery ceases to beat.

## Jonas Hanway

*British traveller and philanthropist, died 1786.*
If you think it will be of service to your practice or to anyone who may come after me, I beg you to have my body opened. I am willing to do as much good as possible.

## Will Hay

*British comic actor, died 1949.*
*A passage in a book he was reading when he died and one which was carved on his gravestone...*
For each of us there comes a moment when death takes us by the hand and says – it is time to rest, you are tired, lie down and sleep.

## Reginald Heber

*British clergyman and hymn writer, Bishop of Calcutta, died 1826.*
*Written on the back of a sermon on confirmation, given earlier the same day...*
Trichinopoly, April 3, 1826.

## John Heckewelder

*Moravian missionary to the Ohio Indians, died 1823.*
Golgotha, Gethsemene.

## Edward Herbert, Baron Herbert of Cherbury,

*British historian, poet and diplomat, died 1648.*
*Making an accurate forecast of his death...*
Then an hour hence he shall depart

## Abram S. Hewitt

*American industrialist and politician, died 1903.*
*Removing the oxygen tube from his mouth...*
And now I am officially dead.

## John Hilton

*British broadcaster, died 1943.*
*Swallowing a few drops of tea...*
That was very good.

## Ludwig Holty

*German poet, died 1776.*
I am very ill. Send for Zimmermann. In fact, I think I'll die today.

## Walter Farquhar Hook

*British clergyman and church historian, died 1875.*
I am old, 78, and very infirm. My contemporaries are passing away and I expect soon to receive my summons. Pray for me.

## Julia Ward Howe

*American author and lecturer; composer*
of 'The Battle Hymn of the Republic', died 1910.
God will help me...I am so tired.

## William Dean Howells

*American litterateur, died 1920.*
*Writing about Henry James...*
Our walks by day were only in one direction and in one region. We were always going to Fresh Pond, in those days a wandering space of woods and water where people skated in winter and boated in summer.

## William H. Hudson

*British author, naturalist and ornithologist, died 1922.*
Goodbye.

## Isaac Hull

*American admiral during the War of 1812, died 1843.*
I strike my flag.

## David Hume

*British philosopher, died 1776.*
*A final letter...*
I go very fast to decline and last night had a small fever, which I hoped might put a quicker period to this tedious illness; but, unluckily, it has, in a great measure, gone off. I cannot submit to your coming over here on my account, as it is possible for me to see you so small a part of the day; but Dr. Black can better inform you concerning the degree of strength which may, from time to time, remain with me. Adieu.

## Anne Hyde

*Duchess of York, died 1671.*
Truth! Truth!

## Douglas Jerrold

*British playwright and satirist, an early contributor to Punch, died 1857.*
I feel like one who is waiting and waited for.

## John G. Johnson

*American lawyer and art collector, died 1917.*
Goodnight, I'm going to sleep now.

## Maurus Jokal

*Hungarian novelist, died 1904.*
I want to sleep.

## Al Jolson

*American singing superstar, died 1950.*
This is it. I'm going, I'm going.

## John Paul Jones

*American patriot, died 1792.*
*The final paragraph of his will...*
I revoke all other testaments or codicils which I may have made before the present, which alone I stand by as containing my last will.

## Christian Jacob Kraus

*German professor of political science, died 1832.*
Dying is different from what I thought.

## Jerome Lalande

*French astronomer known for his tables of the planetary positions, died 1807.*
Withdraw, I no longer have need of any thing.

## Félicité Robert de Lamennais

*French priest and philosopher, died 1854.*
*Watching the sun streaming through his bedroom window...*
Let it come – it is coming for me.

## Franklin K. Lane

*American Secretary of the Interior, died 1921.*
But for my heart's content in that new land, I think I'd rather loaf with Lincoln along a river bank. I know I could understand him. I would not have to learn who were his enemies, what theories he was committed to and what against. We could just talk and open out our minds, and tell our doubts and swap the longings of our hearts that others never heard of. He wouldn't try to master me nor make me feel how small I was. I'd dare to ask him things and know that he felt awkward about them, too. And I know I would find, I know I would, that he had hit his shin

on those very stumps that had hit me. We'd talk of men a lot – the kind they call the great. I would not find him scornful. Yet boys that he knew in New Salem would somehow appear larger in their souls than some of those that I had called the great. His wise eyes saw qualities that weighed more than smartness. Yes, we would sit down where the bank sloped gently to the great stream and glance at the picture of our people the negroes being lynched, the miners' civil war, labor's holdups, employers' ruthlessness, the subordination of humanity to industry…

## Pierre Laplace
*French astronomer, best known for his investigations into the stability of the solar system, died 1827.*
What we know is not much, what we do not know is immense.

## Sir Wilfred Laurier
*Canadian Prime Minister, died 1919.*
It is finished.

## Franz Lehar
*Hungarian composer of operettas whose greatest work was 'The Merry Widow', died 1948.*
Now I have finished with all earthly business, and high time too. Yes, yes, my dear child, now comes death.

## Ellis Lewis
*American lawyer and Chief Justice of Pennsylvania, died 1854.*
I believe I am dying now.

## George Lippard
*Died 1854.*
Is this death?

## S.S.Lusitania
*American liner, torpedoed by a German submarine, 1916.*
*Last message, tossed over the side in a bottle...*
Still on deck with a few people. The last boats have left. We are sinking fast. The orchestra is still playing bravely. Some men near me are praying with a priest. The end is near. Maybe this note will…

## Katherine Mansfield (Katherine Murry)
*New Zealand short story writer, died 1923.*

I believe…I'm going to die. I love the rain. I want the feeling of it on my face.

## Captain Frederick Marryat
*British novelist of the sea, author of Mr. Midshipman Easy, died 1848.*
*Dictating his last thoughts...*
After years of casual, and, latterly, months of intense thought, I feel convinced that Christianity is true, and the only religion that can be practised on this earth; that the basis of Christianity is love; and that God is love. To attempt to establish any other creed will only, in the end, be folly. But Christianity must be implanted in the breast of youth; there must be a bias towards it given at an early age. It is now half past nine o'clock. World, adieu!

## Charles Matthews
*British comic actor, died 1836.*
I am ready.

## Catherine de Médicis
*Consort of Henri II of France, died 1589.*
Ah, my God, I am dead!

## Theodore Parker
*British abolitionist clergyman, died 1869.*
It is all one.

## Harry St. John Philby
*Explorer and orientalist and father of the spy Kim Philby, died 1960.*
God, I'm bored!

## Felix Mendelssohn
*German composer, died 1847.*
Weary, very weary.

## Désiré Joseph Mercier
*Belgian cardinal, died 1926.*
*After hearing the 'Profiscere'...*
Now there is nothing more to be done, except to wait.

## Prosper Mérimée
*French novelist and dramatist, died 1870.*
Goodnight now, I want to go to sleep.

## Helmuth von Moltke
*Prussian general, died 1891.*
*Asked 'Uncle Helmuth, are you ill?'...*
What?

## Lola Montez (Marie Dolores Rosanna Gilbert)
*Irish adventuress and 'Spanish' dancer, mistress of King Ludwig I of Bavaria, died 1861.*
I am very tired.

## Gouverneur Morris
*American politician, died 1816.*
Sixty-four years ago it pleased the Almighty to call me into existence here on this spot, in this very room, and now shall I complain that he is pleased to call me hence?

## Oliver Morton
*American politician, died 1877.*
I am dying. I am worn out.

## Alfred de Musset
*French poet, died 1857.*
Sleep! At last I am to sleep.

## Johann Neander
*German church historian, died 1850.*
I am weary. I will now go to sleep. Goodnight.

## Sir Isaac Newton
*British philosopher and mathematician, died 1727.*
I don't know what I may seem to the world. But as to myself, I seem to have been only a boy playing on the seashore and diverting myself in now and then finding a smoother pebble or prettier shell than the ordinary, whilst the great ocean of truth lay all undiscovered before me.

## Barthold George Niebuhr

*German historian, died 1831.*
*Noticing that his medicine was reserved only for terminal cases...*

What essential substance is this? Am I so far gone?

## Hermann Nothnagel

*German professor of internal medicine and teacher of Sigmund Freud, died 1905.*
*Reporting on his own condition...*

Paroxysms of angina pectoris, with extremely violent pains. Pulse and attacks completely different, sometimes slow, about 36-60, entirely regular, very intense, then again accelerated, 80-90, rather even and regular, finally completely arhythmic, entirely unequal, now palpitating, now slow, with differing intensity. The first sensations of these attacks date several – three or four – years back, in the beginning rather weak, becoming slowly more and more definite. Properly speaking attacks with sharp pains have appeared only within the last five or six days. Written on July 6, 1903, late in the evening, after I had three or four violent attacks.

*Henry Purcell, died 1695.*

## Titus Oates

*Anglican priest and instigator of the 'Popish Plot' of 1678, died 1705.*

It is all the same in the end.

## John Palmer

*British actor, died on stage 1798.*
*Palmer had just delivered this line from his play The Stranger.*

There is another and a better world.

## Dorothy W. Pattison ('Sister Dora')

*Philanthropist, died 1878.*

I have lived alone, let me die alone, let me die alone.

## Henry Charles Peterson

*Australian politician.*

My life has been faulty, but God will judge me by my intentions.

## Orville H. Platt

*American politician, died 1905.*

You know what this means, Doctor, and so do I.

## Plotinus

*Neo-Platonic philosopher, died 270 BC.*

I am making my last effort to return that which is divine in me to that which is divine in the universe.

## Alexander Pope

*British satirist, author of 'The Rape of the Lock', died 1744.*

I am dying, sir, of one hundred good symptoms.

## Henry Purcell

*British composer, died 1695.*
*The final words of his will...*

And I do hereby constitute and appoint my said loving wife my sole executrix of this my last will and testament, revoking all former wills. Witness my hand this day.

## John Quick

*British actor, died 1831.*

Is this death?

## James Quin

*British actor, died 1766.*

I could wish this tragedy were over, but I hope to go through it with becoming modesty.

## Horace Traubel

*American author and socialist, friend and biographer of Walt Whitman, died 1919.*

I am tired, damned tired.

## August Strindberg

*Swedish dramatist, author of Miss Julie and The Ghost Sonata, died 1912.*

Everything is atoned for.

## Maurice Ravel

*French composer, died 1937.*
*Looking at his bandaged head in a mirror...*

I look like a Moor.

## Walter Reed

*American Army bacteriologist, died 1902.*
*Reacting to his promotion to Colonel...*

I care nothing for that now.

## Kenneth Rexroth

*American painter, poet and champion of the Beat movement, died 1982.*
*Remembering his father's last words...*

He said he was dying of fast women, slow horses, crooked cards and straight whiskey.

*Maurice Ravel, composer, died 1937.*

**Armand-Jean du Plessis, Cardinal Richelieu**
*French statesman, died 1642.*
I have no enemies save those of the State.

**'Rob Roy' Macgregor**
*Scottish chieftain and outlaw, died 1734.*
Now all is over. Let the piper play 'Return No More'.

**John Wilmot, Earl of Rochester**
*British poet and libertine, died 1680.*
The only objection to the Bible is a bad life.

**George Brydges, first Baron Rodney**
*British admiral, died 1792.*
I am very ill indeed.

**Salvator Rosa**
*Italian artist, died 1673.*
To judge by what I now endure, the hand of death grasps me strongly.

**Claudius Salmasius (Claude de Saumaise)**
*French classical scholar, died 1653.*
Oh sirs, mind the world less and God more. Had I but one more year it should be spent in studying David's Psalms and Paul's Epistles.

**Franz Schubert**
*Austrian composer of 'lieder' and chamber music, died 1828.*
Here, here is my end.

**Adam Smith**
*Scottish political economist, author of The Wealth of Nations, died 1790.*
I believe we must adjourn the meeting to some other place.

**Al Smith**
*American politician, died 1944.*
Start the Act of Contrition.

**Charles Proteus Steinmetz**
*German-born American electrical engineer and pioneer of the alternating current, died 1923.*
All right. I'll lie down.

**Laurence Sterne**
*British novelist, author of Tristram Shandy, died 1768.*
Now it has come.

**Johann Strauss**
*Austrian composer, celebrated as the 'waltz king', died 1899.*
On receiving advice to get some sleep...
I will, whatever happens.

**Herman Strodtman**
*German murderer, hanged at Tyburn 1701. Strodtman was working in London as an apprentice when he killed Peter Woltyer, his fellow apprentice.*
The lord's will be done! I am willing to die, only I beg of God that I may not (as I deserve) die an eternal death, and that, though I die here for my most heinous and enormous crimes, yet I may, for the love of Christ, live eternally with him in heaven. God bless the King and all my honourable judges: they have done me no wrong, but it is I that have done great wrong. The lord be merciful to me, a great sinner, else I perish.

**John Millington Synge**
*Irish dramatist, author of 'The Playboy of the Western World', died 1909.*
It is no use fighting death any longer.

*Adam Smith, political economist, died 1790.*

*Johann Strauss, 'waltz king', died 1899.*

*Laurence Sterne, author, died 1768.*

### Zachary Taylor
*President of the United States, died 1850.*
I am about to die, I expect the summons soon, I have endeavoured to discharge all my official duties faithfully. I regret nothing, but am sorry that I am about to leave my friends.

### William Tennant
*Scottish Presbyterian divine, died 1777.*
I am sensible of the violence of my disorder, and that it is accompanied by symptoms of approaching dissolution, But, blessed be God, I have no wish to live if it should be His will to call me hence.

### Baron Edward Thurlow
*Lord Chancellor of England, died 1806.*
I'll be shot if I don't believe I'm dying!

*Facing page: Edward Wilson (seated left) photographed during Scott's Expedition to the antarctic. Scott himself (see page 33) stands in the centre and Captain Oates (see page 40) is at Scott's left.*

### Anthony Trollope
*British novelist, author of* The Barchester Chronicles, *died 1882.*
*The final lines of his autobiography...*
Now I stretch out my hand, and from the further shore I bid adieu to all who have cared to read any among the many words I have written.

### John Tyler
*President of the United States, died 1862.*
I am going. Perhaps it is for the best

### Lucilio Vanini
*Italian philosopher, burned in 1619 for giving natural explanations of 'miracles'.*
There is neither God nor devil: for if there were a God, I would pray him to send a thunderbolt on the Council, as all that is unjust and iniquitous; and if there were a devil I would pray him to engulf it in the subterranean regions; but since there is neither one nor the other, there is nothing for me to do.

### Thorstein Veblen
*American economist, died 1929.*
*A farewell note...*
It is also my wish, in case of death, to be cremated, if it can be conveniently done, as expeditiously and inexpensively as may be, without ritual or ceremony of any kind; that my ashes be thrown loose into the sea, or some other sizeable stream running to the sea; that no tombstone, inscription or monument of any name or nature, be set up in my memory or name in any place or at any time; that no obituary, memorial portrait, or biography of me, nor any letters written to or by me be printed or published, or in any way reproduced or circulated.

### Sam Ward
*American bandit, died 1884.*
I think I am going to give up the ghost.

### James Watt
*British engineer, pioneer of steam power, died 1819.*
*To the friends gathered at his bedside...*
I am very sensible of the attachment you show me, and I hasten to thank you for it, as I feel that I am now come to my last illness.

### Carl Maria von Weber
*German composer, died 1826.*
Now let me sleep.

### Thurlow Weed
*American politician, died 1852.*
I want to go home!

### Joseph Blanco White
*British theologist, died 1841.*
Now I die.

### Christof Wieland
*German dramatist, died 1813.*
To sleep...to die.

### Edward Wilson
*British doctor and explorer, killed 1912. Wilson was lost with Scott's Antarctic Expedition; this letter was left for his wife...*
God knows I am sorry to be the cause of sorrow to anyone in the world, but everyone must die and at every death there must be some sorrow. All the things I hoped to do with you after this Expedition are as nothing now, but there are greater things for us to do in the world to come. My only regret is leaving you to struggle through your life alone, but I may be coming to you by a quicker way. I feel so happy now in having got time to write to you. One of my notes will surely reach you. Dad's little compass and Mother's little comb are in my pocket. Your little testament and prayer book will be in my hand or in my breast pocket when the end comes. All is well.

### William Woodville
*British physician and botanist, died 1805. Advising the carpenter who was measuring him for his coffin...*
I shall not live more than two days, therefore make haste.

### Francisco Ximenes de Cisneros
*Spanish Cardinal, died 1774.*
This is death.

### Wilhelm Waiblinger
*German poet, died 1830.*
Addio!

### Count Ferdinand von Zeppelin
*Inventor of the airship, died 1917.*
I have perfect faith.

### Zeno
*Stoic philosopher, died 257 BC.*
Earth, do you demand me? I am ready.

### John von Zimmermann
*Swiss doctor, died 1795.*
I am dying. Leave me alone.

# ACROSS THE GREAT DIVIDE

*If you've got to go, go now.*

## Charles Abbott
*First Lord Tenterden and Lord Chief Justice, died 1832.*
*Addressing an imaginary jury...*
Gentlemen, you are all dismissed.

## John Abernethy
*British surgeon, died 1831.*
Is there anybody in the room?

## Alexander Adam
*British schoolmaster, died 1809.*
*Imagining that he was still teaching his old class...*
That Horace was very well said, you did not do it so well. But it grows dark, very dark. But it grows dark, boys you may go; we must put off the rest till tomorrow.

## John Adams
*President of the United States, died 1826.*
Thomas Jefferson still survives.

## William Ainsworth
*British editor and novelist, died 1882.*
*His last letter...*
Dr. Holman thought me much wasted since I last saw him and so I am in no doubt.
Your affectionate cousin...

## William Allingham
*British poet, died 1889.*
I am seeing things that you know nothing of.

## Eugene Aram
*British murderer, executed 1759.*
*Aram left this suicide note in his cell. His efforts to cheat the gallows failed: he had slashed his wrist and arm, but missed the artery. Thus saved, he was still hanged...*
My dear friend, Before this reaches you I shall be no more a living man in this world, though at present in perfect bodily health; but who can describe the horrors of mind which I suffer at this instant? Guilt – the guilt of blood shed without any provocation, without any cause but that of filthy lucre pierces my conscience with wounds that give the most poignant pains! 'Tis true the consciousness of my horrid guilt has given me frequent interruptions in the midst of my business or pleasures; but yet I have found means to stifle its clamours, and contrived a momentary remedy for the disturbance it gave me by applying to the bottle or the bowl, or diversions, or company, or business; sometimes one, and sometimes the other, as opportunity offered: but now all these, and all other amusements, are at an end, and I am left forlorn, helpless, and destitute of every comfort; for I have nothing now in view but the certain destruction both of my soul and body. My conscience will now no longer suffer itself to be hoodwinked or browbeat; it has now got the mastery; it is my acenser, judge, and executioner; and the sentence it pronounced against me is more dreadful than that I heard from the bench, which only condemned my body to the pains of death, which are soon over; but Conscience tells me plainly that she will summon me before another tribunal, where I shall have neither power nor means to stifle the evidence she will there bring against me; and that the sentence which will then be denounced will not only be irreversible, but will condemn my soul to torments that will know no end. 'Oh! had I but hearkened to the advice which dearbought experience has enabled me to give, I should not now have been plunged into that dreadful gulf of despair which I find it impossible to extricate myself from; and therefore my soul is filled with honour inconceivable. I see both God and man my enemies, and in a few hours shall be exposed in a public spectacle for the world to gaze at. Can you conceive any condition more horrible than mine? O, no! it cannot be! I am determined, therefore, to put a short end to trouble I am no longer able to bear, and prevent the executioner by doing his business with my own hand, and shall by this means at least prevent the shame and disgrace of a public exposure, and leave the care of my soul in the hands of eternal mercy. Wishing you all health, happiness, and prosperity, I am, to the last moment of my life, yours, with the sincerest regard, Eugene Aram.

## Ludovico Ariosto
*Italian romantic poet, died 1533.*
This is not my home.

## Dr. Thomas Arnold
*Headmaster of Rugby School, the 'Doctor' of the school story* Tom Brown's Schooldays, *died 1842.*
*Hearing that his death was not far off...*
Ah, very well.

*Facing page: Collette... 'curves and spheres and circles'.*

*Ludovico Ariosto.*

### George C. Atcheson
%%%%%? Died in a plane crash, ????
As the plane plunged towards the ocean...
Well, it can't be helped.

### Jane Austen
British writer, author of 'Pride and Prejudice' and 'Sense and Sensibility', died 1817.
Asked what she required...
Nothing but death.

### Marie Bashkirtseff
Russian diarist, died 1884.
As she watched a candle go out by her bed...
We shall go out together.

### Lord Beaverbrook
Canadian-born press magnate, died 1964.
His last public statement...
This is my final word. It is time for me to become an apprentice once more. I have not settled in which direction. But somewhere, sometime, soon.

### Henry Ward Beecher
American divine and religious author, died 1887.
Now comes the mystery.

### Claude Bernard
French physiologist, died 1878.
Commenting on a travelling rug that had been spread over his knees...
This time it will serve me for the voyage from which there is no return; the voyage of eternity.

### Jacob Boehm
German mystic, died 1624.
Do you hear the music?
Now I go hence.

### Simón Bolívar
'The Great Liberator' of Latin America, died 1830.
Mourning the fact that he was dying in exile...
Let us go, these people don't want us in this land. Let us go, boys! Take my baggage on board the frigate.

*Simon Bólívar: great liberator... and great cigar?*

### Charles Bonnet
Swiss naturalist and philosophical writer, died 1793.
Bonnet believed one of his servants was stealing from him; his wife persuaded one to 'confess' and humour his delusion...
So he repents. Let him come in and all will be overlooked.

### Andrew Bradford
American magazine publisher, died 1742.
His American Magazine, published in 1741, was the first ever such publication to appear in the then colony.
Oh Lord, forgive the errata!

### William Cullen Bryant
American poet and newspaper editor, died 1878.
Bryant tripped fatally in the street and the blow to his head disorientated him...
Whose house is this? What street is this? Would you like to see Miss Fairchild [his niece]?

### Francis Buckland
British naturalist and Inspector of Fisheries, died 1880.
I am going on a long journey. I shall see many strange animals on the way. God is so good, so good to the little fishes, I do not believe He would let their Inspector suffer shipwreck at last.

### Henry Buckle
British historian, died 1862.
Poor little boys.

### Charles Burney
English music historian and father of Fanny Burney, died 1796.
All this will soon pass away as a dream.

### John Burroughs
American essayist and naturalist, died 1921.
How far are we from home?

### Robert Burton
British scholar, writer and Anglican clergyman, author of The Anatomy of Melancholy, died 1640.
Be not solitary, be not idle.

### Marshal Pierre Cambronne
French soldier and commander of the Old Guard at Waterloo, died 1842.
Ah mademoiselle, man is thought to be something, but he is nothing.

### Admiral Richard Carter
British sailor, died 1692.
Fight the ship. Fight the ship as long as she can swim.

### John J. Chapman
American essayist, died 1784.
I want to take it away!
I want to take it away!
Asked, did he mean the pillow?...
No, no! The mute, the mute I want to play on the open strings!

### G.K.Chesterton
British essayist, critic, novelist and poet, died 1936.
The issue now is clear: it is between light and darkness and everyone must choose his side.

### Talbot Clifton
British explorer, died 1928.
Oh, I offer it.

### Colette (Sidonie-Gabrielle Colette)
French novelist, died 1954.
To reach completion is to return to one starting point. My instinctive bent which takes pleasure in curves and spheres and circles.

### Alfred Cookman
American divine, died 1871.
I am sweeping through the gates, washed in the blood of the Lamb!

### Thomas Coryat
British explorer, died 1617.
Dying in delirium at Surat in Persia...
Sack, sack! Is there any such thing as sack? Pray you give me some sack!

### William Cowper
British poet, died 1800.
What does it signify?

### David Cox
British painter, died 1859.
What does it signify?

### Stephen Crane
American author, died 1900.
When you come to the hedge that we must all go over, it isn't so bad. You feel sleepy, you don't care. Just a little dreamy anxiety, which world you're really in, that's all.

### Marion Crawford
American novelist, died 1909.
I love to see the reflection of the sun on the bookcase.

### Isapwo Muksika Crowfoot
American Indian chief, died 1890.
A little while and I will be gone from among you. Whither I cannot tell. From nowhere we come, into nowhere we go. What is life? It is the flash of a firefly in the light. It is the breath of the buffalo in the wintertime. It is as the little shadow that runs across the grass and loses itself in the sunset.

### Clementine Cuvier
Daughter of the French zoologist and statesman Baron Georges Cuvier.
You know we are sisters for eternity There is life. It is only there that there is life.

### Jacques David
French painter, died 1825.
Checking a print of one of his own paintings...
Too dark...too light...the diminishing of the light is not well enough indicated...this place is blurred...however I must admit, that is a unique head of Leonidas.

## Edouard Dekker ('Multatuli')

*Dutch radical writer, died 1887.*
Writing to his postal chess opponent.

That you are still not crushed, I admit, but that will come a little later. And if this is too difficult for you, let it go if you like. The game can wait.

D. DIDEROT

## Denis Diderot

*French philosopher, encyclopedist and critic, died 1784.*

The first step towards philosophy is incredulity

## Frederick Douglass

*American Black civil rights campaigner, died 1895.*

Why, what does this mean?

## Eleanora Duse

*Italian actress, died 1924.*

We must stir ourselves. Move on! Work, work! Cover me! Must move on! Must work! Cover me!

## Thomas Alva Edison

*American inventor, died 1931.*
Among other inventions Edison pioneered the record-player, the carbon-button transmitter for the telephone speaker, the incandescent lamp, an experimental electric railway and key elements of motion-picture apparatus.

It is very beautiful over there.

## Johann Faust

*A wandering German conjurer and subject of works by Goethe and Marlowe, died 1541.*
As portrayed in Goethe's *Faust* he died on seeing a vision of beauty appear...

Ah, stay, thou art so fair.

## Adam Ferguson

*Scottish professor of philosophy, died 1816.*
He promised his attendant daughters...

There is another world.

## Robert Fergusson

*Scottish poet, died insane 1774.*
To an asylum warder...

What ails ye? Wherefore sorrow for me, sirs. I am very well cared for here, I do assure you. I want for nothing, but it is cold, it is very cold. You know, I told you, it would come to this at last, yes, I told you so. Oh, do not go yet, mother. I hope to be soon, oh, do not go yet, do not leave me!

## Kate Field

*American lecturer and explorer, died 1896.*

The Amherst Eclipse Expedition!

## Solomon Foot

*American Senator, died 1866.*

What, can this be death? Is it come already? I see it, I see it! The gates are wide open. Beautiful, beautiful.

## Rear Admiral Andrew Hull Foote

*American sailor, died 1863.*

We will have them, North and South. The coloured people, yes, we will have them. We must have charity, charity, charity...

## Archibald Forbes

*British war correspondent, died 1900.*
Remembering the horrors of the Zulu Wars...

Those guns, man, those guns! Don't you hear those guns?

## Sir Bartle Frere

*British colonial official, died 1884.*

If they would only read The Further Correspondence, they would surely understand. They must be satisfied.

## Friedrich Froebel

*German educator who was founder of the kindergarten, died 1852.*
Asking to be taken out into his garden...

My friend, I have peeked at lovely Nature all my life. Permit me to pass my last hours with this enchanting mistress.

## Frederick J. Furnivall

*British scholar, one-time editor of the Oxford English Dictionary and founder of innumerable literary and social clubs, died 1910.*
Asked how be wished to be remembered.

I want the Club...

## Pierre Gassendi

*French scientist, mathematician and philosopher, died 1655.*

You see what is man's life.

## Thomas Goffe

*British poet, died 1629.*
He had been told by one Thomas Thimble that his wife would break his heart...

Oracle, oracle, Tom Thimble.

## Henri Gregoire

*French clergyman and Bishop of Blois, died 1831.*

His mind was lost in delirium... Monsieur Baradère, I have been tormented for eight days. I see a whole population of blacks isolated on an island which serves as their refuge. They are going to die of hunger! I was told that some Protestants and Jews came to see me; although they are not of my church, I desire to make acknowledgements of them. Let someone send theological books to Haiti. The poor Haitians! I see that my last hour is come. Do not desert me in my last moments!

*Thomas Edison, inventor extraordinary, died 1931.*

### Mrs Henrietta Hamlin
*American missionary in Turkey, died late 19th century.*

What child is this? Is it little Carrie? Yes! It is little Carrie, and the room is full of them.

### Kasper Hauser
*A mysterious German youth who was killed mysteriously in 1833.*
Hauser's enigmatic appearance in Germany fascinated Europe. Some claimed he was the son of the Grand Duke of Baden, put aside to favour a relation. No-one ever discovered the truth...

I didn't do it myself. Many cats are the sure death of a mouse.

### Rev. John Henley ('Orator Henley')
*British preacher, died 1756.*
He could apparently see some heavenly vision...

Stay! Stay! Stay!

### O. Henry (William S. Porter)
*American short story writer, died 1910.*

Turn up the lights. I don't want to go home in the dark.

### Thomas Hobbes
*British political theorist, author of Leviathan, died 1679.*

I am about to take my last voyage. A great leap in the dark.

### Charles Hodge
*American theologian, died 1878.*
My work is done. The pins of the tabernacle are taken Out.

### A. E. Housman
*British classical scholar and poet, author of A Shropshire Lad, died 1936.*
Hearing a joke as he lay dying...

I'll tell that story on the golden floor.

### Victor Hugo
*French poet, novelist, and dramatist, author of Notre-Dame de Paris and Les Misérables, died 1885.*

I see the black light!

### Vicente Blasco Ibáñez
*Spanish writer and politician, author of The Four Horsemen of the Apocalypse and Blood and Sand, died 1928.*

My garden, my garden!

### Henry James
*American novelist, author of Washington Square, Daisy Miller and The Portrait of a Lady, died 1916.*

So here it is at last, the distinguished thing.

### Don John of Austria
*Spanish general, died 1578.*
Speaking in a child's high-pitched voice...

Aunt, Aunt! My lady Aunt!

### Edmund Kean
*British actor, died 1833.*
In a delirium...

Give me another horse... Howard!

### 'Cholly Knickerbocker' (Maury Paul)
*New York gossip columnist, died 1942.*
Oh Mother, how beautiful it is.

### Charles Lee
*American Revolutionary War general, died 1782.*
His last words were spoken in his final delirium...
Stand by me, my brave grenadiers.

### General Robert E. Lee
*Confederate general in the American Civil War, died 1870.*
Strike the tent!

### Charles, Prince de Ligne
*French aristocrat, died 1814.*
He was raving at some unseen horror...
Back, thou accursed phantom!

### Franz Liszt
*Hungarian piano virtuoso and composer, best-known for his 'Faust Symphony' and a number of piano concertos, died 1886.*
Tristan!

### Gustav Mahler
*Austrian-Jewish composer and conductor noted for his ten symphonies and various songs with orchestra, died 1911.*
Mozart!

*Right:
Gustav Mahler
died in 1911...
but not in Venice.*

### Matthew Maury
*American naval officer, pioneer hydrographer, and one of the founders of oceanography, died 1873.*

Bear me through the pass where the laurels bloom. Are my feet growing cold? Do I drag my anchors? All's well.

### General George Gordon Meade
*American Civil War commander, died 1872.*

I am about crossing a beautiful wide river and the opposite shore is coming nearer and nearer.

### Herman Melville
*American author, best-known for Moby Dick, died 1891.*
The writer quoted another of his great creations, Billy Budd...

God bless Captain Vere!

### Jules Michelet
*French historian, died 1874.*
The nurse to change his linen...

Linen, doctor, you speak of linen. Do you know what linen is? The linen of the peasant, the worker...linen is a great thing, I want to make a book of it.

### Silas Weir Mitchell
*American neurologist, died 1914*
As he died the doctor relived an emergency operation on a Civil War battlefield...

That leg must come off.
Save the leg... lose the life!

### Dwight Lyman Moody
*American evangelist, died 1899.*
*With his partner Ira D.Sankey, a hymn writer,*
*he became the most successful evangelist*
*of the 19th century.*
I see earth receding. Heaven is opening. God is calling me.

### Laurence Oliphant
*British author, traveller and mystic, a*
*pioneer of efforts to establish a Jewish*
*state in Palestine, died 1888.*
More light!

### Edwards Park
*American educator and scholar, died 1899.*
These passages may be found on the following pages...

### Sir William Parry
*British arctic explorer, died 1855.*
The chariots and the horses!

### Rev. Edward Payson
*British divine, died 1827.*
Faith and patience hold out. I feel like a mote in a sunbeam.

### Luigi Pirandello
*Italian dramatist, author of* Six Characters
in Search of an Author, *died 1936.*
The hearse, the horse, the driver and – enough!

### Bishop Beilby Porteous
*British clergyman, author of the* Porteusian
Index, *a censored reading of the Bible,*
*died 1808.*
Oh, that glorious sun!

### Thomas De Quincey
*British writer, author of* Confessions of an
Opium Eater, *died 1859.*
*In his final delirium...*
Sister, sister, sister.

### John Raymond
*British scholar.*
How easy to glide from the work here to the work there.

### Charles Reade
*British social reformer and dramatist,*
*died 1884.*
Amazing, amazing glory! I am having Paul's understanding.

### Jean-Paul Richter
*German romantic novelist, died 1825.*
My beautiful flowers, my lovely flowers.

### Robbie Ross
*British writer and critic; he was the*
*companion of Oscar Wilde, died 1918.*
*Punning on Keats' famous farewell lines...*
Here lies one whose name was written in hot water.

### Rev. Samuel Rutherford
*British divine, died 1779.*

*Franz Liszt*

If he should slay me ten thousand times, ten thousand times I'll trust him. I feel, I feel, I believe in joy and rejoice. I feed on manna. Oh for arms to embrace him! Oh for a well-tuned harp!

### Jean-Jacques Rousseau
*Swiss-born political theorist, author of*
The Social Contract, *died 1778.*
See the sun, whose smiling face calls me, see that immeasurable light. There is God! Yes, God himself, who is opening His arms and inviting me to taste at last that eternal and unchanging joy that I had so long desired.

### Auguste Saint-Gaudens
*French sculptor, died 1907.*
*He was watching a sunset...*
It's very beautiful, but I want to go farther away.

### Jules Ami Sandoz
*American pioneer.*
The whole damn sandhills is deserted, the cattlemen are broke, the settlers about gone. I got to start all over, ship in a lot of good farmers in the spring, build up, build, build...

### Johann Christoph Friedrich von Schiller
*German dramatist and poet, died 1805.*
Many things are growing plain and clear to my understanding. One look at the...

### Mary-Anne Schimmelpenninck
*German author of children's books,*
*died 1856.*
Oh, I hear such beautiful voices, and the children are the loudest.

### Friedrich von Schlegel
*German literary historian, died 1829.*
But the consummate and perfect knowledge…

### 'Dutch Schultz' (Arthur Fleigenheimer)
*Chicago gangster, shot 1935.*
Police stenographers recorded the Dutchman's last ravings. They could make little sense of the lengthy diatribe that ended…
Turn your back to me, please Henry, I am so sick now. The police are getting many complaints. Look out I want that G-note. Look out for Jimmy Valentine, for he's a friend of mine. Come on, come on, Jim. OK, OK, I am all through. I can't do another thing. Look out mamma. Look out for her. Police, mamma, Helen, please take me out. I will settle the incident. Come on, open the soak duckets; the chimney sweeps. Talk to the sword. Shut up, you got a big mouth! Please help me to get up. Henry! Max! Come over here. French Canadian bean soup. I want to pay. Let them leave me alone.

### George Augustus Selwyn
*English clergyman, Bishop of Lichfield, died 1878.*
It is all light.

### Louise Serment ('The Philosopher')
*French writer, died 18th century.*
Soon the light of the skies
Will be gone from my eyes.
Soon the black night will creep,
Bringing smooth dreamless sleep. Gone – the struggle and strife of the sad dream of life.

### William Sharp ('Fiona McLeod')
*Scottish poet, died 1905.*
Oh, the beautiful 'Green Life' again. Ah, all is well.

### Joanna Southcott
*Religious fanatic and mystic, died 1814.*
Southcott died of brain disease, still convinced of her supernatural powers, though when her famous 'Box' of prophecies was opened in 1927 it was found to contain nothing of interest.
If I have been deceived, doubtless it was the work of a spirit. Whether the spirit was good or bad I do not know.

### Henry Morton Stanley
*American explorer and 'discoverer' of the missing missionary Dr. David Livingstone, died 1904.*
Four o'clock. How strange. So that is time. Strange. Enough!

*Alfred, Lord Tennyson.*

---

### Louise Turck Stanton
*American socialite, died 1933.*
Two weeks after her beloved husband had been killed in a car crash Stanton flew her plane out over the Atlantic and vanished. She left a last letter.
I'm just going out into space to find out what it's all about; if there isn't anything that will be OK too.

### Myra Belle Starr
*American horse thief, died 1889.*
The 'Bandit Queen' of the Old West, beloved of romantic myth-makers, perpetuated the illusions on her gravestone.
Shed not for her the bitter tear
Nor give the heart to vain regret.
'Tis but the casket that lies here
The gem that fills it sparkles yet.

### Gertrude Stein
*American writer and patron of the arts, died 1945.*
Stein's last conversation was recorded by Duncan Sutherland. Just before she died she asked, 'What is the answer?' No answer came. She laughed and said…
In that case, what's the question?

### Jane Taylor
*British children's author, died 1823.*
Are we not children, all of us?

### Alfred, Lord Tennyson
*British Poet Laureate, died 1892.*
Whether Tennyson referred to a package, or something more mysterious, was not established…
I have opened it.

### Saint Teresa of Avila
*Religious reformer and mystic, died 1582.*
Over my spirit flash and float in divine radiancy the bright and glorious visions of the world to which I go.

### William Terriss
*British murder victim, killed 1897.*
I shall come back…
He then seemed to die, but added…
Can any man be so foolish as to believe there is no afterlife?

### William Makepeace Thackeray
*British novelist, author of Vanity Fair, died 1863.*
And my heart throbbed with an exquisite bliss.

---

### Theodore Thomas
*German-born conductor, died 1905.*
I have had a beautiful vision, a beautiful vision.

### Henry David Thoreau
*American radical ascetic and writer, author of Walden, died 1862.*
Asked whether he had finally made his peace with God…
We never quarrelled. Moose… Indian…

### Hideko Tojo
*Japanese politician and soldier, died 1948.*
Oh look, see how the cherry blossoms fall mutely.

### Leo Nicolayevitch Tolstoy
*Russian novelist, author of War and Peace, Anna Karenina and The Death of Ivan Ilyich, died 1910.*
The truth,…I care a great deal…how they…

### J. M. W. Turner
*British artist, died 1851.*
The Sun is God.

### Mark Twain (Samuel Clemens)
*American humorous novelist, author of Tom Sawyer and Huckleberry Finn, died 1910.*
Twain's deathbed memorandum read…
Death, the only immortal, who treats us all alike, whose peace and whose refuge are for all. The soiled and the pure, the rich and the poor, the loved and the unloved.

### Jonah Ustinov ('Klop')
*Russian father of actor and raconteur Peter Ustinov, died 1962.*
I will remember you in my dreams.

### Daniel Webster
*American lawyer and politician, died 1852.*
Well children, doctor, I trust on this occasion I have said nothing unworthy of Daniel Webster. Life – life. Death – death. How curious it is.

### Sarah Wesley
*Wife of Methodist founder John Wesley.*
Open the gates! Open the gates!

### Victor Yvart
*Belgian writer, died 1831.*
Nature, how lovely thou art.

### Florenz Ziegfeld
*American impresario, died 1932.*
Dying in his apartment Ziegfeld imagined himself once more at a 'Follies' first night…
Curtain! Fast music! Lights! Ready for the last finale! Great! The show looks good, the show looks good!

# NEARER MY GOD

*Never mind, we'll all be with our maker soon.*

### Bishop Abbot
*British clergyman, died 1633.*
Come Lord Jesu, come quickly. Finish in me the work that Thou hast begun. Into Thy hands oh Lord I commend my spirit, for Thou hast redeemed me, oh God of truth. Save Thy servant who hopes and confides in Thee alone. Let Thy mercy, oh Lord, be shown unto me. In Thee have I trusted, Oh Lord, let me not be confounded for ever.

### Madame Adélaide
*Duchess of Luxembourg.*
Her aunt Madame de Maintenon promised her that she would be with God...
Yes, Aunt.

### Albert, Margrave of Brandenburg
*German aristocrat, died 1170.*
Lord Jesus.

### Georges d'Amboise
*French cardinal and chief minister of state under Louis XII, died 1510.*
I believe.

### Fisher Ames
*American politician, died 1808.*
I have peace of mind. It may arise from stupidity, but I think it is founded on a belief of the gospel. My hope is in the mercy of God.

### James Andrew
*British Methodist bishop and President of the East India Company's Military Seminary, died 1833.*
God bless you all.

### Eusebius Andrews
*British divine and supporter of the exiled Charles II, beheaded for treason 1650.*
Lord Jesus receive me!

### Anéglique Arnauld ('Mère Angélique')
*Jansenist reformer and nun, died 1661.*
Oh Jesus, oh Jesus, you are my God, my justice, my strength, my all.

### Earl of Arundel
*British Catholic aristocrat, beheaded for treason 1580.*
Jesus, Mary!

### Roger Ascham
*British humanist and gambler, died 1568.*
I desire to depart and be with Christ.

### Cardinal d'Astros
*French clergyman, died 1851.*
Neither life, nor death, nor any being can separate us from Him.

### Cardinal d'Aste
*French clergyman, died @@@@@???.*
I wish to die sitting, in tribute to the most worshipful will of my good and precious Jesus.

### Dr. Frederick Baedeker
*German Missionary, died 1906.*
I am going in to see the King in all His beauty.

### John Bannister
*British comic actor, died 1836.*
My hope is in Christ

### Richard Baxter
*British Presbyterian divine, died 1691.*
I have pain there is no arguing against sense but I have peace. I have peace! I am almost well.

### Cardinal David Beaton (or Bethune)
*Scottish statesman and clergyman, Archbishop of St. Andrews, died 1546.*
I am a priest Fie, fie! All is gone!

### Rev. Joseph Beaumont
*British clergyman, Master of Peterhouse, Cambridge, and poet, died 1699.*
Beaumont collapsed in the pulpit after announcing the next hymn...
Then, while the first Archangel sings, He hides his face beneath His wings.

### The Venerable Bede
*English historian, author of The History of the English Church and People, died 735.*
It is brought to an end. Take my head in your hands for it is very pleasing to me to sit facing my holy place where I have been used to pray, so that I may sit and call upon my Father. Gloria Patri et Filio et Spiritu Sancto.

### Bishop Bedell
*Irish clergyman, Bishop of Kilmore and Ardagh, died 1642.*
I have kept the faith once given to the Saints for which cause I have also suffered these things, but I am not ashamed for I know whom I have believed and I am persuaded that he is able to keep that which I have committed to him against that day.

*Facing page:*
*In 1492 Columbus sailed the ocean blue. In 1506 he died.*

### Bergerus
*Councillor to Emperor Maximilian, died 16th century.*
Farewell, oh farewell all earthly things. And welcome heaven.

### Charles, Duc de Berry
*French aristocrat, died 1820.*
Blessed Virgin, have mercy.

### Cardinal de Berulle
*French clergyman, died 1629.*
I do bless…Jesus, Mary, bless, rule and govern.

### Johann Bessarion
*German humanist, died 1472.*
Thou art just, oh Lord, and just are Thy decrees, but Thou art good and merciful and Thou wilt not recall our failings.

### Edward Bickersteth
*British evangelical divine, died 1850.*
The Lord bless thee, my child, with overflowing grace, now and forever.

### John Blackie
*Scottish man of letters, died 1895.*
The Psalms of David and the Songs of Burns, but the Psalmist first. Psalms…poetry…

### Ambrosius Blaurel
*Swabian reformer.*
Oh my Lord Jesus, this made you in your great thirst desire nothing, but you were given gall and vinegar.

### Charles James Blomfield
*Bishop of London, died 1857.*
I am dying.

### Johann Bluntschli
*Swiss jurist, died 1881.*
Glory be to God in the highest. Peace on earth, good will to all men.

### Herman Boerhaave
*Dutch doctor, died 1738.*
He that loves God ought to think nothing desirable but what is pleasing to the Supreme Goodness.

### Henry, Viscount Bolingbroke
*British philosopher and politician, died 1751.*
*A letter to Lord Chesterfield…*
God who placed me here will do what He pleases with me hereafter and He knows best what to do. May He bless you.

### Auguste Bouvier
*French Protestant theologian, died 1564.*
My God, my God!

### Robert Boyle
*Anglo-Irish chemist and natural philosopher noted for his pioneering experiments on the properties of gases, died 1691.*
We shall there desire nothing that we have not, except more tongues to sing more praise to Him.

### David Brainerd
*British missionary, died 1747.*
I am almost in eternity. I long to be there. The watcher is with me. Why tarry the wheels of his chariot? Lord, now let Thy servant depart in peace.

### Johann Breitinger
*Swiss critic, died 1776.*
Living or dying, we are the Lord's.

### Frederika Bremer
*Swedish novelist, Sweden's 'Jane Austen', died 1865.*
Ah, my child, let us speak of Christ's love…the best, the highest love.

### Arthur Brisbane
*British journalist, died 1836.*
*He died quoting Voltaire's Candide…*
This is the best of all possible worlds.

### Bishop Brooks of Massachusetts
*American clergyman, died 1893.*
There is no other life but the eternal.

### Eldridge Brooks
*American editor, died 1902.*
My head is pillowed on the bosom of the dear Lord.

### John Brown
*Scottish preacher, died 1787*
My Christ!

### Robert Bruce
*Scottish theologian, died 1631.*
Now God be with you, my dear children, I have breakfasted with you and shall sup with my Lord Jesus Christ

### Martin Bucer
*German Protestant reformer, died 1551.*
He pointed three fingers to the sky. He governs and disposes all.

### George Bull
*British theologian, died 1710.*
Amen.

### William Bull
*British Congregationalist, died 1814.*
Bless the Lord!

### John Bunyan
*Religious writer, author of The Pilgrim's Progress, died 1688.*
*Bunyan quoted the burial service…*
Weep not for me but for yourselves. I go to the Father of our Lord Jesus Christ who will, no doubt, through the mediation of His blessed Son, receive me, though a sinner. Where I hope that we, ere long, shall meet to sing the new song and remain everlastingly happy, world without end.

### Major-General Andrew Burn
*British soldier, died 1824.*
*Asked if he would like to see anyone…*
Nobody, nobody but Jesus Christ. Christ crucified is the stay of my poor soul.

### Lady Isabel Burton
*Wife of the explorer Sir Richard Francis Burton, died 1896.*
Thank God.

### Horace Bushnell
*Congregational minister and controversial theologian, the 'father of American religious liberalism', died 1876.*
Well, now we are all going home together and I say, the Lord be with you and in grace and in peace and love. And that is the way I have come along home.

### Simeon Calhoun
*American missionary, died 1876.*
Were the church of Christ what she should be, twenty years would not pass away without the story of Christ being uttered in the ear of every living person.

### Antonio Canova
*Italian sculptor, died 1822.*
Pure and amiable spirit.

### William Carstares
*Scottish statesman and divine, died 1715.*
I have peace with God through our Lord Jesus Christ.

## William Caxton
*The first British printer, died 1491.*

God then give us His grace and find in us such a house that it may please Him to lodge therein, to the end that in this world He keeps us from adversity spiritual and in the end of our days He brings us with Him into His realm of heaven for to be partners of the glory eternal which grant to us the Holy Trinity.

## Thomas Charles of Bala
*Welsh preacher and writer, died 1814. Offered a glass of Madeira...*

Yes, if the Lord pleases.

## Mathias Claudius
*German poet, died 1815.*

Lead me not into temptation, deliver me from evil. Goodnight.

## Margaret Clitheroe, 'The Martyr of York'
*English religious martyr, executed 1586. Accused of harbouring a Roman Catholic priest, she was pressed to death by the 'peine forte et dure'...*

Jesu, Jesu, have mercy on me.

## Thomas Cobden-Sanderson
*British designer and book-binder, died 1922.*
*The last entry in his diary...*

Every day, every day my Guide says to me 'Are you ready?' And I say to my guide 'I am ready'. And my Guide says 'March'. And to the end one day more I march, Everyday am I ever on the ever-diminishing way to the end.

## Sir Edward Coke
*British judge and legal writer, died 1633.*

Thy kingdom come,
Thy will be done.

## Giovanni Columbini
*Founder of the Jesuate Order, died 1367.*

Father, into Thy hands I commend my spirit.

## Christopher Columbus
*Italian explorer, European discoverer of the Americas, died 1506.*

Into Thy hand, Oh Lord, I commit my spirit.

## Edward Copleston
*British clergyman, Bishop of Llandaff, died 1849.*

I expect soon to die and I die in the firm faith of the redemption wrought by God in man through Christ Jesus, assured that all who believe in Him will be saved.

## John Cosin
*British, Bishop of Durham, died 1672.*

Lord.

## Mandell Creighton
*British scholar, historian, and bishop successively of Peterborough and London, died 1901.*

God.

## Howard Crosby
*American scholar, died 1891.*

My heart is resting sweetly with Jesus and my hand is in His.

## Bishop Cummings
*British clergyman, died 1876.*

Jesus! Precious Saviour!

## Ernst Curtius
*German archaeologist who directed the excavation of Olympia, died 1896.*

As the bird with the day's last gleam
Wearily sings itself asleep.
As it twitters in its dream
Ever fainter comes its peep.
So my songs scarce reach the ear,
Overtaken by my night.
But the loud ones will burst clear
When it comes another light!

## Varina H. Davis
*Wife of Confederate President Jefferson Davis, died 1898.*

Oh Lord, in Thee have I trusted. Let me not be confounded.

## Wentworth Dillon
*Earl of Roscommon, died 1684.*
*His own translation of the Dies Irae...*

My God, my Father and my Friend, do not forsake me in the end.

## Duchesse de Dondeauville
*French aristocrat.*
*Asked if she loved God...*

Yes.

## Paul L. Dunbar
*American poet, died 1906.*

Through the valley of the shadow.

## Mary Baker Eddy
*American evangelist, founder of the Christian Science Church, died 1910.*

God is my life.

## Richard Lovell Edgeworth
*British writer, died 1817.*

I die with the soft feeling of gratitude to my friends and submission to the God who made me.

## Jonathan Edwards
*American Puritan theologian and philosopher, died 1758.*

Trust in God and you need not fear.

## Dwight D. Eisenhower
*American president, died 1969.*

I want to go. God take me.

## Desiderius Erasmus
*Dutch scholar, the most learned and influential European intellectual of his era and a pioneer of Humanism, died 1536.*

Dear God!

## Thomas Erskine of Linlathen
*Scottish theologian, died 1639.*

You there! To the end! Oh Lord, my God. Jesus, Jesus Christ! Love. The peace of God, for ever and ever, for Jesus' sake, Amen and Amen.

## Jeremiah Evarts
*Missionary, died 1831.*

Wonderful, wonderful glory. We cannot understand, we cannot comprehend, wonderful glory, I will praise Him. Who are in the room? Call all in, call all, let a great many come. I wish to give directions, wonderful glory, Jesus reigns.

## Marchesa Giulietta Faletti
*Italian prison reformer.*

May the will of God be done in me and by me in time and for eternity.

## John Fawcett
*British Baptist theologian, died 1817.*

Come Lord Jesus, come quickly! Oh receive me to Thy children!

### Abbé Edgeworth de Firmont

*French clergyman, guillotined 1793.*
*Supposed words to Louis XVI of France as the Abbé mounted the scaffold...*
Son of Saint Louis, ascend to heaven.

### James Elroy Flecker

*American poet, died 1915.*
Lord, have mercy on my soul.

### John Foster

*British essayist, died 1876.*
I commend you to the God of mercy, and very affectionately bid you Farewell.

### Samuel Fothergill

*British Quaker, died 1772.*
All is well with me. Through the mercy of God, in Jesus Christ, I am going to a blessed and happy eternity. My troubles are ended. Mourn not for me.

### George Fox

*British founder of the Quaker movement, died 1691.*
I am glad I was here. Now I am clear, I am fully clear. All is well. The Seed of God reigns over all and over death itself. And though I am weak in body yet the power of God is over all and the Seed reigns over all disorderly spirits.

### Henry Watson Fox

*British missionary, died 1848.*
Jesus, Jesus must be first in the heart.
*Asked whether he was first in Fox's...*
Yes, He is.

### August Francke

*German scholar, died 1727.*
*Asked if Christ were still with him.*
Yes.

### James A. Froude

*British historian, died 1894.*
Shall not the Judge of all the earth do right?

### Elizabeth Fry

*British prison reformer, died 1845.*
Oh dear Lord, help and keep Thy servant.

### Andrew Fuller

*Founder of the American Baptist Missionary Society, died 1815.*
I have no religious joys, but I have a hope in the strength of which I think I could plunge into eternity.

### Edward Gibbon

*British historian, author of* The History of the Decline and Fall of the Roman Empire, *died 1794.*
Mon dieu! Mon dieu!

### George Gilfillan

*British writer and Presbyterian clergyman, died 1878.*
I am dying, doctor? O the will of the Lord be done... Yes, I believe in God, in Christ.

### Frédéric Godet

*Swiss theologian, died 1850.*
*To his assembled family...*
I have carried you in my heart all my life, and I hope it will still be permitted to do the same up there.

### William Godfrey

*Cardinal and archbishop of Westminster, died 1963.*
The Church gave me everything. [He was promptly answered: 'You gave everything to the Church.']

### John Mason Good

*British doctor and writer, died 1827.*
Which taketh away the sins of the world.

### Stephen Grellet

*Quaker missionary, died 1855.*
Not my will, but Thine be done.

### Robert Haldane

*British Evangelist, died 1842.*
Forever with the Lord. For ever, for ever.

### John Vine Hall

*Religious writer best known for his tract* The Sinner's Friend, *died 1860.*
Passing away, passing away. Jesus, Jesus! He is, he is! Pray. Amen!

### Wilhelm Hauff

*German novelist and poet, died 1827.*
Father, into Thy hands I commend my immortal spirit.

### Francis Havergal

*British poet and hymn writer, died 1879.*
He...

### Robert Hawker

*British poet, died 1875.*
His banner over me was love.

### Rev. Lemuel Haynes

*British divine, died 19th century.*
I love my wife, I love my children. But I love my Saviour better than all.

### Father Isaac Hecker

*Founder of the Paulists, died 1888.*
*Insisting on doing his own blessing...*
No, I will.

### Felicia Hemans

*British author, died 1835.*
I feel as if I were sitting with Mary at the feet my Redeemer, hearing His voice and learning of Him to be meek and lowly.

### Ebenezer Henderson the Elder

*Scottish missionary to Iceland, died 1858.*
My flesh and my heart faileth, but God is the strength of my heart and my portion for ever.

### James Hervey

*British divine, died 1758.*
Precious Salvation.

### Helius Eobanus Hessus

*German humanist, died 1133.*
I want to ascend to my Lord.

### Peter Heylin

*British divine, died 1662.*
I go to my God and Saviour.

### Francis Hodgson

*British schoolmaster, Provost of Eton College, died 1852.*
Charming... God's mercy.

### James Hope

*British physician, died 1841.*
I thank God.

### William Hunter

*British Protestant martyr, burnt 1555.*
Lord, Lord receive my spirit!

### Dean William Inge

*British clergyman, known as 'The Gloomy Dean' for his consistently pessimistic opinions, died 1954.*
*In an interview shortly before his death.*
If I could live my life over again I don't think I would be a clergyman. I know as much about the afterlife as you do. I

don't even know if there is one…in the sense that Church teaches.

## Rev. Edward Irving
*Scottish divine, died 1834.*
If I die, I die unto the Lord. Amen.

## John Angell James
*British Independent minister, died 1859.*
*He spoke to his doctor, quoting Jesus…*
Inasmuch as thou hast done it unto one of the least of these, thou hast done it unto Me.

## William Jennings Bryan
*American politician, died 1925.*
With hearts full of gratitude to God.

## Bishop Jewell
*Bishop of Salisbury, died 1571.*
This day let me see the Lord Jesus.

## Sir Henry Jones
*British professor of moral philosophy, died 1939.*
The Lord reigneth, let the earth rejoice.

## Joseph
*Biblical patriarch.*
I die. And God will surely visit you and bring you Out of the land unto the land which he sware to Abraham, Isaac and Jacob. God will surely visit you and ye shall carry my bones up from hence.

## Thomas Ken
*Bishop of Bath and Wells, died 1711.*
God's will be done.

## Johannes Kepler
*German astronomer and astrologer, died 1630.*
*Asked how he expected to be saved…*
Solely by the merits of Jesus Christ, Our Saviour.

## Martin Luther King
*American Black civil rights leader, assassinated 1968.*
*The night before he gave what would prove his last, prophetic speech…*
I have been to the top of the mountain and I have seen the promised land. Now I am happy, happy I am not afraid. Mine eyes have seen the glory of the coming of the Lord!

## Charles Kingsley
*British writer and pioneer of 'muscular Christianity', died 1875.*
*Kingsley quoted from the Episcopal funeral service…*
Thou knowest, Oh Lord the secrets of our hearts. Shut not Thy merciful ears to our prayers, but spare us, oh Lord most holy, oh God most mighty, oh holy and merciful Saviour, Thou most worthy judge eternal, suffer us not at our last hour, from any pains of death to fall from Thee.

## Friedrich Klopstock
*German epic and lyric poet, died 1803.*
*Recited the words of his own ode, 'Der Erbarmer'…*
Can a woman forget her child that she should not have pity on the fruit of her womb? Yes, she may forget, but I will not forget Thee!

## Meta Klopstock
*First wife of the poet Friedrich.*
*To her sister…*
It is over! The blood of Jesus Christ cleanse thee from all sin!

## John Knox
*Scottish Protestant reformer, died 1572.*
*Asked whether he had heard prayers…*
I wish to God you had heard them as I have heard them, and I praise God of that heavenly sound.

## William Henry Krause
*Irish divine, died 1852.*
I am so restless I can hardly think, but the Lord's hand is not shortened.

## Henri Lacordaire
*French Roman Catholic ecclesiastic, died 1861.*
My God, open to me!

## Adrienne Lecouvreur
*French actress, died 1730.*
*Asked by her priest to repent, she pointed to a bust of the Comte de Saxe…*
There is my universe, my hope, my deity.

## John Locke
*British philosopher and pioneer of the Enlightenment in England, died 1704.*
Oh, the depths of the riches and the goodness of the knowledge of God.

## Henry Luce
*American publishing entrepreneur, founder of Time and Life magazines, died 1967.*
Oh Jesus!

## Mary Lyon
*American educator, died 1849.*
I should love to come back to watch over the seminary, but God will take care of it.

## Cyrus Hall McCormick
*American inventor of the mechanical reaper, died 1884.*
It's all right, it's all right. I only want heaven.

## John Mcloughlin
*American pioneer, died 1857.*
*Asked 'Comment allez-vous?' (literally 'How do you go?') he punned…*
To God.

## Richard Mansfield
*British actor, died 1907.*
God is love.

## Margaret of Angoulême
*Queen consort of Henry II of Navarre and a major figure of the French Renaissance, died 1549.*
Jesus, Jesus, Jesus!

## Mother Marianne
*Dutch abbess of Molokat, died 1900.*
Now, Sister, to my room.

## Jaques Marquette ('Père Marquette')
*French Jesuit missionary and explorer, he made the first expedition down the Mississippi River, died 1675.*
Jesus, Mary.

## Mary, Countess of Warwick
*British aristocrat, died 1678.*
*To her attendants…*
Well ladies, if I were but one hour in heaven, I would not again be with you, much as I love you.

### John F. D. Maurice
*British scholar and socialist, died 1872.*
The knowledge of the love of God, the blessing of God Almighty, the Father, the Son and the Holy Ghost be amongst you, amongst us and remain with us forever.

### Giuseppe Mazzini
*Italian patriot, died 1872.*
Yes, yes! I believe in God.

### Aaron 'The Gambling Man' Mitchell
*American criminal, the last man to die on the San Quentin death row, 1967*
*He stood naked on a landing the night before his death, slashed his wrist and exclaimed…*
Do you know that I am going to die just like Jesus Christ did? I will die to save you guys.

### Sir Moses Montefiore
*British-Jewish magnate and philanthropist, died 1885.*
Thank God, thank heaven.

### Charles-Louis de Secondat, Comte de Montesquieu
*French political philosopher, died 1755.*
I am conscious of the greatness of God and the littleness of man.

### John Newton
*British divine, once a slaver, latterly a friend of the poet Cowper, died 1807.*
I am satisfied with the Lord's will.

### Katherine Norton
*Scottish gentlewoman, died, 1746.*
*She died after witnessing the execution at the stake of her betrothed the Jacobite rebel James Dawson. He was tried and convicted of high treason and executed on a day that, had he been pardoned, was to have been that of their marriage.*
My dear, I follow thee I follow thee! Sweet Jesus, receive both our souls together.

### Margaret Ogilvy
*Mother of Sir James Barrie, died 1895.*
God… love…

### Margaret Oliphant
*Scottish novelist, died 1897.*
I seem to see nothing but God and our Lord.

### John Owen
*British nonconformist divine and epigrammatist, died 1622.*
*Told by Rev. William Payne that the first sheet of his Meditations on the Glory of Christ was being printed…*
I am glad to hear it. But, oh Brother Payne, the long-wished for day is come at last, in which I shall see that glory in another manner than I have ever, or was capable of doing in this world.

*Joseph Priestley.*

### Blaise Pascal
*French mathematician and moralist, died 1662.*
May God never forsake me.

### Coventry Patmore
*British poet, died 1896.*
*Embracing his wife…*
I love you dear, but the Lord is my life and my light.

### Captain James Paton
*Scottish Covenanter, hanged in Edinburgh in 1684.*
*His last words from the scaffold…*
Farewell sweet scriptures, preaching, praying, reading, singing and all duties. Welcome, Father, Son and Holy Spirit. I desire to commit my soul to Thee in well-doing. Lord, receive my spirit.

### William Penn
*British-born founder of Pennsylvania, died 1718.*
To be like Christ is to be a Christian.

### Pope Pius IX
*Italian pontiff, creator of the doctrine of papal infallibility, died 1878.*
Death wins this time.

### John Preston
*British Puritan divine, died 1628.*
Blessed be God. Though I change my place I shall not change my company, for I have walked with God while living and now I go to rest with God.

### Joseph Priestley
*British minister and chemist, died 1804.*
I am going to sleep like you, but we shall all awake together and, I trust, to everlasting happiness.

### Edward Pusey
*British Anglican theologian, scholar and a leader of the High Church 'Oxford Movement', died 1882.*
My God!

### Francis Quarles
*British aphorist and religious poet, died 1644.*
What I cannot utter with my mouth, oh Lord, accept from heart and soul.

### William Romaine
*British theologian, died 1795.*
Holy, holy, holy blessed Lord Jesus. To Thee be endless praise.

### Pierre Royer-Collard
*French monarchist statesman and philosopher, prime exponent of the 'philosophy of perception', died 1845.*
There is nothing solid and substantial in the world but religious ideas.

### Charles Russell
*Lord Russell of Killowen, Lord Chief Justice of England, died 1900.*
My God, have mercy upon me.

### Samuel Rutherford
*Scottish Principal of St. Mary's College, St. Andrews, died 1661.*
Glory, Glory dwelleth in Emmanuel's land

### Rev. Thomas Rutherford
*Regius professor of divinity at Cambridge, died 1771.*
He has indeed been a precious Christ to me and now I feel him to be my rock, my strength, my rest, my hope, my joy, my all in all.

### Boéton de Saint-Laurent d'Airgorse
*Protestant and leader of the Camisard rebellion in France, broken on the wheel 1705.*
*To the executioner who was discussing whether he had yet suffered enough for a coup de grâce…*
My friend, you think that I am suffering, and you are not mistaken. I am suffering indeed, but he who is with me and for whom I suffer, gives me strength to endure my suffering with joy.
*Then to the watching crowd…*
My dear brethren, let my death aid you by its example to maintain the purity of the Gospel, and be ye my witness that I die in the religion of Christ and his blessed apostles.

### Lawrence Saunders
*British Protestant martyr, burnt 1555.*
Welcome the cross of Christ. Welcome everlasting life.

## Etienne Senancour
*French romantic novelist, died 1846.*
Eternity, be thou my refuge.

## Elizabeth Seton
*Founder of the American Sisters of Charity, died 1821.*
Soul of Christ sanctify me, body of Christ save me, blood of Christ inebriate me, water out of the side of Christ strengthen me Jesus, Mary and Joseph.

## Mary Martha Sherwood
*British children's author, died 1851.*
God is very good. Remember this, my children, that God is love. He that dwelleth in love dwelleth in God, and God in him.

## Franz Von Sickingen
*German nobleman and leader of the Reformation, died 1523.*
To his chaplain...
I have already confessed my sins to God.

## Mrs. Jane Lothrop Stanford
*American philanthropist and wife of the millionaire, died 1905.*
My God forgive my sins.

## Sir James Stonhouse
*British physician and divine, died 1795.*
Precious salvation!

## Baron Strathcona and Mount Royal
*Builder of the Canadian-Pacific Railway, died 1914.*
Oh God of Bethel, by whose hand Thy people still are fed.

## Simon of Sudbury
*Archbishop of Canterbury, killed 1381.*
Attacked by the mob during the Peasants' Revolt, he was horribly mutilated by the axe, and was not actually killed until the eighth blow. The treasurer and two others were slain with him. Sudbury's head was placed on a pole, with a cap nailed upon it to distinguish it from the others.
Ah! It is the hand of God.

## Frederick Swartz
*German missionary, died 1798.*
Had it pleased my Lord to spare me longer I should have been glad. I should have been able to speak yet a word to the sick and the poor. But His will be done. May He in mercy receive me. Into Thy hands I commend my spirit. Thou hast redeemed me, oh Thou faithful God.

## Roger B. Taney
*American jurist, died 1864.*
Lord Jesus, receive my spirit.

## Torquato Tasso
*Italian Renaissance poet, courtier and mystic, died 1595.*
Lord, into Thy hands I commend my spirit.

## Edward Taylor
*American preacher, died 1871.*
*Asked if Jesus was precious...*
Why, certainly, certainly.

## Jeremy Taylor
*British Bishop of Down and Connor, and administrator of Dromore, died 1667.*
My trust is in God.

## Kateri Tekakwitha ('The Lily of the Mohawks')
*The first native American to be canonised, died 1680.*
I am leaving you. I am going to die. Remember always what we have done together since we first met. If you change I shall accuse you through the tribunal of God. Take courage, despise the discouragings of those who have not the faith. If they ever try to persuade you to marry, listen only to the Fathers. If you cannot serve God here, go to the Mission at Lorette. Don't give up your mortifications. I shall love you in heaven. I shall pray for you. I shall aid you.

## Hester Lynch Thrale
*English writer and friend of Dr. Johnson, died 1821.*
I die in the trust and fear of God.

## Dudley Tyng
*British clergyman, died 18th century.*
His father, who asked him if he knew Jesus, provided the keynote for a great hymn...
Know him? He is my Saviour and my all. Father, stand up for Jesus!

## Mr. Underhill
*British Protestant martyr, burnt to death under Queen Mary for heresy, and refusing to abandon Protestantism.*
Dear Father, I beseech Thee to give once more to this realm the blessing of Thy word, with godly peace. Purge and purify me by this fire in Christ's death and passion through Thy spirit, that I may be an acceptable burnt-offering in Thy sight. Farewell dear friends. Pray for me and pray with me.

## James Ussher
*Irish clergyman, Archbishop of Armagh and chronologist of the Old Testament, died 1656.*
Among many other writings, he calculated that the day of creation was October 23, 4004 BC and that of the Great Flood November 25, 2348 BC.
Lord forgive my sins. Especially my sins of omission.

## Cornelius Vanderbilt
*American millionaire, died 1885.*
I'll never give up trust in Jesus. How could I let that go.

## Richard Whately
*British logician and theologian, died 1863.*
Whately backed his chaplain's altered reading of the text 'Our vile body' from Philippians iii, 21 to 'this body of our humiliation'.
That's right. Not 'Vile'. Nothing that He made is vile...

## George Whitfield
*British evangelist and preacher, died 1770.*
The last words of his final sermon, preached the night before he died...
My body fails, my spirit expands. How willingly I would live forever to preach Christ. But I die to be with him!

## Jonathan Wild
*British thief, 'thief taker' and receiver of stolen goods, died 1725.*
Wild's death-bed repentance hardly rings true when faced with his record...
Lord Jesus receive my soul.

## Frances Willard
*American temperance campaigner, died 1898.*
How beautiful to be with God.

## John Woolman
*Quaker preacher and anti-slavery campaigner, died 1772.*
I believe my being here is in the wisdom of Christ I know not as to life or death.

## Brigham Young
*American religious leader, president of the Mormon church, died 1877.*
Amen.

# HOLIER THAN THOU

*Saints and martyrs take the stairway to heaven.*

### Saint Achard
*French saint, died 1170.*

No suffering can expiate hate; it is not redeemed by martyrdom. It is a stain that all the blood in us would fail to wash. So I go to join my fathers. Place my body in the sepulchres of our brethren.

### Saint Agatha
*Sicilian noblewoman and Christian martyr, killed 251.*
*Her breasts were cut off as part of the torture...*

Cruel tyrant, do you not blush to torture this part of my body, you that sucked the breasts of a woman yourself?

### Saint Agathon
*Greek saint, died third century AD.*

Show me your charity and speak not to me for I am fully occupied.

### Saint Ambrose
*Italian bishop and biblical critic, died 397.*
*Choosing Bishop Simplicitas as his successor...*

Old though he be, he is the best of all.

### Saint Andrew
*Apostle of Galilee, crucified 235.*

Oh cross most welcome, most looked for; with a willing mind, joyfully and desirously I come to thee, being the scholar of Him which did hang on thee, because I have always been thy lover and have coveted to embrace thee.

### Saint Anselm of Canterbury
*Italian-born British scholar, Archbishop of Canterbury and founder of Scholasticism, died 1109.*

Yes, if it be His will I shall obey it willingly. But were He to let me stay with you a little longer till I had resolved a problem about the origin of the soul, I would gladly accept the boon, for I do notknow whether anyone will work it out when I am gone. If I could but eat I think I should pick up a little strength. I feel no pain in any part of my body, only I cannot retain nourishment and that exhausts.

### Saint Antony of Egypt
*Christian hermit and founder of monasticism, died 356.*

To Athanasius the bishop give one of my sheepskins and the cloak under me, which was new when he gave it to me and has become old by my use of it, and to Serapion the Bishop give the other sheepskin and do you have the haircloth garment. And for the rest children, farewell, for Antony is going and is with you no more.

### Saint Thomas Aquinas ('Doctor Angelicus')
*Italian theologian, author of* Summa Theologic, *died 1274.*

I receive Thee, redeeming price of I my soul Out of love for Thee have I studied, watched through many nights and exerted myself. Thee did I preach and teach. I have never said aught against Thee. Nor do I persist stubbornly in my views. If I ever expressed myself erroneously in the sacrament I submit myself to the judgement of the Holy Roman Church, in the obedience of which I now part from this world.

### Saint Bernadette Soubirous of Lourdes
*French saint, died 1879.*

Blessed Mary Mother of God pray for me a poor sinner. A poor sinner.

### Saint Bernard
*French Cistercian monk and mystic, the founder of Clairvaux Abbey and one of the most influential churchmen of his time, died 1153.*

I know not to which I ought to yield. To the love of my children which urges me to stay here or the love of God which draws me to Him.

*Facing page:*
*St. Ambrose*
*Enthroned by*
*Alvise Vivarini in*
*the Church of the*
*Frari, Venice.*

### Saint Boniface
*British martyr, died 754, by having hot lead poured down his throat.*

I thank the Lord Jesus, Son of the living God.

### Saint Carlo Borromeo
*Cardinal and archbishop, leader of the Counter-Reformation in Italy, died 1584. Asked if he wished to receive the viaticum...*

At once.

### Saint John Bosco
*Italian educator of the poor and founder of the Salesian Fathers, died 1888.*

Thy will be done.

### The Buddha (Prince Gautama Siddhartha)
*Founder of Buddhism, died 483 BC. Aged 80, his final words were to his monks...*

Transient are all conditioned things. Try to accomplish your aim with diligence.

### Saint Catherine of Siena (Caterina Benincasa)
*Dominican tertiary, mystic and patron saint of Italy, died 1380.*

No, I have not sought vain glory. But only the glory and praise of God.

### Saint Cecilia
*The patroness of music and a Christian martyr, killed 230. She supposedly survived attempts to burn her and was then beheaded. Her last words were to Bishop Urban...*

I obtained three days' delay that I might commend myself and all these to thy beatitude and that thou might consecrate this my house as a church.

### Saint Christodole
*Greek saint. When deciding where to be buried...*

My children, do not be ungrateful to the desert isle of Patmos, where we have laboured so hard.

### Saint Christopher
*Greek saint, killed third century. A miracle cure that worked...*

I know O King that I shall be dead on the morrow. When I am dead, O tyrant, make a paste of my blood, rub it on your eyes and you shall recover your sight.

### Saint Chrysogonus
*Roman Christian martyr, killed 304. To the Roman Emperor Diocletian, a leading antagonist of Christianity...*

I adore the One God in heaven and spurn your proffered dignities as clay.

### Saint Columba
*Irish founder of Celtic monasticism, died 597.*

Here I cease. Have peace and love.

### Saint Cuthbert
*Scottish Bishop of Lindisfarne Abbey and one of the most venerated saints, died 687.*

For I know that although during my life some have despised me, yet after my death you will see what sort of a man I was and that my doctrine was by no means worthy of contempt.

### Saint Cyprian
*Early Carthaginian Christian theologian and the first bishop-martyr of Africa, killed 258. On hearing his sentence of death...*

Thanks be to God.

### Saint Dominic
*Spanish monk and founder of the Order of Friar-Preachers, died 1221. When asked where he wanted to he buried...*

Under the feet of my friars.

### Saint Elizabeth
*Died 1st century.*

The time is already arrived, wherein God has called those that are His friends to the heavenly espousals!

### Saint Eloi
*Bishop of Noyan, died 659.*

And now, O Christ, I shall render up my last breath in confessing loudly Thy name; receive me in Thy great mercy, and disappoint me not in my hope; open to me the gate of life and render the Prince of Darkness powerless against me. Let Thy clemency protect me, Thy might hedge me, and Thy hand lead me to the place of refreshment and into the tabernacle Thou hast prepared for Thy servants and them that stand in awe of Thee.

### Saint Francis of Assisi
*Italian founder of the Franciscan orders and leader of the church reform move-ments of the early 13th century, died 1226.*

Welcome, sister death.

### Mohandas Karamchand Gandhi ('Mahatma Gandhi')
*Architect of Indian independence, assassinated 1948.*

Hari Rama! Hari Rama!

### Saint Goar
*Hermit and patron saint of the River Rhine, died 575.*

Here shall my Saviour be known in all the simplicity of His doctrines. Ah, would that I might witness it, but I have seen these things in a vision. But I faint! I am weary! My earthly journey is finished. Receive my blessing. Go and be kind to one another.

### Saint Maria Goretti ('The Martyr of Purity')
*Italian martyr, killed 1902. She was only eleven when she was stabbed to death, resisting the unwanted advances of a 19-year-old youth.*

May God forgive him; I want him in heaven.

### Saint Hilda
*British nun, abbess of Whitby, died 680. Her final words were to her fellow-nuns...*

Handmaids of Christ, maintain the peace of the gospel with each other and with all.

### Saint Ignatius of Antioch
*Bishop of Antioch, thrown to the lions 110 AD.*

Let me enjoy these beasts, whom I wish much more cruel than they are; and if they will not attempt me, I will provoke and draw them by force. I am God's wheat and I am ground by the teeth of wild beasts that I may be found pure bread for Christ.

## James the Apostle

*Christian martyr and one of the Twelve Apostles, beheaded 43 AD.*
*James, beheaded by order of King Herod Agrippa I of Judaea, is the only Apostle whose martyrdom is recorded in the New Testament. His last words accompanied a kiss for a fellow martyr...*

Peace be to thee, brother.

## Saint James the Less

*Christian martyr, stoned to death, 44 AD.*

O Lord God, Father I beseech Thee to forgive them, for they know not what they do.

## Saint James the Dismembered

*Tortured to death, 421AD.*

O Lord of lords, Lord of the living and the dead, give ear to me who am half dead. I have no fingers to hold out to Thee, O Lord, nor hands to stretch forth to Thee. My feet are cut off and my knees demolished, wherefore I cannot bend the knee to Thee, and I am like to a house that is about to fall because its columns are taken away. Hear me, O Lord Jesus Christ, and deliver my soul from its prison!

## Saint Jean Baptiste de la Salle

*French philanthropist, educator, and founder of the Brothers of the Christian Schools ('The Christian Brothers'), died 1719.*
*When asked if he accepted his sufferings with joy.*

Yes, I adore in all things the designs of God in my regard.

## Saint Jerome of Prague

*Czech religious reformer, burnt 1416.*

Bring thy torch hither. Do thine office before my face. Had I feared death I might have avoided it.

## Jesus of Nazareth

*Dissident Jewish prophet and Christian Messiah, crucified 33 AD.*

It is finished.

## Saint Joan of Arc

*French heroine during the Hundred Years War, burnt to death by the English 1431.*

Ah Rouen, I have great fear that you are going to suffer by my death. Jesus, Jesus!

## Saint John the Abbot

*Died 813.*

Never have I done my own will, and never have I taught others to do what I had not first done myself!

## Saint John the Almoner

*Died 616.*

I thank Thee, O my God, that Thy mercy has granted the desire of my weakness, which was that at my death I should possess naught but a single penny. And now this penny too can be given to the poor!

## Saint John of the Cross (Juan de Yepes y Élvarez)

*Spanish poet and mystic, reformer of Spanish monasticism, and co-founder of the contemplative order of Discalced Carmelites, died 1591.*

Into Thy hands, O Lord, I commend my spirit.

## Saint John Chrysostom

*Early Church Father, biblical interpreter, and archbishop of Constantinople, killed 407.*

Glory be to God in all things.

## Saint John the Evangelist

*Author of the fourth Gospel, died 104.*

Thou hast invited me to Thy table, Lord; and behold I come, thanking Thee for having invited me, for Thou knowest that I have desired it with all my heart.

## Saint Lawrence

*Archbishop of Rome and Christian martyr, roasted to death on a gridiron 258.*

This side is roasted enough, turn up, oh tyrant great, assay whether roasted or raw thou thinkest the better meat.

## Saint Leger

*Christian martyr, executed 678.*
*As he was being led away to be beheaded...*

There is no need to weary yourselves longer, brothers! Do here the bidding of him that sent you!

## Saint Ignatius Loyola

*Spanish theologian and founder of the Society of Jesus (the Jesuits), died 1556.*

Tell him that my hour has come and that I ask his benediction. Tell him that if I go to a place where my prayers are of any avail, as I trust, I shall not fail to pray for him, as I have unfailingly, even when I had most occasion to pray for myself.

## Saint Lucy

*Italian Christian, virgin and martyr, died c.300.*

I make known to you that peace is restored to the Church! This very day Maximian has died, and Diocletian has been driven from the throne. And just as God has bestowed my sister Agatha upon the city of Catania as its protectress, so He has this moment entitled me to be the patroness of the city of Syracuse.

## Saint Margaret

*Queen consort of Malcolm III Canmore and patroness of Scotland, died 1093.*
*Her last letter...*

I am of noble birth, and was called Margaret in the world; but in order safely to cross the sea of temptation, I called myself Pelagius, and was taken for a man. I did this not for a lie and a deception, as my deeds have shown. From the false accusation I have gained virtue, and have done penance albeit I was innocent. Now I ask that the holy sisters may bury me, whom men have not known; and that my death may show forth the innocence of my life, when women acknowledge the virginity of one whom slanderers accused as an adulterer.

## Saint Margaret of Antioch

*Virgin martyr and one of the most venerated saints during the Middle Ages, executed 304.*
*According to legend she told her executioner...*

Brother, draw thy sword now, and strike!

## Saint Mark the Evangelist

*Author of the second Gospel, died 75 AD.*

Into Thy Hands I commend my spirit.

*Saint Mark the Evangelist.*

### Saint Martin of Tours

*Patron saint of France and the first great leader of Western monasticism, died 370. Seeing the Devil near him...*

Why standest thou here, horrible beast? Thou hast no share in me. Abraham's bosom is receiving me.

### Mohammed (Abu al-Qasim Muhammad ibn 'Abd Allah ibn 'Abd al-Muttalib ibn Hashim)

*The founder of Islam, died 632.*

Oh Allah, be it so.

### Saint Monica

*Mother of Saint Augustine, died 387.*

Lay this body wherever it may be. Let no care of it disturb you: this only I ask of you that you should remember me at the altar of the Lord wherever you may be.

### Saint Oswald

*Anglo-Saxon king of Northumbria, who introduced Christianity to his kingdom, killed at the battle of Maserfeld 642.*

Lord have mercy on their souls.

### Saint Pancratius

*Roman Christian martyr, killed at the age of 14, first century.*
*To the Roman emperor Diocletian, chief persecutor of early Christianity...*

In body I am a child, but I bear a man's heart: and by grace of my Master Jesus Christ, thy threats seem as vain to me as this idol which stands before me. And as for the gods whom thou desirest me to adore, they are naught but imposters, who sully the women of their own household, and spare not their own kin. If thine own slaves today behaved as these gods, thou wouldst be in haste to put them to death. And it wonders me much that thou dost not blush to adore such gods!

### Saint Paul

*Christian missionary and one of the most influential of the early Fathers of the Church, died 67 AD.*
*Written in the 2nd epistle to Timothy...*

Do thy diligence to come before winter. Eubulus greeteth thee, and Pudens, and Linus, and Claudia, and all the brethren. The Lord Jesus Christ be with thy spirit. Grace be with you. Amen.

### Saint Paulinus

*Bishop of Nola, died 431.*

Thy word is a lantern unto my feet, and a light unto my paths.

### Saint Pelagia of Antioch

*Aged 15, she threw herself from a housetop to save her chastity c.311.*

Hast thou a bishop?...Let him pray the Lord for me, for he is a true apostle of Christ.

### Pembo the Hermit

*Christian anchorite.*

Thank God that not a day of my life has been spent in idleness. Never have I eaten bread that I have not earned. I do not recall any bitter speech that I have made for which I ought to repent now.

### Saint Perpetua

*Christian martyr, killed in the arena by a cow 203.*

Continue firm in the faith, love one another and do not be scandalised by our sufferings.

### Saint Peter

*The leader of Christ's disciples and recognised by Roman Catholics as the first Pope, crucified c. 67 AD.*
*His last words were to his wife, as he was led out to die...*

Oh thou, remember the Lord Jesus Christ.

### Saint Peter Martyr

*Inquisitor, preacher and religious founder; he was assassinated by members of the heretical Cathar sect 1252.*
*Bludgeoned over the head, he wrote his last words on the ground with his own blood before being fatally stabbed in the heart.*

I believe in God

### Saint Polycarp

*Greek bishop of Smyrna who was the leading second century Christian figure in Roman Asia, burnt 166.*
*He refused the executioner's demand to nail him to the stake...*

He who gives me the power will grant me to remain in the flames without the security you will give by the nails.

### Saint Prisca

*Roman martyr, killed 250.*

My courage and my mind are so firmly founded upon the firm stone of My Lord Jesus Christ that no assault can move me. Your words are but wind, your promises are but rain, your menaces are passing floods, and however hardly these things hurtle at the foundation of my courage, they cannot change me.

### Saint Protasius

*Christian martyr, executed 352.*

I bear thee no anger, Count, for I know that thou art blind in thy heart, but rather do I pity thee, for thou knowest not what thou dost. Cease not to torture me, that I may share with my brother

the good countenance of our Master.

### Saint Savina

*Died 311.*

O Lord who hast ever preserved me in chastity, suffer me not longer to be wearied with journeying! Command me not to go beyond this place! Let my body here find rest! I commend to Thee my servant, who has borne so much for me, and let me be worthy to see my brother in Thy kingdom, whom I have not seen here!

### Saint Savinianus

*Christian martyr, killed 275.*

Fear not to strike me down; and do ye bear away some drops of my blood to the emperor, that he may receive his sight, and acknowledge the power of God.

### Saint Secundus

*Christian martyr, tortured to death 119.*
*Prior to having boiling pitch and lead poured into his mouth he declared...*

How sweet are Thy words to my palate, more than honey to my mouth!

### Sixtus

*Christian bishop, killed 258.*
*To Saint Lawrence, who was awaiting his own death by torture...*

Cease weeping, you will soon follow me!

### Saint Stephen

*First king of Hungary and founder of the Hungarian state, killed 1038.*

Lord lay not this sin to their charge.

### Saint Theodora

*Christian martyr, executed 867.*
*Her words were spoken to the child she was falsely accused of being the father of, when she was arrested disguised as a monk...*

Sweet my son, the end of my life approaches, and I leave thee to

God, who shall be thy Father and thy Helper. Sweetest son, persevere in fasting and prayer, and serve thy brethren devoutly.

## Saint Theodore

*Seventh archbishop of Canterbury and the first of the whole English Church, died 690.*

With my Christ I was, and am, and will be.

## Saint Thomas ('Doubting Thomas')

*One of the Apostles and the first person to acknowledge Christ's divinity, died 53 AD.*

I adore, but not this metal; I adore, but not this graven image; I adore my Master Jesus Christ in Whose name I command thee, demon of this idol, to destroy it forthwith!

## Saint Vincent de Paul

*French saint, founder of the Congregation of the Mission for preaching missions to the peasantry and for training a pastoral clergy, died 1680.*

Jesus.

## John Whitgift

*Archbishop of Canterbury, a major figure in the early Anglican church, died 1604.*

Pro ecclesi Dei, pro ecclesi Dei.

## William Whittle

*British religious fanatic, hanged 1766. Whittle had killed his own wife and children for their alleged apostasy against the Catholic faith; asked on the scaffold why he had killed his own children, he responded...*

The mother had carried them to the church of the heretics: so they would have been damned if I had not killed them. But now they are in purgatory and in time they will go to heaven. [After his death the attending clergyman, one Dr. Oliver, received this note: 'Sir, I make bold to acquaint you, that your house, and every clergyman's that's in the town, or any black son of a bitch like you for you are nothing but heretics and damned souls. If William Whittle, that worthy man, hangs up in ten days, you may fully expect to be blown to damnation'.]

## Saint Francis Xavier

*Roman Catholic missionary who helped establish Christianity in India, the Malay Archipelago and Japan, died 1552*

In Thee, O Lord, have I hoped, let me never be confounded!

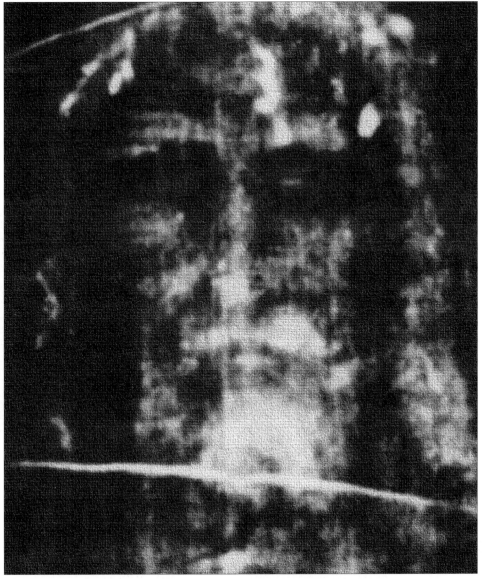

*Jesus of Nazareth? The Turin Shroud, now proved by carbon dating not to be Christ's winding sheet, may be the world's first photograph...even a self-portrait by Leonardo da Vinci.*

# SOMEBODY HELP ME

*Like it or not, death remains a solo adventure.*

### Henry Adams
*American author, died 1918.*
*To his secretary...*
Dear child, keep me alive.

### Diane de France, Duchess of Angoulême.
*French wit and beauty, possibly the illegitimate daughter of Diane de Poitiers, who was highly influential at the courts of Henri III and IV, died 1619.*
My God, I am going to beg pardon for my sins. Help thy humble servant in this moment which is to be decisive for me for all eternity.

### Quintus Aurelius
*Roman patrician, committed suicide. The Emperor suspected him of treason...*
Woe is me, my Alban farm has informed against me.

### Don Carlos of Austria
*Pretender to the Spanish throne, died 1909.*
God be propitious to me, a sinner.

### Max Baer
*German heavyweight boxier, died 1959.*
Oh God, here I go!

### Louis Barthou
*French politician, killed 1934. The French Foreign Minister was accompanying King Alexander I of Yugoslavia when fascist assassins killed them both...*
I can't see what's happening now. My eyeglasses, where are my eyeglasses?

### Sam Bass
*American outlaw, killed 1878. Refusing to talk to the lawman who shot him...*
Let me go, the world is bobbing around.

### Aubrey Beardsley
*British artist and illustrator, died 1898. The imminence of death appeared to trouble the hitherto sedulously decadent artist. Fortunately, this last demand went unheeded...*
I am imploring you burn all the indecent poems and drawings.

### Henry Beaufort
*Bishop of Winchester, died 1447. After so saintly a life, did Beaufort see the devil on his death bed?...*
And must I die? Will not all my riches save me? I could purchase the kingdom if that would save my life. What, is there no bribing of death…?
*He then apparently saw an awful vision...*
Away! Away! Why thus do you look at me? I pray you all pray for me…

### General Ludwig Beck
*German army officer, executed 1944. After the Stauffenberg plot to assassinate Hitler failed, ageing General Beck tried to shoot himself. Two attempts failed and a soldier had to finish him off...*
If it doesn't work this time, then please help me.

### William Beckford
*British eccentric, author of the horror novel Vathek and builder of Fonthill Abbey, the most sensational building of the English Gothic revival, died 1844. Writing to his daughter...*
Come quick, quick!

### Judah Benjamin
*American lawyer, died 1884.*
What I require is warmth. Will it never come?

### Joseph Bodwell
*American Governor of Maine. Asking to be helped back into a chair...*
Get me there quickly!

### Junius Brutus Booth
*American actor-manager and father of John Wilkes Booth, assassin of President Lincoln, died 1852.*
Pray, pray, pray.

### Lucrezia Borgia
*Italian intriguer, died 1519. To Pope Alexander VI, her father...*
Most Holy Father and Honoured Master. With all respect I kiss your Holiness' feet and commend myself in all humility to your holy mercy. Having suffered for more than two months, early in the morning of the 14th. present, as it pleased God, I gave birth to a daughter and hoped then to find relief from my sufferings. But I did not and shall be compelled to pay my debt to nature. So great is the favour that our merciful Creator has shown me, that I approach the end of my life with pleasure, knowing that in a few

*Facing page: Brian Jones of the Rolling Stones, found dead in his swimming pool in 1969.*

hours, after receiving for the last time all the sacraments of the church, I shall be released.

### David G. Broderick
*American politician, died 1859.*
I die. Protect my honour.

### Guillaume Dode de la Brunérie
*French general, died 1851.*
The doctors still assert that the enemy is retreating. I believe, on the contrary, that we are, as it were, on the eve of a battle. God knows what tomorrow will bring.

### George Villiers, second Duke of Buckingham
*Favourite of Charles II, died 1687.*
My distemper is powerful. Come and pray for the departing soul of poor, unhappy Buckingham.

### Sir George Burns
*British shipowner, died 1896.*
Lord Jesus, come, come…I am waiting, I am ready. Home, home. Give me patience to wait thy time, but Thou knowest what I suffer.

### Robert Burns
*Scottish national poet, died 1796.*
Don't let the awkward squad fire over me.

### Sir Richard Burton
*British explorer and writer, 1890.*
*His rigidly puritanical wife refused to give him any medicines without the presence of a doctor…by which time it was too late…*
Quick Puss! Chloroform, ether…or I am a dead man!

### Arthur Capel, Lord Capel of Hadham
*British aristocrat and supporter of King Charles I, beheaded 1649.*
God Almighty staunch this blood. God Almighty staunch this issue of blood. This will not do the business. God Almighty, find another way to do it.

### Enrico Caruso
*Italian opera singer, died 1921.*
Doro, I can't get my breath!

### Phoebe Cary
*American poet, died 1871.*
Oh God, have mercy on my soul.

### Rufus Choate
*American politician, died 1859.*
I don't feel well. I feel faint.

### Charles Coffin
*American war correspondent, died 1916.*
If it were not for this pain I should get up and write.

### Lady Jane Colquhoun
*British author of religious tracts, died 1846.*
Looking for her grandson. Where is he? I can't see him!

### Henri I de Bourbon, Prince de Condé
*French Huguenot leader, died of wounds 1588.*
Hand me my chair, I feel extremely weak.

### Uriel Acosta
*Spanish freethinker and rationalist, died 1640.*
*Born a Marrano, or Christianised Spanish Jew, Acosta fled Spain for Holland and embraced Judaism. But his freethinking beliefs proved that this religion, like others, preferred ideology to tolerance.*
There you have the true story of my life. I have shown you what role I played in this vain world-theatre and in my unimportant and restless life. Now fellow men, make your just and dispassionate judgement speaking freely according to the truth as becomes men who are really men. If you find something which arouses your sympathy, then realise and mourn the sad lot of Man which you share. And let there be no confusion about this: the name that I bore as a Christian in Portugal was Gabriel da Costa. Among the Jews – would that I had never got involved with them – I was known, by a small change, as Uriel.

### Rev. Benjamin Cutler
*American clergyman.*
Lift me up, lift me right up.

### Jefferson Davis
*President of the American Confederacy, died 1889.*
*Refusing a dose of medicine…*
Please excuse me, I can't take it.

### Sir James Radcliffe, Earl of Derwentwater
*Jacobite rebel, beheaded 1716.*
*To his executioner…*
I am but a poor man. There's ten guineas for you. If I had more I would give it to you. I desire you to do your office so as to put me to the least misery you can.

### Charles Dickens
*British novelist, died 1870.*
*To his friends who were trying to lay him on a sofa…*
On the ground!

### Henry H. Dixon
*American sportswriter, died 1870.*
Oh God, I thank thee. I could not bear much more.

### Flix-Antoine-Philibert Dupanloup
*French clergyman and Roman Catholic Bishop of Orléans, died 1878.*
*When people offered to pray for him…*
Yes, yes…

### Madame Dupin
*Mother of Georges Sand, died 1865.*
Comb my hair.

### John Eliot
*Missionary to the American Indians, died 1600.*
*To a friend…*
You are welcome to my very soul, Please retire into my study for me and give me leave to be gone.

### Henry Fawcett
*British statesman, died 1884.*
The best things to warm my hands with would be my fur gloves. They are in the pocket of my coat in the dressing-room.

### 'Big Jim' Fisk
*American financial speculator, assassinated 1872.*
*Fisk was killed by his ex-partner Med Stokes. Despite his appeal, no-one came to his rescue…*
For God's sake, will nobody help me?

### Andrew Fletcher of Saltoun
*Scottish patriot, died 1716.*
*Asked by Lord Sunderland for any last wishes...*
I have a nephew who has been studying the law. Make him a judge when he is fit for it.

### John Ford
*American movie director, died 1973.*
May I please have a cigar?

### Henry Fuseli (Johann Heinrich Fuessli)
*Swiss-born British artist, died 1825.*
Is Lawrence come, is Lawrence come?

### David Garrick
*British actor, the greatest thespian of his era, died 1779.*
Oh dear…

### Paul Gauguin
*French artist, died 1903.*
*Alone on his tropical paradise Gauguin sent off a note to a nearby missionary, but he was dead before it could arrive...*
Would it be too much to ask you to come and see me? My eyesight seems to be going and I cannot walk. I am very ill.

### Baron Louis de Geer
*Swedish statesman, died 1896.*
My God, have pity on me. Do not visit on me suffering beyond my strength… Oh Christ! Thou hast suffered still more for me.

### Johann Wolfgang von Goethe
*German poet and dramatist, author of The Sorrows of Young Werther, Faust and Egmont, died 1832.*
More light!

### Joseph Goldberger
*American medical researcher, died 1929.*
*To his wife...*
Mary, don't leave me. You have always been my rock, my strength. Mary, we must have patience.

### Ulysses S. Grant
*American President, died 1885.*
Water!

### Benjamin Harrison
*American President, died 1901.*
*To his wife...*
Are the doctors here?

### Ferdinand Rudolph Hassler
*German engineer, died 1843.*
My children! My papers!

### Lafcadio Hearn
*American writer, translator, and teacher who introduced the culture and literature of Japan to the West, died 1904.*
Ah, because of sickness.

### W. E. Henley
*British poet and editor, died 1903.*
*A letter to Charles Whibley...*
Dear Boy, I'd give much to see you just now. When can you come? I can't get to town, being kind of broken-hearted or I'd tryst you there. But I want your advice and, if I can get it, your help. And I want the first of these soon. The sooner the better.

### Henry the Lion
*Duke of Saxony and Bavaria, died 1195.*
God be merciful to me a sinner.

### Wilhelm Hey
*German poet, died 1854.*
*A last poem for the two men who had assisted him...*
So you my nurses dear
In these last difficult days,
In bitter parting here,
Show me your loving ways.
The love so tenderly given
And yet such strength behind,
A brief foretaste of heaven,
Is what it brings to mind.

### Fitz-Greene Halleck
*American poet, died 1867.*
*To his wife...*
Maria, hand me my pantaloons if you please.

### Thomas Halyburton
*British theologian, died 1712.*
Pray! Pray!

### Cyrus Hamlin
*American missionary, died 1900.*
*Hamlin wanted to sit one last time in the chair he had sat in as a boy...*
Put me there.

### Warren Gamaliel Harding
*American President, died 1923.*
That's good. Go on. Read some more. Almost home.

### Benjamin Hill
*American politician, died 1882.*
Almost home.

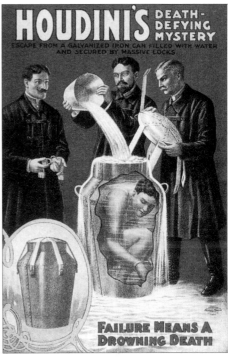

### Harry Houdini (Erich Weiss)
*American escapologist, died 1926.*
I am tired of fighting. I guess this thing is going to get me.

### Robert Housman
*British divine, died 1838.*
*Receiving a gift of violets...*
I shall never again see the spot where those flowers grew. Give him my thanks for the present.

### Baron Friedrich von Hugel
*German Catholic theologian, died 1925.*
*To his nurse...*
Pray for me.

### Thomas Hutchinson
*Governor of Massachusetts, died 1780.*
*Hutchinson's stringent administration helped precipitate the American Revolution.*
Help me!

### Brian Jones
*British rock musician, drowned 1969.*
*A final telegram before the co-founder of the Rolling Stones died in his swimming pool...*
Don't judge me too harshly.

### 'Josélito' (José Gomez)
*Spanish bullfighter, killed 1920.*
Mother, I'm smothering!

### Adoniram Judson
*American linguist and Baptist missionary in Burma, died 1850.*
*Judson was worried about the hot Burmese climate affecting his body...*
Brother Ranney will you bury me? Bury me? Quick, quick!

*Goethe…*
*'More light!'.*

*David's portrait of the dead Marat*

### Joseph Karge
*Linguist, died 19th century.*
Karge had been reading about death on his travels...
I have but one desire concerning it...that it come suddenly and without warning.

### John Kitto
*British theologian, died 1854.*
Pray God to take me soon.

### Théophile Laennec
*French physician and inventor of the stethoscope, died 1826.*
The doctor took off his rings before he lay down to die...
It would be necessary soon that another do me this service. I do not want anyone to have the bother of it.

### Sidney Lanier
*American poet, died 1881.*
Refusing a soothing drink...
I can't.

### D. H. Lawrence
*British novelist, author of Lady Chatterley's Lover and Sons and Lovers, died 1930.*
I think it is time for morphine.

### Giacomo Leopardi
*Italian poet and scholar, died 1837.*
I can't see you any more.

### Amy Lowell
*American poet, died 1925.*
Pete...a stroke! Get Eastman!

### William H. McGuffey
*American author of primary readers, died 1873.*
Oh that I might once more speak to my dear boys. But Thy Will be done.

### Sarah Malcolm
*British laundress, hanged 1733.*
On the gallows the murderess called on the man she had killed...
Oh my master, my master, I wish I could see him!

### Sir Horace Mann
*British diplomat, died 1786.*
To his wife...
Sing to me, if you have the heart.

### Cardinal Henry Manning
*British cardinal and priest, died 1892.*
To Sir Andrew Clark...
Is there any use in your coming tomorrow? Then mind you, Sir Andrew, come at nine tomorrow.

### Jean Paul Marat
*French Revolutionary, assassinated 1793.*
As his killer Charlotte Corday struck her blows, Marat called to his companion...
Help, my dear, help!

### John Churchill, first Duke of Marlborough
*British soldier and statesman, died 1722.*
When it was suggested he should go to bed...
Yes.

### Lorenzo de' Medici
*Ruler of Florence, died 1492.*
Asked whether he still liked his food...
As a dying man always does.

### 'Owen Meredith' (Edward Bulwer Lytton)
*British poet, died 1891.*
I feel thirsty and I should be glad to drink something.

### Joaquin Miller
*American poet, died 1913.*
Take me away, take me away.

### John A. Morehead
*American Lutheran leader, died 1866.*
On the day of his wife's burial...
Will you do me a favour? Will you kindly ask my physician how long before I shall join my Nellie?

### John Pierpoint Morgan
*American millionaire, died 1913.*
Don't baby me so!

### Daniel O'Connell
*Irish nationalist leader, died 1847.*
My dear friend, I am dying. Jesus, Jesus, Jesus...

### 'Ouida' (Marie Louise de la Ramée)
*British novelist, died 1908.*
I have been very ill these days and my maid is of the opinion that I shall never get well. The weather is intensely cold and at San Remo it is so warm and brilliant. It is odd that there should be so great a difference. Excuse this rough word...I am ill and cannot write.

### Jan Paderewski
*Polish musician and statesman, died 1941.*
Asked if he would like some champagne.
Please.

### Thomas Nelson Page
*American author who specialised in romantic legends of Southern plantation life, died 1922.*
Here Alfred, take this spade.

### Louis Pasteur
*French chemist and microbiologist, died 1895.*
Offered a glass of milk...
I cannot.

### John Payne
*British publisher and translator, died 1800.*
Have you got the sheets? Did you get the pillowcases?

### Boies Penrose
*American politician, died 1921.*
To his valet...
See here, William, see here. I don't want any of your damned lies. How do I look? Am I getting any better? The truth now... All right, William. When you go to church tomorrow, pray for me too.

### Peponila
*Wife of the Gallic rebel Sabinus, died first century AD.*
Pleading with Emperor Vespasian to spare her family...

These little ones, Caesar, I bore and reared in the monument [where Sabinus had hidden] that we might be a greater number to supplicate you.

### Claretta Petacci
*Mistress of the Italian dictator Benito Mussolini, killed with her lover 1945.*

Mussolini must not die!

### Marshal Pétain
*French soldier, a national hero during World War I, but seen as a traitor for his leadership of the collaborationist Vichy government in World War II, died in prison 1951.*

Do not weep, do not grieve.

### Joseph Pulitzer
*American newspaper owner, died 1911.*
To the friend who was reading to him...

Softly, quite softly.

### Jeanne-Antoinette Poisson ('Madame de Pompadour')
*Mistress of Louis XV of France and a patron of the arts, died 1764.*
As the priest was leaving her room.

One moment, M. le Curé', and we will depart softly...

### Anne Radcliffe
*British 'Gothic' novelist, author of* The Mysteries of Udolpho, *died 1823.*
Taking a little food...

There is some substance in that.

### Richard III
*Killed at the battle of Bosworth Field, 1485.*
According to Shakespeare's Richard III...

A horse, a horse, my kingdom for a horse!

### W. Graham Robertson
*British author, died 1948.*
His final instructions...

I should like the ashes to be buried or otherwise disposed of at the cematorium, with no tombstone nor inscription to mark the place of burial. No funeral, no mourning, no flowers. By request. If these arrangements are carried out one may perhaps manage to die without making a public nuisance of oneself.

### John Rodgers
*American naval officer, died 1882.*

Butler, do you know the Lord's Prayer? Then repeat it for me.

### Franklin Delano Roosevelt
*American President, died 1945.*

I have a terrific headache.

### Theodore Roosevelt
*American President, died 1919.*

Please put out the light.

### Nicholas Rubinstein
*Founder of the Moscow Conservatory and brother of the pianist, Anton, died 1881.*

Oysters! Nothing will do me as much good as a dozen cold oysters and an ice afterwards.

### José de San Martin
*Argentine soldier, statesman and national hero, died 1850.*
To his brother...

Mariano...back to my room!

### Friedrick H. Schleiermacher
*German theologian, died 1834.*

Now I can hold out here no longer. Lay me in a different posture.

### Olive Schreiner
*South African writer died 1920.*
A final letter...

I long to see the stars and the veldt. One day I will go up to Matjesfontein just for a day, if there is someone to take me. It doesn't seem to me that this is Africa. A Happy New Year, my dear one.

### General Winfield Scott
*American soldier, died 1866.*
Peter, take good care of my horse.

*The Right Honorable Anthony Ashley Cooper Earl of Shaftesbury Baron Ashley of Winbourn S. Giles, & Lord Cooper of Pawlett.*

### Anthony Ashley Cooper, seventh Earl of Shaftesbury
*British philanthropist, died 1885.*
Handed something by his valet...
Thank you.

### John Sherman
*American politician, died 1900.*
I think you had better send for the doctor. I feel so faint.

### Sir Stanley Spencer
*British artist, died 1959.*
To the nurse who had just given him an injection...
Beautifully done.

### Count Friedrich Stolberg
*German poet, died 1821.*
To his doctor...
Tell me, will it truly be all over tomorrow or the next day? Praise God Thanks, thanks! I thank you with all my heart! Jesus be praised!

### Jeremy Taylor
*British Bishop of Dromore, died 1667*
Bury me at Dromore.

### Samuel Tilden
*American politician, died 1886.*
Water!

*Facing page: Booker T. Washington, black rights activist.*

### Henry Timrod
*American divine, died 1867.*
Failing to swallow a drink on his deathbed.
Never mind. I shall soon drink of the river of eternal life.

### Gitanillo de Triano
*Spanish matador, killed in the bullring in 1931.*
Tell them to moisten my mouth. Moisten my mouth a little.

### Paul Verlaine
*French poet, died 1896.*
Don't sole the dead man's shoes yet.

### Alfred de Vigny
*French poet, died 1863.*
Pray for me.
Pray to God for me.

### James J. Walker
*American politician, died 1946.*
A staunch Democrat he resisted his nurse's advice to lie back until she admitted to sharing his party beliefs...
In that case I shall abide by the wishes of a fair constituent.

### Robert Walker
*American politician, died 1951.*
Following this request Walker received a shot of sodium amytal which induced a coma and, in due course, death...
I feel terrible, doc.
Do something quick!

### Booker T. Washington
*Campaigner for black rights, died 1915.*
Take me home. I was born in the South, I have lived and laboured in the South, and I wish to die and be buried in the South.

### John Lee 'Sonny Boy' Williamson
*American blues musician, murdered on his way home from a blues bar 1948.*
Lord have mercy.

*Right: Sonny Boy Williamson, the original. After his death, his name and reputation were hijacked by another.*

### William C. Whitney
*American politician, died 1904.*
Don't get angry nurse. I love my son and daughter. It does me good to chat with them.

### Charles Wolfe
*Irish poet and clergyman, died 1823.*
Close this eye. The other is closed already. Now farewell.

### Rev. John Wood
*British naturalist, died 1889.*
Give me a large cup of tea.

### Elinor Wylie
*American poet, died 1928.*
Offered a glass of water...
Is that all it is?

### William L. 'Cap'n Bob' Yancey
*American lawyer, died 1863.*
I will just lie here for a few minutes. I will stay here a little while just to please you. Don't leave me, little lady. I love to watch your bright, young face. Two things in this world I have always loved...a bright, young face and walking in the sunshine.

### 'Abd Allah ibn az-Zubayr
*Arab rebel against the Umayyad dynasty, killed in battle 692.*
No-one need ask where 'Abd Allah is. Whoever wants him will meet him in the first ranks. Oh Lord, the troops of Syria are assailing me in great numbers and have already torn aside veils that cover thy sanctuary. Send my phalanxes to my aid!

Dear Friend:
Here is the picture of KING BISCUIT TIME you asked us for.
Reading from left to right: Sonny Boy Williamson, announcer Sam Anderson, Robert Junior Lockwood.
We hope you'll keep on listening to KING BISCUIT TIME on Station KFFA at 12:45 and you'll keep on using KING BISCUIT FLOUR.
Sincerely,
Sonny Boy and Robert Junior
INTERSTATE GROCER CO.
HELENA, ARK.

# FEAR AND LOATHING

*There must be some way out of here, said the joker to the priest.*

### Pierre Abelard
*Founder of scholastic theology, died 1142.*
I don't know! I don't know!

### Anonymous longtime hedonist
*Raving in his last delirium.*
Now for the dice! That's mine! More wine, damn you, more wine! Oh, how they rattle. Fiends, fiends assail me! I say you cheat! The cards are marked! Now the chains rattle! Oh death, oh death!

### Jeanne Bécu, Comtesse du Barry
*The last mistress of Louis XV of France, guillotined 1793.*
You are going to hurt me! Oh, please, do not hurt me!

### Frédéric Bastiat
*French economist, died 1850.*
I am not able to explain myself.

### William Battie
*British physician, died 1776.*
Young man, you have heard, no doubt, how great are the terrors of death, this night will probably offer you some experience. But you may learn, and may you profit by the example, that a conscientious endeavour to perform his duties will ever close a Christian's eyes with comfort and tranquillity.

### Ludwig van Beethoven
*German composer, died 1827.*
*Refusing a glass of wine which he had just asked for...*
Too bad, too bad! It's too late!

### Arnold Bennett
*British novelist, playwright and man of letters, died 1931.*
Everything has gone wrong my girl!

### Pierre Béranger
*French poet, died 1857.*
Today, on the day of his Epiphany, my Lord Jesus Christ will appear to me: either for glory, as I in my repentance should like, or for condemnation, as others would hope and as I fear.

### Georges Bizet
*French composer, died 1875.*
I am in a cold sweat. It is the sweat of death. How are you going to tell my father?

### Mary Blandy
*British murderess, hanged for poisoning her own father 1752.*
Gentlemen, don't hang me high for the sake of decency… I am afraid I shall fall.

### Anne Boleyn
*Second wife of Henry VIII and mother of Elizabeth I, beheaded for her alleged adultery 1536.*
The executioner is, I believe, an expert…and my neck is very slender. Oh God, have pity on my soul!

### Cesare Borgia
*Duke of the Romagna and captain general of the armies of the church, killed in battle 1507.*
I die unprepared.

### Jacques Bossuet
*French clergyman and writer, died 1704.*
I suffer the violence of pain and death, but I know whom I have believed.

### Prince Louis de Bourbon
*French nobleman, killed 1560.*
*The Prince's request was ignored by his captor...*
Mercy, mercy, mercy My Lord of Chemberg. I am your prisoner.

### George Briggs
*Governor of Massachusetts, died 1861.*
*To his son...*
You won't leave me again, will you?

*Facing page: Siamese twins Chang and Eng.*

### Charlotte Brontë
*British novelist, died 1855.*
*She had only been married one year...*
Oh, I am not going to die, am I? He will not separate us, we have been so happy.

### Rev. Abel Brown
*American abolitionist, killed by a pro-slavery mob.*
Must I be sacrificed? Let me alone, every one of you!

### Georg Büchner
*German dramatist, author of Woyzeck and Danton's Death, died 1837.*
We do not suffer too much. We suffer too little. For it is through suffering that we attain God. We are death, dust and ashes. How should we dare to complain?

### Saul Budgen
*American merchant, died 1851.*
Oh dear…

### Hans von Bülow
*German musician, died 1894.*
*Asked how he felt...*
Bad.

### George S. Cadoudal
*A plotter against Napoleon, executed 1804.*
*Rejecting advice to repeat the 'Hail Mary' so as to protect himself 'now and at the hour of our death'...*
For what? Isn't this the hour of my death?

### John Calvin
*Swiss Protestant reformer, died 1564.*
Thou bruisest me, Oh Lord, but it is enough for me to feel that it is Thy hand.

### George Campbell
*American outlaw, killed 1881.*
*To Marshall Dallas Stoudenmire who shot him in the 'Battle of Keating's Saloon', in El Paso...*
You big sonofabitch, you murdered me!

### Roger Casement
*Irish patriot, shot as a spy 1916.*
*From his last letter to his sister...*
It is a cruel thing to die with all men misunderstanding.

*Chopin in 1849, shortly before his death aged 39.*

### Frédéric Chopin
*Polish composer, died 1849.*
*His last written request...*
The earth is suffocating. Swear to make them cut me open, so I won't be buried alive.

### Augustin-Louis, Baron Cauchy
*French mathematician who pioneered the theory of 'substitution groups', died 1857.*
No, I do not suffer much… Jest Mary and Joseph!

### Chang and Eng
*The famous Siamese twins, died 1874.*
*Chang died first, followed three hours later by his brother. As ever they were bickering...*
*Chang:* I don't want to go to bed.
*Eng:* [on seeing that his brother was dead…] My last hour is come. May the Lord have mercy on my soul.

### Elizabeth Chivers
*British murderess, hanged 1712.*
*She had committed 'the murder of her bastard child' by drowning it in a pond, her last words were to an attendant clergyman.*
Oh, sir! I am lost. I cannot pray, I cannot repent, my sin is too great to be pardoned. I did commit it with deliberation and choice, and in cold blood. I was not driven to it by necessity. The father had all the while provided for me and for the child, and would have done so still, had not I destroyed the child, and thereby sought my own destruction.

### Thomas Colley
*British chimney-sweep, hanged for murder 1751.*
*Colley was hanged for ducking John and Ruth Osborne, whom he and a mob had accused of witchcraft. He had then taken money off the rest of the mob in payment for what he called the 'sport'.*
Good people, I beseech you all to take warning by an unhappy man's suffering, that you be not deluded into so absurd and wicked a conceit as to believe that there are any such beings upon earth as witches. It was that foolish and vain imagination, heightened and inflamed by the strength of liquor, which prompted me to be instrumental (with others as mad as myself) in the horrid and barbarous murder of Ruth Osborne, the supposed witch, for which I am now so deservedly to suffer death. I am fully convinced of my former error, and, with the sincerity of a dying man, declare that I do not believe there is such a thing in being as a witch, and pray God that none of you, through a contrary persuasion, may hereafter be induced to think that you have a right in any shape to persecute, much less endanger the life of, a fellow-creature. I beg of you all to pray to God to forgive me. and to wash clean my polluted soul in the blood of Jesus Christ, my Saviour and Redeemer. So exhorteth you all, The dying Thomas Colley.

### Nicolo Coviello
*London music teacher, died 1926.*
*Visiting a nephew in Coney Island, he was listening to a jazz band...*
This isn't music. Stop it.

### Robert Damiens ('Robert the Devil')
*Assassin of Louis XV, tortured to death 1717.*
*Damiens was chained to a red-hot steel 'bed' and his entrails were slowly torn out...*
Oh death, why art thou so long coming. May God have pity on me, and Jesus deliver me!

### Hart P. Danks
*Died 20th century.*
*An unfinished note...*
Its hard to die alone and…

### Engelbert Dollfuss
*Chancellor of Austria, assassinated 1934.*
Children, you are so good to me. Why aren't the others? I have only desired peace. We have never attacked anybody. We have always fought to defend ourselves. May God forgive them.

### Gaston Doumergue
*President of the French Republic, assassinated 1937.*
*Daumergue refused to see a doctor, fearing that...*
He put me in the discard.

### 'George Eliot' (Mary Ann Evans)
*British novelist, author of* The Mill on the Floss, *died 1880.*

Tell them I have a great pain in the left side.

### Ebenezer Elliott
*British radical poet, known as 'The Corn Law Rhymer', died 1849.*

A strange sight, sir … an old man unwilling to die.

### Henry Venn Elliott
*British evangelical clergyman, died 1865.*

Suffer me not from any pains of death to fall from Thee.

### Eliza Fenning
*British murderess, hanged 1815. She had allegedly killed her employers, the Turner family, although popular opinion had found her innocent.*

Before the just and almighty God, and by the faith of the holy sacrament I have taken, I am innocent of the offence with which I am charged.

### Marshall Field II
*American merchant, died accidentally 1906.*

I do not know how this happened. I can account for it in no way. It was an accident. What are the chances of my recovery, Doctor?

### Benjamin Franklin
*American diplomat and inventor, died 1790.*

A dying man can do nothing easy.

### Melvin Fuller
*American jurist, died 1910.*

I am very ill.

### Captain Allen Gardiner
*British missionary, died 1851. Starving to death, he wrote his last letter…*

My dear Mr. Williams, The Lord has seen fit to call home another of our little company. Our dear departed brother left the boat on Tuesday at noon, and has not since returned. Doubtless he is in the presence of his Redeemer, whom he served so faithfully. Yet a little while, and through grace we may join that blessed throng to sing the praises of Christ throughout eternity. I neither hunger nor thirst, though five days without food. Marvellous loving kindness to me a sinner! Your affectionate brother in Christ…

### Piers Gaveston
*Favourite of King Edward II of England, killed 1312. Gaveston was killed by a group of nobles who resented his influence…*

Oh noble Earl, spare me!

### Vincent Van Gogh
*Dutch painter, committed suicide 1890.*

Now I want to go home. Don't weep. What I have done was best for all of us. No use. I shall never get rid of this depression.

### Ben Hall
*Australian bushranger, shot dead 1865. The 'King of the Bushrangers' demanded…*

I'm wounded, for the love of God, shoot me dead!

### Richard Halliburton
*British sailor, lost at sea 1939. His last message…*

Southerly gales, squalls, lee rail under water, wet bunks, hard tack, bully beef. Wish you were here, instead of me.

### Henry Hammond
*British royalist divine, died 1660.*

Lord make haste!

### Robert Hare
*British antiquary and benefactor to the University of Cambridge, died 1611.*

There is a long dreary lane in every life, called 'Suffering', which I now seem to have entered.

### Warren Hastings
*British Governor-General of India, died 1818.*

Surely at my age it is time to go. God only can do me good. My dear, why wish me to live to suffer thus? None of you know what I suffer.

### Benjamin Haydon
*British historical painter, committed suicide 1846.*

God forgive me. Amen.

### Philip Henry
*British nonconformist divine and diarist, died 1696.*

O death where is thy…

### Saint Hilary
*Roman clergyman, Bishop of Poitiers and later Pope, died 468.*

Soul, thou hast served Christ these seventy years and art thou afraid to die? Go out soul go out!

### Reverend Rowland Hill
*British preacher and missionary, died 1833.*

Christ also hath suffered for sins, the just for the unjust, that he might bring us unto God.

### Sidney Hillman
*British Labour leader, died 1946.*

I feel like hell. I'm going to lie down again.

### Katsushika Hokusai
*Japanese painter, best known for his 'Thirty-six Views of Mount Fuji', died 1849.*

If heaven had only granted me five years more, I could have become a real painter.

### Thomas Holcroft
*British novelist and playwright, died 1809. Talking about his pain…*

How tedious. My affections are strong.

### John Holloway
*British murderer, hanged 1807.*

The excution was witnessed by a great mob, some hundred of whom were found dead or dying when the crowds dispersed. I am innocent, innocent, by God! Innocent, innocent, innocent! Gentlemen! No verdict! No verdict! Gentlemen! Innocent, innocent!

### Vicomtesse d'Houdetot

I am sorry for myself.

### Henrik Ibsen
*Norwegian playwright, author of* A Doll's House, Hedda Gabler *and* The Master Builder, *died 1906. Rejecting those who said he might get better…*

On the contrary!

*Following page: A self-portrait by Hokusai.*

天保六乙未年四月
齢七十六前北齊爲一改
更狂老人卍筆

### Washington Irving
*American essayist, acknowledged as 'the first American man of letters', died 1859.*

Well, I must arrange my pillows for another night. When will this end?

### Friedrich Jacobs
*German classical philologist, died 1819.*
*He recited Latin verses...*

Who would wish, indeed, to prolong pain, the breath failing all too gradually? Better to die, than to drag out a dead life, the senses buried in the limbs.

### William Jay
*British dissenting minister, died 1853.*

Oh, none of you know what it is to die.

### Richard Jefferies
*British naturalist, novelist and essayist, author of Bevis: The Story of a Boy, died 1887.*

Yes, yes, that is so. Help, Lord, for Jesus' sake. Darling, goodbye. God bless you and the children, and save you all from such great pain.

### Lord Francis Jeffrey
*British jurist and critic, died 1850.*
*He was writing about a dream he had had about political journals...*

I read the ideal copies with a good deal of pain and difficulty, owing to the smallness of the type, but with great interest and, I believe, often for more than an hour at a time, forming a judgement of their merits with great freedom and acuteness, and often saying to myself 'This is very cleverly thought out, but there is a fallacy in it, for so and so…'

### Stone Johnson
*Twentieth-century American professional footballer, killed in a game.*

Oh my God, oh my God! Where's my head? Where's my head?!

### Julian the Apostate (Flavius Claudius Julianus)
*Roman scholar and soldier, killed in battle 363.*
*A lifetime pagan, his words referred to Christiantity and its founder...*

You have conquered, O Galilean.

### Joseph Lakanal
*French educator, who reformed the French educational system during the French Revolution, died 1845.*
*To his doctor...*

Your attentions will not save me. I feel that there is no more oil in the lamp.

### Charles Lamb
*British poet and essayist, author of The Essays of Elia, died 1834.*

My bedfellows are cramp and cough … we three all in one bed.

### Julie de Lespinasse
*French beauty and courtesan, died 1776.*

Am I still alive?

### Mrs. Linn Linton
*British novelist, died 1898.*

I am very forlorn at the present moment and wish I was at Malvern. Oh, don't I just!

### Henry Longfellow
*American poet, the most popular of his era and best remembered for The Song of Hiawatha, died 1881.*
*To his sister...*

Now I know that I must be very ill, since you have been sent for.

### Jean-Baptiste Lully
*Composer and director of the Paris Opéra, died 1687.*

Sinner, thou must die.

### Madame de Maintenon
*Second wife of Louis XIV of France, died 1719.*
*Asked to bless her 'daughters', the children of Louis XIV to whom she had been governess...*

I am not worthy.

### Manolete (Manuel Laureano Rodruiguez Sanchez)
*Spanish bullfighter, killed in the bullring 1947.*

I can't feel anything in my right leg. I can't feel anything in my left leg. Doctor, are my eyes open? I can't see!

### Jules Mazarin
*Cardinal and Prime Minister of France, died 1661.*

Oh my poor soul, what is to become of thee? Whither wilt thou go?

### Hortense Mazarin
*Sister of the Cardinal, died 1699.*
*After she died her creditors seized her corpse.*

Debt!

### George Meredith
*Novelist and poet, author of The Ordeal of Richard Feverel, died 1909.*
*Mentioning his doctor's opinion.*

I'm afraid Sir Thomas thinks very badly of my case.

### Honoré-Gabriel Riqueti, Comte de Mirabeau
*One of the leaders of the French Revolution, died 1791.*

Are you not my doctor and my friend? Did you not promise to save me from the pain of such a

*Comte de Mirabeau*

death? Do you wish me to carry away regret for having given you my confidence?

### Maria Montessori
*Italian educator and originator of the educational system that bears her name, died 1952.*

Am I no longer of any use, then?

### 'Mad' Daniel Morgan
*Australian bushranger, 'The Murrumbidgee Terror', shot in the back by police 1865.*

Why didn't you give me a chance instead of shooting me in the back like a dog?

### John Motley
*British diplomat and historian, died 1877.*

I am ill, very ill. I shall not recover.

### Frédéric Moyse
*French murderer, executed by the guillotine.*
*Moyse had killed his own son...*

What! Would you execute the father of a family?

### Modest Petrovich Mussorgsky
*Russian composer, best known for his opera Boris Godunov, died 1881.*

It is the end.
Woe is me!

### James Naylor

*British Quaker, self-appointed 'Messiah', died 1660.*

I have fellowship therein with them who live in dens and desolate places in the earth.

### Harriet Newell

*British missionary, died 1812.*

The pain, the groans, the dying strife. How long, oh Lord, how long?

### Francis Newport

*Militant British atheist, died 1692.*

Oh, the insufferable pangs of hell and damnation!

### Charles Nodier

*French man of letters, died 1844.*

It is very hard, my children, I no longer see you. Remember me, love me always.

*Dorothy Parker.*

### Phil Ochs

*American folksinger, committed suicide 1975.*

*A message from the stage at his last concert...*

One day you'll read about it. Phil Ochs, A Suicide at 35.

*Phil Ochs on stage a few months before his death, with close friend Bob Dylan.*

### Francis Oliver

*Chancellor of France, died 1560. Oliver condemned many innocents on the orders of the corrupt Cardinal Lorrain...*

Cardinal, thou wilt make us all be damned.

### Amelia Opie

*British novelist and poet, died 1853. Sending a message to anyone who asked after her...*

Tell them, I have suffered great pain, but I think on Him who suffered for me. Say that I am trusting in my Saviour and ask them to pray for me.

### Dorothy Parker

*American poet, writer and wit, died 1967. Asked to compose her own epitaph...*

Excuse my dust.

### William Pattison

*British poet, died 1727. Starving to death he sent this last appeal for help...*

Sir, if you was ever touched with a sense of humanity, consider my condition. What I am, my proposals will inform you. What I have been, Sidney College in Cambridge can witness, but what I shall be some few hours hence, I tremble to think. Spare my blushes ... I have not enjoyed the common necessaries of life for these two days and can hardly hold to subscribe myself.

### Brian Piccolo

*American professional footballer, died of cancer 1968.*

*To his girlfriend...*

Can you believe it Joy? Can you believe this shit?

### Edgar Allan Poe

*American writer, best known for his* Tales of Mystery and Imagination, *died 1849.*

Lord help my poor soul.

## William Pope
*British atheist, died 1797.*
*Pope led an atheistic cult who delighted in desecrating religious places and objects and at whose meetings a Bible was ritually kicked around the floor.*

I have done the damnable deed. The horrible damnable deed. I cannot pray God will have nothing to do with me. I will not have salvation at his hands. I long to be in the bottomless pit, the lake which burneth with fire and brimstone. I tell you I am damned. I will not have salvation. Nothing for me but hell. Come eternal torments! Oh God do not hear my prayers for I will not be saved. I hate everything that God has made!

## Mrs. Mary Price
*British housewife, murdered by her husband 1738.*
As he throttled her with his whip...

My dear! my dear! For God's sake if this is your love, I will never trust you more!

## Lieutenant Prochaska
*Polish soldier, committed suicide.*
He killed his wife, children and himself after being told that another lieutenant had made advances to his wife...

Let the lieutenant now make love to my wife if he pleases.

## John Randolph of Roanoke
*American politician, died 1833.*
Traditionally he ordered a secretary...
Write that word 'remorse' and show it to me.
But in reality said...
Dying. Home…Randolph and Betty, my children, adieu! Get me to bed at Chatham or elsewhere, say Hugh Mercer's or Minor's. To bed I conjure you all!

## Louis, Duc de Richelieu
*French aristocrat, died 1789.*
Dying on the eve of the French Revolution...
What would Louis XIV have said?

## Rainer Maria Rilke
*German poet, author of the* Duino Elegies *and* Sonnets to Orpheus, *died 1926.*

I still think of the world, poor shard of a vessel that remembers being of the earth. But how it abuses our senses and their dictionary the pain that turns their pages.

## José Rizal y Alonso
*National hero of the Philippines, executed by a Spanish firing squad 1896.*
Oh Father, how terrible it is to die. How one suffers! Father, I forgive everyone from the bottom of my heart. I have no resentment against any one, believe me, your reverence.

## Frederick Robertson
*British divine, died 1853.*
I cannot bear it. Let me rest. I must die. Let God do his work.

## Louis François, Duc de Rohan-Chabot
*French Archbishop of Besançon, died 1648.*
I am nothing, nothing, less than nothing!

## Anthony de Rosa
*British murderer, hanged 1752.*
*He had stabbed his victim to death during a mugging, the bloody knife proving his guilt...*
I am as an innocent as a child unborn. Would you have me own myself guilty of what I know no more of than you do? I know, if I be guilty and deny it, I must send my soul to the bottom of hell, which I hope I know better than to do.

## Anton Rubinstein
*Polish-American virtuoso pianist and composer, died 1894.*
I am suffocating. A doctor! Quick! A doctor!

## John Ryland
*British Baptist minister, died 1825.*
No more pain.

## Raphael Sabatier
*French surgeon, died 1811.*
To his son...
Contemplate the state to which I am fallen and learn to die.

## Donatien Alphonse François, Marquis de Sade
*French philosopher, died 1814.*
*The conclusion of his will demanded that...*
The ground over my grave shall be sprinkled with acorns so that all traces of my grave shall disappear so that, as I hope, this reminder of my existence may be wiped from the memory of man.

## Richard Savage
*British poet and vagrant, died 1743.*
To his gaoler...
I have something to say to you, sir…'Tis gone!

## Thomas Scott
*American congressman, died 1887.*
To the priest...
Begone, you and your trumpery! Until this moment I believed that there was neither a God nor a hell. Now I know and feel that there are both and that I am doomed to perdition by the just judgement of the Almighty.

## Richard Brinsley Sheridan
*British dramatist, author of* The Rivals *and* The School for Scandal, *died 1816.*
I am absolutely undone.

## Siward
*Danish adventurer, later Earl of Northumberland, died 1055.*
Shame on me that I did not die in one of the many battles that I have fought, but am reserved to die with the disgrace of the death of a sick cow! At least put on my armour of proof, gird the sword by my side, place the helmet on my head, let me have my shield in my left hand and my axe in my hand, that the bravest of soldiers may die in a soldier's garb.

## Peter Spengler
*Martyr, died 16th century.*
It is all one, for shortly I must have forsaken this skin, which already hangeth to my bones. I know well that I am a mortal and a cor-ruptible worm, and have nothing in me but corruption. I have long time desired my latter day, and have made my request that I might be delivered out of this mortal body, to be joined with my Saviour Christ. I have deserved, through my manifold sins committed against my Saviour Christ, my cross, and my Saviour Christ hath borne the cross, and hath died upon the cross, and for my part I will not glory in any other thing, but only in the cross of Jesus Christ.

*Far left: Rilke, from a 1906 portrait by his friend, Expressionist painter Paula Modersohn-Becker.*

### Baruch Spinoza
*Dutch-Jewish philosopher, the foremost exponent of seventeenth-century Rationalism, died 1677.*

God have mercy upon me and be gracious to me…a miserable sinner.

### Edmund Clarence Stedman
*British poet and editor, died 1908.*

Twenty-seven letters! What is the use!

### Robert Louis Stevenson
*Scottish novelist and travel writer, died 1894.*

My head, my head!

### Erich von Stroheim
*Austrian film director, died 1957.*
He was still berating Hollywood on his deathbed…

This isn't the worst. The worst is

*Composer Sir Arthur Sullivan.*

that they stole twenty-five years of my life.

### Sir Arthur Sullivan
*British composer, the Sullivan of 'Gilbert and Sullivan', died 1900.*

My heart, my heart!

### Francis Talma
*French actor, died 1826.*

The worst is, I cannot see.

### Matthew Tindall
*British militant atheist, died 1733.*

Oh God, if there be a God, I desire thee to have mercy on me!

### William Eyton Tooke
*British philosopher, committed suicide nineteenth century.*
Obsessed with researches into moral and political philosophy which had become too demanding, he started repeating over and over…

This subject is too much for me. My head is distracted.

### Rev. Augustus Toplady
*British composer of hymns, including 'Rock of ages cleft for me', died 1778.*
Asked whether he was in pain…

It is delightful.

### Bérénger de Tours
*French theologian, died 1088.*
His writings had been banned by the Vatican…

I shall not long hesitate between conscience and the Pope, for I shall soon appear in the presence of God to be acquitted, I hope, to be condemned, I fear.

### Gaston Truphène
*French merchant, murdered 1928.*
Truphène was trying to collect a debt when his killer, the Parisian jeweller Mestorino, smashed his skull with a mandrel, used for holding jewellery for engraving or cutting.

There are 300,000 francs, you can take them all!
And to Mestorino's sister-in-law who stood by and watched…
Suzanne, I have a sister like you. Take pity on me!

### Ivan Turgenev
*Russian author, died 1883.*
Ending a letter to fellow-writer Leo Tolstoy…

I can neither walk, eat nor sleep. It tires me even to mention all this. My friend, great writer of the Russian land, heed my request. Let me know whether you receive this sheet and permit me once more closely, closely to embrace you, your wife and all yours. I can no more. I am tired.

### William H. Vanderbilt
*American millionaire, died 1899.*

I have had no real gratification or enjoyment of any sort more than my neighbour down the block who is worth only half a million.

### Leonardo da Vinci
*Milanese draughtsman, anatomist, scientist and artist, died 1519.*

I have offended God and mankind because my work did not reach the quality it should have.

### General Joseph Wall
*British Governor of Goree (Senegal), he had a man flogged to death and was hanged as a murderer in 1802.*

I do not wish to be pulled by the heels.

### Gus Wernicke
*Australian bushranger, shot by the police 1879.*

Oh God, I'm shot! And I'm only fifteen!

### John Greenleaf Whittier
*American poet and abolitionist, died 1892.*

No, no!

### Dr. John Wolcot
*British satirist who wrote as Peter Pindar, died 1819.*
Asked what could be done to help him…

Give me back my youth.

### Giacomo Zane
*Italian poet, died 1560.*

I should like to live.

### David Zeisberger
*American missionary, died 1808.*

I have reviewed my whole life and found that there is much to be forgiven.

*Facing page: Self-portrait by Leonardo… 'my work did not reach the quality it should have'.*

# LOOK BACK IN ANGER

*Death is one thing, but there's nothing quite like bad temper.*

### Agrippina
*Mother of the Roman Emperor Nero, killed 59 AD.*
Smite my womb!

### Gabriele D'Annunzio
*Italian poet and novelist, died 1938.*
I'm bored, I'm bored!

### Aratus
*Greek poet, poisoned 213 BC.*
Staring at the blood he was coughing up...
These, Oh Cephalon, are the wages of a King's love.

### Antoine Barnave
*French politician, guillotined 1793.*
This, then, was my reward.

### Alexander Graham Bell
*Scottish inventor of the telephone and educator of the deaf, died 1922.*
So little done, so much to do.

### Alban Berg
*Australian composer, died 1936.*
Advised to relax...
But I have so little time!

### Bestoujeff
*Russian revolutionary, hanged 1926.*
He was hanged alongside Count Pestel (see page 56) and his rope also broke...
Nothing succeeds with me. Even here I meet with disappointment.

### Elisa Bonaparte
*Sister of Napoleon, died 1820.*
Told that nothing was as certain as death...
Except taxes.

### Pauline Bonaparte
*Napoleon's favourite sister, died 1825.*
I always was beautiful.

### Tycho Brahe
*Danish astronomer, died 1601.*
Let me not seem to have lived in vain.

### Richard Brocklesby
*British physician, died 1797.*
To those who were helping him undress...
What an idle piece of ceremony this buttoning and unbuttoning is to me now.

### Stopford Augustus Brooke
*Irish divine and man of letters, died 1916.*
Hearing the news read to him...
It will be a pity to leave all that.

### Marcus Junius Brutus
*Assassin of Caesar, died 42 BC.*
Quoting the Greek playwright Euripedes...
Oh wretched virtue! Thou art a bare name. I mistook thee for a substance, but thou thyself are the slave of fortune.

### Robert Burns
*Scottish poet, died 1796.*
Receiving a bill sent to his death bed...
That damned rascal!

### Caius Cassius
*Leader of the plot to kill Julius Caesar, committed suicide 42 BC.*
Through too much fondness for life I have lived to endure the sight of my friend taken by the enemy before my face.

### Paul Cézanne
*French painter, died 1906.*
Recalling the name of the director of the Museum at Aix who had once refused to exhibit his works...
Pontier! Pontier!

### Roch Chamfort
*French writer, died 1794.*
Ah, my friend, I am about to leave this world where the heart must either be broken or be brass.

### Charles Churchill
*British poet and satirist, died 1764.*
What a fool I have been.

*Facing page:
James Dean...
his 'fun days' were over in 1955.*

*Cézanne...
on his way to work.*

139

## Grover Cleveland
*American President, died 1908.*
I have tried so hard to do right.

## Rev. Dr. John Colbatch
*British lawyer, died 1748*
*He remembered a far-off legal wrangle over a Latin tag...*
Arrogat, my lord!

## Auguste Comte
*French philosopher, died 1857.*
What an incomparable loss.

## Ann Coppola
*American wife of gangster 'Trigger Mike' Coppola, committed suicide 1962. Her suicide note...*
Mike Coppola…Someday, somehow, a person, or God, or the law shall catch up with you, you yellow-bellied bastard. You are the lowest and biggest coward I have ever had the misfortune to meet.

## Crato of Thebes
*Greek Philosopher, died 300 BC.*
*Referring to his crooked back...*
Ah, poor humpback. Thy many long years are at last conveying thee to the tomb. Thou shalt soon visit the palace of Pluto.

## Thomas Danvers
*British builder of 'Danvers Folly', a small castle on the Thames.*
*He committed suicide after a string of misfortunes. His note ran...*
Descended from an ancient and honourable family, I have, for fifteen years past, suffered more indigence than ever a gentleman submitted to. Neglected by my acquaintance, traduced by my enemies, and insulted by the vulgar, I am so reduced, worn down and tired, that I have nothing left but that lasting repose, the joint and dernier inheritance of all.
'Of laudanum an ample dose
Must all my present ills compose
But the best laudanum of all
I want (not resolution) but a ball.'
Advertise this. T.D.

## Henry Stewart, Earl of Darnley
*English nobleman, second husband of Mary, Queen of Scots, killed 1567.*
*Supposed killed on the Queen's order, he quoted the Sixtieth Psalm against the Queen...*
It is not an open enemy that has done me this dishonour, for then I could have borne it. It was even thou, my companion, my guide and my own familiar friend.

## James Dean
*American film star, killed in a car crash 1955.*
*Dean was talking shortly before his fatal crash...*
My fun days are over.

## John Dennis
*British poet, died 1734.*
*Told on his deathbed that someone had published a book of poems under his name...*
By God! That could be no-one but that fool [Richard] Savage!

## John Denton
*British nonconformist divine, died 1709.*
I wish I could once more recall
That bright and blissful joy.
And summon to my weary heart
The feelings of a boy.
But now on scenes of past delight
I look and feel no pleasure.
As misers on their bed of death
Gaze coldly at their treasure.

## Camille Desmoulins
*One of the leaders of the French Revolution, guillotined 1794.*
Oh my poor wife. Poor people… how they have deceived you.

## Denis Diderot
*French philosopher, died 1784.*
*Taking an apricot that his wife had offered...*
But what the devil do you think that will do to me?

## Alexandre Dumas
*French dramatist and novelist, died 1870.*
*'Dumas Père' died complaining to his son that he would never find out how The Count of Monte Cristo ended...*
I shall never know how it all comes out.

## Marquis Joseph Dupleix
*French colonialist, died 1763.*
*In a letter to the French government...*
I have sacrificed my youth, my fortune, my life to enrich my nation in Asia. Unfortunate friends, too weak relations, devoted all their property to the success of my projects. They are now in misery and want. I have complied with all the judiciary forms. I have demanded, as the last of the creditors, that which is due to me. My services are treated as fables, my demand is denounced as ridiculous, I am treated as the vilest of mankind. I am in the most deplorable indigence. The little property that remains to me has been seized. I am compelled to ask for decrees for delay in order not to be dragged to prison.

## James B. Eads
*American engineer, died 1887.*
I cannot die. I have not finished my work.

## Pope Eugenius IV (Gabriele Condolmere)
*Italian pontiff, died 1447.*
Oh Gabriele, how much better it would have been for thee and how much more it would have promoted thy soul's welfare if thou had never been raised to the Pontificate, but had been content to lead a quiet and religious life in a monastery.

## John Galsworthy
*British popular novelist, author of The Forsyte Saga, died 1933.*
*Beyond speech Galsworthy scribbled a dying note...*
I have enjoyed too pleasant circumstances.

## Stephen Gardiner
*British Protestant bishop, burnt for heresy in 1555.*
*Expressing his sorrow at ever denying the supremacy of the Catholic church...*
I have denied with Peter, I have gone out with Peter, but not yet have I wept with Peter.

### Geronimo

*Chief of the Apache Indians, died 1909.*
*Interviewed before his death...*

I want to go back to my old home before I die. Tired of fight and want to rest I asked the Great White Father to allow me to go back, but he said no.

### Nikolai Gogol

*Russian novelist and dramatist, died 1852.*
*Quoting the Old Testament...*

And I shall laugh a bitter laugh.

### Oliver Goldsmith

*British dramatist, novelist and biographer, died 1774.*
*Asked whether his mind was at rest?...*

No, it is not

### Pope Gregory VII

*Italian pontiff and saint, one of the great reforming popes of the Middle Ages, died 1085.*

I have loved righteousness and hated iniquity, therefore I die in exile.

### Reinier de Groenveld

*Dutch political leader.*

Oh God, what a man I was once and what am I now?... Patience.

### Hugo Grotius (Huig de Groot)

*Dutch jurist, statesman and scholar, a pioneer of international law, died 1645.*

By understanding many things I have accomplished nothing.

### Guang Zhou

*Chinese Emperor, died 1912.*
*His wish was never carried out.*

We were the second son of the Prince Ch'un when the Empress Dowager selected Us for the Throne. She has always hated Us, but for Our misery of the past ten years, Yuan Shiai is responsible and none other. When the time comes I desire that Yuan be summarily beheaded.

### Jaroslav Hašek

*Czech writer, author of* The Good Soldier Schweik, *died 1923.*
*Rebuking the doctor who refused him one final glass of brandy...*

But you're cheating me!

### Georg Friedrich Hegel

*German philosopher, died 1831.*

Now, nobody will ever understand me.

### James Hogg ('The Ettrick Shepherd')

*British poet, died of hiccups 1835.*

It is a reproach to the faculty that they cannot cure the hiccup.

### Oliver Wendell Holmes

*American judge, son of the poet, died 1935.*
*Before his final incarceration in an oxygen tent...*

Lot of damn foolery.

### David Hume

*British philosopher, died 1776.*

I am dying as fast as my enemies, if I have any, could wish, and as cheerfully as my best friends could desire.

### Andrew Jackson

*American President, died 1845.*

I have only two regrets ... that I have not shot Henry Clay or hanged John C. Calhoun.

### Jezebel

*Phoenician princess, died c.843 BC*

Has Zimri peace who slew his master?

### Father Joseph (François-Joseph le Clerc du Tremblay)

*French diplomat and mystic, 'The Grey Eminence', thus named for his behind-the-scenes influence on Cardinal Richelieu, died 1638.*

Render an account!

### James Joyce

*Irish novelist, author of* Ulysses, *died 1941.*

Does nobody understand?

*James Joyce with his portraitist Augustus John.*

### Franz Kafka
*Czech writer, died 1924.*
Demanding that all his papers should be burnt...
There will be no proof that I ever was a writer.

### John Keats
*British poet, died 1821.*
Inscribed on his gravestone...
Here lies one whose name was writ in water.

### William Kidd ('Captain Kidd')
*Scottish-born pirate, hanged 1701.*
Kidd had only surrendered on the sure promise of a free pardon...
This is a very false and faithless generation.

### François de Malherbe
*French poet, died 1628.*
To the priest who was eulogising heaven...
Hold your tongue! Your wretched style disgusts me.

### George Browne Macdonald
*Rudyard Kipling's grandfather, died 1868.*
Lord, what things I lie here and remember.

### Marie Henriette
*18-year-old French suicide.*
Her former lover, defying parental fury they had written their marriage contract in blood, deserted her...
He has dishonoured me, the monster! He deceived me by pretence, which went to my heart! But it is he who is to be pitied, wretch that he is! Look back

### Karl Marx
*German political theorist, died 1883.*
Asked by his housekeeper if he had a last message to the world...
Go on, get out! Last words are for fools who haven't said enough.

### Tommaso Masaniello
*Italian soldier, killed 1646.*
His own troops assassinated him...
Ungrateful traitors.

### H.L. Mencken
*American editor, critic, essayist and philologist, died 1956.*
To James T Farrell...
Remember me to my friends, tell them I'm a hell of a mess.

### Jean Messelier
*Anarchist, died 1733.*
Voltaire published his will.
I should like to see, and this will be the last and most ardent of my desires, I should like to see the last king strangled with the guts of the last priest!

### James Montrose
*Swansea housebreaker, committed suicide in his prison cell 1905.*
I had a hard task to keep from hanging myself while I was awaiting trial for two months, and it was then I made up my determination that the first warder that reported me for any paltry offence I would murder for the purpose of getting hung out of this miserable cure of life. But as I hate the law, and therefore did not wish to die by it, I have changed my mind, and take the curse of life away myself. Rather than have a life in the cursed gaols of England, which are ruled by gangs of brutal tyrants, I would sooner die; and I say again that it were far better to be down in the grave. I am happy in the thought that I will soon be no more.

### Henri Murger
*French author, died 1861.*
Referring to his *Scènes de la vie de Bohème*...
No more music, no more commotion, no more Bohemia.

### Adam Narusewicz
*Polish historian, died 1796.*
Regretting dying with his work incomplete...
Must I leave it unfinished?

### Henry Oxburgh
*Jacobite rebel, executed 1716.*
He was hanged, drawn and quartered at Tyburn, his head being displayed upon one of the spikes on the top of Temple Bar. Last letter...
I might have hoped from the great character [General] Mr. Wills gave me at Preston (when I treated with him for a surrender) of the clemency of the Prince now on the throne (to which, he said, we could not better entitle ourselves than by an early submission) that such as surrendered themselves Prisoners at Discretion, on that Prospect, would have met with more lenity than I have experienced, and I believe England is the only country in Europe where Prisoners at Discretion are not understood to have their Lives saved.

### Pope Pius X
*Italian pope, died 1914.*
The Pope refused to bless the armies of the Holy Roman Empire, then had a fatal heart attack after dismissing the Emperor Franz Joseph...
Get out of my sight! Get out of my sight! Away! Away! We grant blessing to no-one who provokes the world to war.

### Cecil Rhodes
*British colonial administrator, died 1902.*
Turn me over, Jack
Traditionally, he is also to have said...
So little done, so much to do.

### Legh Richmond
*British evangelical divine and author of moral tracts, died 1827.*
It will be all confusion. The church! There will be such confusion in my church!

### Sandro Sandri
*Italian Fascist war correspondent killed reporting the Sino-Japanese war, 1937.*
They've killed me this time. What an end. In another nation's ship, in this country.

### Reginald (Reynold Scott)
*British anti-witche writer, died 1599.*
The last words of his will, referring to his second wife, a widow named Alice Collyar...
Great is the trouble my poor wife hath had with me, and small is the comfort she hath received at my hands, whom if I had not matched withal I had not died worth one groat.

### Sir Ernest Shackleton
*Irish explorer of the Antarctic, died 1922.*
Complaining to his doctor...
You are always wanting me to give up something. What do you want me to give up now?

### 'Suspinianus' (Johann Spiessheimer)

*Viennese humanist, died @@@@@@@@?.*
*To fellow humanist, Johann Brassican...*

That you have not visited me in my grievous and deadly sickness what even strangers do will be noted at the appointed time. Through my man-servant I informed myself of your situation and sent you wine and other good things. By your behaviour you have marked yourself out as a sneak and an intriguer, and I shall see that posterity knows about it. What is another man to you? In order that you may be aware of my intention, even when my hand is a corpse's, I am putting it in writing. Let it be goodbye, then. It goes badly with me, but I am what I always was.

### Hannen Swaffer

*British journalist, died 1962.*
*It is not known to what he referred...*
What a cow!

### Jonathan Swift

*Irish clergyman and satirist, author of*
Gulliver's Travels, *died 1745.*

I am dying like a poisoned rat in a hole. I am what I am!

### Toussaint l'Ouverture

*Haitian revolutionary leader, died 1803.*
*To his gaolers...*
You have taken away my watch and the money I had in my pocket. I hereby serve notice on you that these objects are my personal property and that I will call you to account for them on the day I am executed, when I shall expect you to remit them to my wife and children.

### William Tweed

*'Boss' of Tammany Hall, New York's*
*political 'machine', died 1870.*
*Referring to his old partners and rivals...*
[Samuel] Tilden and Fairchild, they will be satisfied now.

### General Charles de Villars

*French soldier, died 1734.*
*Talking about the Duke of Berwick, who died*
*in battle, while de Villars died in bed...*
I always deemed him more fortunate than myself.

### Henry Wainwright

*British murderer, hanged 1875.*
*Public executions were no longer*
*performed, but Wainwright's death was*
*witnessed by some hundreds of officials,*
*pressmen and friends of the warden...*
You curs! So you have come to see a man die!

### Stephen Ward

*British osteopath, suicide 1963.*
*Scapegoated for the Profumo Affair, he*
*committed suicide during his trial.*
*One of ten notes...*
I'm sorry to disappoint the vultures.

### William Westwood ('Jacky Jacky')

*Australian bushranger, hanged 1846.*
*His last letter, to the prison chaplain...*
Out of the bitter cup of misery I have drunk, the sweetest draught is that which takes away the misery of a living death. It is the friend that deceives no man. All will be quiet. No tyrant will disturb my repose.

*Stephen Ward.*

*Jonathan Swift...*
*'I am what I am!'*

# ALL MY OWN WORK

*Suicide is painless, but that doesn't mean it's silent.*

### Julius Agrestis
*Roman nobleman, committed suicide 69 AD.*
Charged with treason, he proved his loyalty in death...

Since you [Emperor Vitellius] require some decisive proof and I can no longer serve you in any other way, either by my life or death, will give you a proof which you can believe.

### Anonymous
*17-year-old girl who committed suicide. Cited by Dostoevsky...*

I am undertaking a long journey. If I should not succeed, let people gather to celebrate my resurrection with a bottle of Cliquot. If I should succeed, I ask that I be interred only after I am altogether dead, since it is particularly disagreeable to awake in a coffin in the earth. It is not chic!

### Anonymous
*Doctor who committed suicide...*

As if I were free. My heart must be strong. It won't give up. Pulse running well. I feel fine. When will it be over?

### Anonymous
*American worker. His suicide note...*

My small estate I bequeath to my mother, my body to the nearest accredited medical school; my soul and heart to all the girls; and my brain to Harry Truman.

### Anonymous
*Committed suicide. Found on the wall in an empty house in Hampstead London,*

Why suicide? Why not?

### Anonymous
*Hollywood failure. His suicide note...*

I tried so hard to make a comeback. Exit, Act III.

### Anonymous
*Apothecary. Rebuffed by his mistress, he shot himself...*

When a man knows not how to please his mistress, he ought to know how to die.

### Anonymous
*German who committed suicide 1783. He took his scissors and cut first his throat and then the arteries in his wrists. Still alive, he took a knife used for gutting deer and stabbed himself in his heart. His wife returned from church to find him dying. Prior to this, he had concluded his journal...*

My life, such as it is, is a mere animal life, devoid of reason. In my mind a life which stands in opposition to duty is a moral death, and worse than that which is natural. In favour of the few whose life I cannot render happy, it is at least my duty not to become an oppression. I ought to relieve them from a weight which sooner or later cannot fail to crush them.

### Anonymous
*Theatrical hopeful. Finally allowed to act, he was hooted off stage. His suicide note...*

My Dear Mother, All my hopes have been ruined. I fancied myself a man of genius, the reality has proved me to be a fool. I die, because life is no longer to be supported. Look charitably on this last action of my life. Adieu!

### Anonymous Woman
*After claiming that religious principles made suicide impossible, she then used this sophistry to justify her death...*

There are no general rules with exceptions; and I am the precise exception in this case, therefore I commit suicide without violating any religious principles.

### Barney Barnato
*British adventurer, committed suicide by jumping off a ship 1897.*

What is the time?

### Paul Bern
*Husband of film star Jean Harlowe, committed suicide by slashing his wrists 1932. He killed himself two months after their marriage ceremony because of his impotence...*

Dearest Dear, Unfortunately this is the only way to make good the frightful wrong I have done you. And to wipe out my abject humiliation.

*Facing page: Virginia Woolf, suicide by drowning, 1941.*

### Bordeaux

*An otherwise anonymous French soldier's suicide note...*

If we exist after life, and it is forbidden to quit it without permission, I will endeavour to procure a moment to inform you of it. If not, I shall advise all those who are unhappy, which is by far the greater part of mankind, to follow my example. When you receive this letter I shall have been dead at least twenty-four hours.

### Eustace Budgell

*English writer, one of the most prolific contributors to the early* Spectator *magazine, drowned himself 1837. The coroner's jury returned a verdict of lunacy. He left a paper on his desk staring...*

What Cato did and Addison approved Cannot be wrong.

### Thomas Chatterton

*British poet, killed himself with a dose of arsenic, aged 18 in 1770.*

I am about to quit forever my ungrateful country. I shall exchange it for the deserts of Africa where tigers are a thousand times more merciful than man.

### Christine Chubbuck

*American newsreader on station WXLT in Florida, shot herself on screen, aged 29, during her 'Sun Coast Digest', 1974. Her notes for the programme were discovered, the suicide bid was written up in the third person and her condition was described as 'critical'.*

In keeping with Channel 40's policy of bringing you the latest in blood and guts, you are going to see another first: an attempted suicide.

### Robert Clive

*British Governor-General of India, stabbed himself to death 1774. When asked to sharpen a pencil he picked up the penknife and stabbed himself, as he put it...*

To be sure.

### Charles Caleb Colton

*British writer, author of* Lacon, *shot himself 1832. Colton suffered from a painful disease and in his death falsified one of the remarks in 'Lacon', viz. that no one ever committed suicide from bodily pain, though thousands have done so from mental anguish. Colton could not face a threatened operation.*

When life is unbearable, death is desirable and suicide justifiable.

### Gnaius Domitius Corbulo

*Roman nobleman, suicide 67 AD. Ordered to kill himself by the emperor Nero, who suspected him of treason...*

Well deserved.

### Hart Crane

*American writer, committed suicide by jumping off a ship into the Caribbean Sea in 1932.*

Goodbye, everybody!

### René Crevel

*French surrealist painter, committed suicide by gas 1905.*

Is it true…that one commits suicide for love, for fear, for syphilis? It is not true. Suicide is a means of selection. Those men commit suicide who reject the quasi-universal cowardice of struggling against a certain spiritual sensation so intense that it must be taken until further notice as a sensation of truth. Only this sensation permits the acceptance of the most obviously just and definitive of solutions…suicide.

### John Davidson

*British poet, drowned himself 1909. These were his last written words, penned in 'The Testament of John Davidson'. He disappeared from his house at Penzance and threw himelf into the sea*

Men are the universe become conscious; the simplest man should consider himself too great to be called after any name.

### Demosthenes

*Athenian orator, suicide 322 BC. He killed himself rather than be captured by the Macedonians...*

Now, as soon as you please, you may commence the part of Creon in the tragedy, and cast out this body of mine unburied. But, O gracious Poseidon, I for my part while I am still alive will arise and depart out of this sacred place though Antipater and the Macedonians have not left so much as Thy temple unpolluted.

### William Dorrington

*British perjurer. Condemned for perjury, he threw himself from the roof of St Sepulchre's Church, London. This note was found on the roof...*

Oh supreme God, who inhabitest the highest heavens, heal my afflictions, as with the wretched in hell, the joyful in heaven, shew mercy to the guilty.

### George Eastman

*American scientist, committed suicide 1932.*

To my friends: my work is done. Why wait?

### Sergeant Paul Falck

*NCO in the Prussian Reichswehr, committed suicide 1930. He wrote in the official station record book...*

At ten minutes after midnight Sgt. Falck committed suicide by shooting himself. Corporal Junker has been instructed to take over the reveille.

### Florine and Guyon

*A Parisian couple. A rich young woman and her lover, a hussar, found drowned in the river Seine. This was their last note...*

Oh you, whoever you may be, compassionate souls, who shall find these two bodies united; know that we loved each other with the most ardent affection and that we have perished together that we may be eternally united. Know, compassionate souls, that our last desire is that you should place us, united as we are, in the same grave. Man should not separate those whom death has joined.

### James V. Forrestal

*Son of the celebrated American admiral, committed suicide 1949. Quoting Sophocles as his suicide note...*

Woe to the mother in her close of day
Woe to her desolate heart and temples grey
When she shall hear.
Her loved one's story whispered in her ear
'Woe, woe!' will be the cry
No quiet murmur like the tremulous wail.

### M. Gillet

*A French suicide, hanged himself aged 75.*

Jesus Christ has said, when a tree is old and can no longer bear fruit, it is good that it should be destroyed.

### Charlotte Gilman

*American feminist, committed suicide in 1935.*

Human life consists in mutual service. No grief, pain, misfortune or 'broken heart' is excuse for cutting off one's life while power of service remains. But when all usefulness is over,

*Joseph Goebbels and friends, Germany, 1943.*

when one is assured of an unavoidable and imminent death, it is the simplest of human rights to choose a quick and easy death in place of a slow and horrible one.

### Thomas Giltens
*Committed suicide 1916.*
*He killed himself with a shotgun after his son enlisted to fight in World War I.*

Dear Family, forgive me. I cannot live. I have not slept for some time and I am very tired. Heaven and earth forgive me.

### Fanny Godwin
*Illegitimate daughter of Mary Wollstonecraft and William Godwin, committed suicide 1816.*
*Her note...*

I have long determined that the best thing I could do was to put an end to the existence of a being whose birth was unfortunate, and whose life has only been a series of pains to those persons who have hurt their health in endeavouring to promote her welfare. Perhaps to hear of my death may give you pain, but you will soon have the blessing of forgetting that such a creature ever existed.

### Joseph Goebbels
*Hitler's propaganda chief, committed suicide 1945.*
*Goebbels killed himself, his wife and their children shortly before the Russians over-ran Berlin.*

This is the worst treachery of all. The generals have betrayed the Führer. Everything is lost. I shall die together with my wife and family. You will burn our bodies. Can you do that?

### Magda Goebbels
*Wife of Joseph Goebbels, committed suicide alongside her husband (after first killing their children) 1945.*

You see, we die an honourable death. If you should ever see Harald [son from her first marriage, a war prisoner] again, give him our best and tell him we died an honourable death.

### Tony Hancock
*British comedian, drug overdose 1968.*
*His last TV monologue in 1964 proved an ironic farewell...*

What have you achieved? What have you achieved? You lost your chance, me old son. You contributed absolutely nothing to this life. A waste of time you being here at all. No place for you in Westminster Abbey. The best you can expect is a few daffodils in a jam jar, a rough-hewn stone bearing the legend 'He came and he went' and in

between ... nothing! Nobody will even notice you're not here. After about a year afterwards somebody might say down the pub 'Where's old Hancock? I haven't seen him around lately'. 'Oh, he's dead y'know'. 'Oh, is he?'. A right raison d'être that is. Nobody will ever know I existed. Nothing to leave behind me. Nothing to pass on. Nobody to mourn me. That's the bitterest blow of all.

### Hannibal
*Carthaginian general, committed suicide in 183 BC.*

Let us ease the Romans of their continual dread and care, who think it long and tedious to await the death of a hated old man. Yet Titus will not bear away a glorious victory, nor one worthy of those ancestors sent to caution Pyrrhus, an enemy and conqueror too, against the poison prepared for him by traitors.

### Baron James A. Harden-Hickey
*Soldier of fortune.*
*His last note was meant for his wife.*

My Dearest, No news from you, although you have had plenty of time to write; Harvey has written me that he has no-one in view at present to buy my land. Well, I shall have tasted the cup of bitterness to the very dregs, but I do not complain. Goodbye. I forgive you your conduct toward me and trust you will be able to forgive yourself. I prefer to be a dead gentleman to a living blackguard like your father.

### Heinrich Himmler
*German Nazi leader and commander of the S S, committed suicide 1945.*
He cheated the gallows by taking poison.

I am Heinrich Himmler!

### Hugo von Hofmannsthal
*Austrian poet and playwright, died 1929.*
His letter on his son's suicide...

Good friend, I sincerely hope it goes well with you. Yesterday afternoon a great misfortune visited our Rodauner House. During a bad, oppressive thunderstorm our poor Franz took his life with a shot in the temple. The motive for this dreadful deed lies darkly deep: in the depths of character and of fate. There was no external motive. We had eaten together as usual, en famille. There is something infinitely sad and infinitely noble in the way the poor child went. He was never able to share his thoughts. So his departure was silent too ... Raymond is with us. In all friendship, Hugo von Hofmannsthal.

### Judas Iscariot
*Apostle and betrayer of Christ, committed suicide c.AD 33.*

I have sinned in that I have betrayed the innocent blood.

### Malcolm Jamieson
*London plasterer, cut his own neck, 1901.*
Oh my poor head! I'll do it before I leave this earth!

### Rev. Jim Jones
*American leader of the People's Temple, 913 members of which committed mass suicide in Guyana in 1978.*
A final note...

We didn't commit suicide, we committed an act of revolutionary suicide, protesting the conditions of an inhumane world.

### Thornton Jones
*Welsh solicitor, who cut his own throat while asleep 1924.*
He lived for eighty minutes...

Forgive me, forgive me!
Then wrote down...
I dreamt that I had done it; I awoke to find it true.

### Heinrich von Kleist
*German dramatist and poet, committed suicide 1811.*
His suicide letter to his sister...

I cannot die without, contented and serene as I am, reconciling myself with all the world and, before all others, with you, my dearest Ulrike. Give up the strong expressions which you resorted to in your letter to me: let me revoke them; truly, to save me, you have done all within the strength, not only of a sister, but of a man ... all that could be done. The truth is, nothing on earth can help me. And now good-bye: may Heaven send you a death even half equal to mine in joy and unutterable bliss: that is the most heart-felt and profoundest wish that I can think of for you. Your Henry. Stimmung, at Potsdam, on the morning of my death.

### Günther von Kluge
*German Field-Marshal, implicated in the plot to kill Hitler, committed suicide 1944.*
His suicide note was addressed to Adolf Hitler...

I depart from you, my Führer, as one who stood nearer to you than perhaps you realised in the consciousness that I did my duty to the utmost. Heil, my Führer, von Kluge, Field-Marshal, 18 August 1944.

### Richard Kroning
*14-year-old Australian schoolboy, known as 'The Schoolgirl's Pinup', committed suicide 1977.*
One of his girlfriends was pregnant and his mother had left home...

I miss her yelling and screaming and the rest of the noise. I know how much you both love me. I love you both, but I've just got to go. My time is up.

### Carole Landis
*American film star, committed suicide in 1948.*

Dearest Mommie. I am sorry, really sorry to put you through this. But there is no way to avoid it. I love you darling. You have been the most wonderful Mom ever. And that applies to all our family. I love each and every one of them dearly. Everything goes to you. Look in the files and there is a will which decrees everything. Goodbye my angel. Pray for me.

### Dr. Robert Ley
*Nazi war criminal, committed suicide by hanging 1945.*
His suicide note written before hanging himself in his cell, thus cheating his executioner...

The fact that I should be a criminal, that I can't stand.

### Paul and Germaine Lieubaut
*French newlyweds who committed double suicide 1923.*
He was aged 30, she 22; she wore her wedding dress and they had been married just six days...

We are killing ourselves because we are too happy. We do not need money, for we are worth over 30,000 francs. We have good health and a wonderful life before us, but we prefer to die now because we are the happiest people in the world. We adore each other but we would rather descend into the grave together while we are so happy.

### Vachell Lindsay
*American poet, committed suicide 1931.*
He drank a bottle of Lysol...

They tried to get me...I got them first!

### Jesse Livermore ('The Boy Plunger')
*Committed suicide 1933.*
Written in his notebook, immediately prior to shooting himself...

My life has been a failure, my life has been a failure, my life has been a failure.

### Lucan
*Roman poet, committed suicide 65 AD.*
His own verse 'Pharsalia' provided a farewell message...

Asunder flies the man no single wound the gaping rupture seems where trickling crimson flows the tender streams but from an opening horrible and wide a thousand vessels pour the bursting tide at once the winding channel's course was broken where wandering life her mazy journey took.

### M. Malglaive
*A half-pay French officer who had lost what little money he possessed. He and his wife committed suicide through the fumes of a charcoal stove; this note went to a friend...*

When you shall have received this letter my poor Elizabeth and I will be no more. Be so good as to have our door opened, you will find our eyes closed for ever. We are weary of misfortunes and don't see how we can do better than end them. Satisfied of the courage and attachment of my excellent wife, I was certain she

*Facing page: 'I am Heinrich Himmler!'*

would adopt my views and take her share in my design.

### Charlotte Mew
*English poetess, committed suicide 1928.*
Don't keep me, let me go.

### Richard Middleton
*English poet and story writer, committed suicide 1641.*
*His note...*
Good-bye! Harry. I'm going adventuring again, and thanks to you I shall have some pleasant memories in my knapsack. As for the many bitter ones, perhaps they will not weigh so heavy now as they did before. 'A broken and contrite heart, oh Lord, Thou shalt not despise.' Richard.

### Florence Martha Miller
*London dressmaker, committed suicide by coal gas poisoning 1924.*
*This poem was found in her hand. The Coroner noted 'If original it is an excellent example of versifying'...*
Even now my summons echoes
from afar
And grave mists gather round
my star;
I am weary and am travel worn,
My faltering feet are pierced by
many a thorn,
This cruel world has made my
faint heart bleed
When dreamless rest is mine I
shall not need
The tenderness for which I long
tonight.

### Hugh Miller
*Scottish geologist and man of letters, committed suicide 1856.*
*A suicide letter to his wife...*
Dearest Lydia, My brain burns, I must have walked; and a fearful dream rises upon me. I cannot bear the horrible thought God and Father of the Lord Jesus Christ, have mercy upon me. Dearest Lydia, dear children, farewell. My brain burns as the recollection grows. My dear wife, farewell, Hugh Miller.

### Philip Mordaunt
*British aristocrat. Date and death unknown*
*His suicide followed a life distinguished only by his wealth, success and uninterrupted enjoyment. But ennui led to his suicide. He paid his debts, bade farewell to his friends and wrote some verses to commemorate the occasion. Then...*
Life has given me a headache. And I want a good sleep in the churchyard to set me to rights.

*Right: Rommel... from desert war hero to suicide on Hitler's orders.*

### J. F. N.
*An unknown German merchant.*
*After losing his fortune, he starved himself to death; this was his final journal entry.*
I here protest before the all-wise God that, notwithstanding all the misfortunes which I have suffered from my youth, I yet die very unwillingly, although necessity has imperiously driven me to it. Nevertheless I pray for it. Father forgive him, for he knows not what he does. More I cannot write for faintness and spasms, and this will be the last. Dated near the forest, by the side of the Goat public house. J. F. N.

### Emiko Nokita
*A 13-year-old Japanese schholgirl, killed herself in 1977 by throwing herself off a roof in Tokyo.*
*Her final message...*
I wish I had seen the Bay City Rollers.

### Eugene O'Neill Jr.
*American classical scholar, committed suicide at 40.*
His note...
Never let it be said of O'Neill that he failed to empty a bottle. Ave atque vale.

### Major John Oneby
*British murderer, committed suicide 1727.*
Oneby killed his victim in a tavern brawl; he committed suicide in his cell in Newgate but first left a note for his gaolers...
Give Mr. Akerman, the turnkey below stairs, half a guinea, and Jack who waits in my room five shillings. The poor devils have had a great deal of trouble with me since I have been here.

### Jules Pascin
*French artist, committed suicide 1930.*
On the eve of an important one-man show of his work, Pascin hanged himself. He wrote on the wall...
Adieu Lucy.

### Cesare Pavese
*Italian writer, committed suicide by overdose 1950.*
His final diary entry...
The thing most feared in secret always happens; all it needs is a little courage. The more the pain grows clearer and definite, the more the instinct for life reasserts itself and the thought of suicide recedes. It seemed easy when I thought of it. Weak women have done it. It needs humility, not pride. I am sickened by all this. No words. Action. I shall write no more.

### Horace Pitt
*Headmaster of Oakfield School, Monmouth, shot himself at Penarth 1928.*
His document entitled 'My Last Thoughts'...
Wistful, wanton, wayward, wild
Sceptic head yet heart of child,
God, who shaped the land and sea,
Why hast Thou so mismade me?
Tell me, dost Thou sometimes jest?
Ideas, loft practice,
Low mouthing, yes.
But acting no.
Why, o Architect Divine,
Didst Thou warp this mind of mine?
And added...
About 11 pm. The night has fallen...I have lived about forty years in three hours. Thank God for life. It is good to have lived, and for death. I cannot dogmatise but shall know in 60 seconds. Bang.

### Roland de la Platière
*French radical, committed suicide 1793.*
His wife, Madame Roland, was guillotined in 1793...
After my wife's murder, I would not remain any longer in a world so stained with crime.

### Jacques Rigaut
*French surrealist painter, committed suicide, 20th century*
Suicide is a vocation.

### Roman soldier
*After witnessing the emperor Otho's suicide he killed himself too*
Behold in my action an instance of the unshaken fidelity of all your soldiery. There is not one of us but would strive this to preserve thee.

### Erwin Rommel
*German general, committed suicide 1944.*
Explaining his suicide, which was ordered by Hitler, to his son...
To die at the hand of one's own people is hard.

### Solomon Rosbach
*American diamond merchant, committed suicide 1946.*
He killed himself by jumping from the Empire State Building...
No above, no below. So I jump.

### Bourg Saint-Edmé
*French man of letters, committed suicide.*
His suicide note to his children...
At four o'clock or at 4.15 I will carry out my design, if everything goes right. I am not afraid of death, since I am seeking it, since I desire it! But prolonged suffering would be frightful. I walk; all ideas vanish. I think only of my children. The fire is dying out. What a silence all around! Four o'clock. I hear the chimes. Soon comes the moment of sacrifice. I put my snuff box in my desk drawer. Goodbye my dearest daughters! God will pardon my sorrows. I put my spectacles in the drawer. Goodbye, once more, goodbye, my darling children! My last thought is yours, for you are the last flutterings of my heart.

### George Sanders
*American film star, commited suicide from 'ennui' in 1970.*
He left an explanatory note...
Dear World, I am leaving you because I am bored. I am leaving you with your worries. Good luck.

### Jean Seberg
*American film star, committed suicide in 1979.*
I can't live any longer with my nerves.

### Lucius Annaeus Seneca
*Roman philosopher, committed suicide in 65 AD.*
While bleeding, he entered a pool of heated water, with which he sprinkled the nearest of his slaves...
I offer this liquid as a libation to Jupiter the Deliverer.

### Simon
*British monk, committed suicide by poison in 1216.*
He drank poisoned wine in order to get King John of England to drink it...
If it shall like your princely majesty, here is such a cup of wine as ye never drank a better before in all your lifetime; I trust this wassail shall make all England glad.

*George Sanders: died of boredom.*

*Lupe Velez ...yet another Hollywood casualtly.*

### Richard Smith
*British bookbinder, committed suicide 1732. He killed his wife, his child and himself while jailed for debt in the King's Bench prison.*
*This note was left for his landlord...*

He hopes affects enough will be found to discharge his lodgings and recommends to his protection his ancient dog and cat.

### Socrates
*Greek philosopher, committed suicide by drinking hemlock 399 BC*

Crito, I owe a cock to Asclepius. Will you remember to pay the debt?

### Sophonisba
*Wife of Masinissa, committed suicide by poison.*
*Her husband was ordered to surrender her to the Romans, but rather than this fate he sent her a dose of poison which she voluntarily drank...*

*Facing page: Jean Seberg with Jean-Paul Belmondo in 'Breathless', 1960.*

If my husband has for his new wife no better gift than a cup of death, I know his will and accept what he bestows. I might have died more honourably if I had not wedded so near to my funeral.

### Filippo Strozzi II
*Florentine intriguer against the Medicis, committed suicide 1538.*
*He backed a defiant note with a line from Virgil carved with his sword on the prison wall...*

If I have not known how to live, I shall know how to die. May some avenger rise from my bones!

### Gary Swan
*American, committed suicide for love, aged 25, 1977.*
*He went to the local lovers' lane and poured petrol over himself, then lit a match. He left a note for the person who had jilted him...*

Death by burning is supposed to hurt the greatest. You don't burn to death, you die from the shock and the pain. By the time you read this I will be dead. This is my way of proving a point. I love you. C'est la vie.

### Theramenes
*Athenian statesman and general, committed suicide by drinking hemlock 5th century BC.*
*He toasted his accuser...*

This to the health of the lovely Critias!

### Paetus Thrasea
*Roman senator and Stoic, committed suicide 66 in AD.*
*Ordered by Nero to kill himself...*

We pour out a libation to Jupiter the Deliverer. Behold, young man, and may the gods avert the omen, but you have been born into times in which it is well to fortify the spirit with examples of courage.

### Henning von Tresckow
*German general and one of the Stauffenberg plotters against Hitler, committed suicide 1945.*
*He chose suicide rather than execution...*

The worth of a man is certain only if he is prepared to sacrifice his life for his convictions.

### John Upson
*A Suffolk glover, on trial for felony, he committed suicide by hanging himself with a garter 1774.*

Farewell vain road I've had enough of thee. And now I'm careless of what thou say'st of me. Thy smiles I court not, nor thy frowns I fear. My cares are past, my heart lies easy here What faults they find in me take care to shun. And look at home, enough is to be done.

### Jacques Vache
*French surrealist painter, committed suicide, 20th century*
*He fulfilled his wish in all points, killing himself with two university friends...*

I shall die when I want to die. And then I shall die with someone else. To die alone is boring. I should prefer to die with one of my best friends.

### Lupe Velez
*Hollywood film star, committed suicide in 1944.*

To Harald, May God forgive you and forgive me too but I prefer to take my life away and our baby's before I bring him with shame or killing him, Lupe.
*And on the back of this note...*

How could you, Harald, fake such a great love for me and our baby when all the time you didn't want us. I see no other way out for me so goodbye and good luck to you. Love, Lupe.

### James White
*A self-made millionaire who killed himself owing debts of $610,000.*
*A last letter...*

The world is nothing but a human cauldron of greed...it is one dark day after another. My soul is sickened by the homage paid to wealth.

### Virginia Woolf
*English novelist, committed suicide by drowning 1941.*

I have a feeling I shall go mad. I cannot go on any longer in these terrible times. I hear voices and cannot concentrate on my work. I have fought against it but cannot fight any longer. I owe all my happiness to you, but cannot go on and spoil your life.

### Taki Zenzaburo
*Japanese officer of the Prince of Bizen, committed suicide by hara-kiri.*

I, and I alone, unwarrantably gave the order to fire on the foreigners at Kobe, and again as they tried to escape. For this crime I disembowel myself, and I beg you who are present to do me the honour of witnessing the act.

### Stefan Zweig
*Austrian philosopher, committed suicide in 1942.*
*Sickened by the state of Europe under fascism...*

I believe it is time to end a life which was dedicated only to spiritual work, considering human liberty and my own as the greatest wealth in the world. I leave an affectionate goodbye to all my friends.